ADVANCE PRAISE FOR

Intersectionality & Higher Education: Research, Theory, & Praxis, Second Edition

"There is a saying, when you know better, you do better. The second edition of *Intersectionality & Higher Education* will help educators do better around identity development and understanding contexts and institutional power structures that press down upon those most affected by marginalization. The renowned scholars that contributed to this book give readers an accessible way to unpack intersectionality within higher education."

—Bridget Turner Kelly, Associate Professor,
College of Education, University of Maryland;
Executive Editor, *Journal of Student Affairs Research and Practice*

"For those engaged in social justice work as well as those unfamiliar with the interwoven nature of identity and disparities that exacerbate oppression, and the nuances of multiple group memberships, intersectionality is essential in advancing justice and curbing inequities. Too often is the case that scholars, practitioners, and advocates for social justice fall short of illustrating identity markers that are not siloes but routinely converge in fueling prejudice, systemic discrimination, and oppressive conditions. However, the second edition of *Intersectionality & Higher Education* edited by Donald "DJ" Mitchell, Jr. and associates recognizes this constraint subsequently providing breadth and depth on intersectionality. Readers will be informed and enlightened with complex applied theoretical, methodological, and practical intersectional approaches."

—Eboni M. Zamani-Gallaher, Associate Dean & Professor,
The Graduate College, University of Illinois at Urbana-Champaign

Intersectionality
& Higher Education

This book is part of the Peter Lang Education list.
Every volume is peer reviewed and meets
the highest quality standards for content and production.

PETER LANG
New York • Bern • Berlin
Brussels • Vienna • Oxford • Warsaw

Intersectionality & Higher Education

Research, Theory, & Praxis, Second Edition

Donald "DJ" Mitchell, Jr., Editor

with Jakia Marie & Tiffany L. Steele, Associate Editors

Foreword by D-L Stewart

PETER LANG
New York • Bern • Berlin
Brussels • Vienna • Oxford • Warsaw

Library of Congress Cataloging-in-Publication Data

Names: Mitchell, Donald, Jr., editor.
Title: Intersectionality & higher education : research, theory, & practice /
Donald "DJ" Mitchell, Jr., editor with Jakia Marie &
Tiffany L. Steele, associate editors; foreword by D-L Stewart.
Description: Second Edition | New York: Peter Lang, 2019.
Identifiers: LCCN 2018055362 | ISBN 978-1-4331-6535-1 (paperback: alk. paper)
ISBN 978-1-4331-6527-6 (ebook pdf)
ISBN 978-1-4331-6528-3 (epub) | ISBN 978-1-4331-6529-0 (mobi)
Subjects: LCSH: Minorities—Education (Higher)—United States.
Education, Higher—Social aspects—United States.
Multicultural education—United States.
Identity (Psychology)
Racism in education—United States.
Educational equalization—United States.
Classification: LCC LC3731 .I566 2019 | DDC 378.1/9820973—dc 3
LC record available at https://lccn.loc.gov/2018055362
DOI 10.3726/b15089

Bibliographic information published by **Die Deutsche Nationalbibliothek**.
Die Deutsche Nationalbibliothek lists this publication in the "Deutsche
Nationalbibliografie"; detailed bibliographic data are available
on the Internet at http://dnb.d-nb.de/.

© 2019 Peter Lang Publishing, Inc., New York
29 Broadway, 18th floor, New York, NY 10006
www.peterlang.com

Contents

Figures AND Tables

FIGURES

TABLES

Foreword

D-L STEWART

Kimberlé Crenshaw, the original midwife for bringing the concept of intersectionality into academic discourse, said the following in a printed interview:

> What's exciting is that I really don't remember a time when a political academic concept generated by people of [C]olor—and particularly a concept that is the home of women of [C]olor—has gotten this much elite attention. There's a way in which the mad attention on intersectionality by the left and the right—the fight over what it means, the fight over how it gets deployed, who gets to use it—is a recognition that we're sitting on some valuable conceptual real estate, and we just need to double down and figure out how to develop and protect it. (Guobadia, 2018, para. 13)

The concept of intersectionality in higher education and student affairs has reflected the phenomenon that Crenshaw notes above. Slow to the conceptual party—as fields such as critical legal studies, feminist studies, and ethnic studies had been entrenched in the use of and debates about intersectionality for nearly two decades—the field of higher education and student affairs has grabbed ahold of intersectionality and as a core idea in theory and practice. Broached in the early 2000s in higher education research by me, Susan Jones, and Charmaine Wijeyesinghe, intersectionality quickly became a "buzzword" bandied about in conference spaces, academic research, and graduate preparation classrooms.

Despite its ever-increasing popularity in the field, a certain "illiteracy" as Crenshaw noted accompanies its misuse generally (Guobadia, 2018, para. 9) as being merely about recognizing the multiple identities of individual students leading to critiques of intersectionality as representing excessive tribalism. Unfortunately, the misuse of intersectionality by student affairs researchers and practitioners has added fuel to the general illiteracy about the concept whose origins lay in the intellectual thought of Black women.

Due to an insular approach, some reviews of intersectionality begin with the work of White scholars in higher education, despite what those scholars have written themselves. Missing are its roots in the writing of nineteenth and early twentieth-century Black women, such as Anna Julia Cooper, let alone the academic work of Kimberlé Crenshaw and Patricia Hill Collins, or even later scholars such as Lisa Bowleg and Leslie McCall—all writing prior to the boom of intersectionality research in higher education and student affairs. Theoretical literature that seeks to employ an intersectional analysis has been misinterpreted and taught as being merely about multiple identities, while the label of intersectionality is applied inappropriately to theory and practice involving merely the convergence of multiple identities for individuals and student groups.

In contrast to these abuses, this text seeks to "double down and figure out how to protect and develop" (Guobadia, 2018, para. 13) intersectionality, defined by Crenshaw as

> [S]imply a prism to see the interactive effects of various forms of discrimination and disempowerment. It looks at the way that racism, many times, interacts with patriarchy, heterosexism, classism, xenophobia—seeing that the overlapping vulnerabilities created by these systems actually create specific kinds of challenges. (Guobadia, 2018, para. 6)

From this starting point, how can intersectionality be useful in higher education theory and practice and why is it necessary? As Crenshaw noted, the interlocking systems and structures of oppression create overlapping vulnerabilities that are particularly felt for people at the crossroads of multiple minoritized social groups. These interlocking systems are apparent in higher education and student affairs as well. Here are just three examples.

First, at some institutions, students who sign up for mandatory on-campus housing well after the deadline for priority consideration, often end up in the oldest residence halls with the fewest amenities. From a neoliberal perspective, this is simply good business and should incentivize on-time submission of housing applications. From a single-lens perspective, perhaps only classism would be put at the forefront. However, when we consider that these students also tend to be people of Color, first-generation, *and* low-income, it becomes evident that no single-issue analysis will be sufficient to resolve the current situation. Not only classism is at play, but rather the intersection of neoliberalism, classism, racism, and college knowledge work to put these students in a unique predicament where there are certain sections of campus residences that are called "ghettos," "the projects," and worse.

Second, a building's third-floor bathrooms are closed down for renovations. On that floor is the only ADA-compliant, all gender bathroom in the building.

Initially, no plan is in place to provide bathroom access in the building for people with disabilities, people who need relief assistance, and transgender people made unsafe in gendered restroom facilities. The closest ADA-compliant and all gender restrooms are in the building across the center mall. This is no mere oversight, but rather the function of interlocking systems and structures of ableism and trans-antagonism. These oppressive systems pull together not only two social groups, but also those who overlap across those groups.

Third, some institutions still close down the dining halls during holiday breaks and require an extra fee per night for those students who remain in the residence halls. Often international students are thought of as harmed by this policy and they are, yet initiatives are often put in place for those students to have home stays with local families. However, for low-income, emancipated foster youth, who are often racially minoritized, queer, and/or transgender, this policy creates a unique precarity. It is assumed that domestic students can go "home" during the break and have their housing and dining needs met by parents, other relatives, or other guardians. The interlocking systems of neoliberalism, classism, racism, and heteronormativity intersect in this case.

These three examples demonstrate that no single oppressive system creates inequitable and unjust conditions in higher education. Rather, if we are to build a truly socially just movement we must attend to the -isms within the -ism that may be our focus. As Crenshaw noted,

> So when racial justice doesn't have a critique of patriarchy and homophobia, the particular way that racism is experienced and exacerbated by heterosexism, classism etc., falls outside of our political organizing. It means that significant numbers of people in our communities aren't being served by social justice frames because they don't address the particular ways that they're experiencing discrimination. (Guobadia, 2018, para. 7)

There is much research in higher education and student affairs that focuses on either racism or classism as the main issue that policymakers and college administrators need to address. Yet, to adapt Crenshaw, a class analysis that does not critique racism, heteronormativity, and neoliberalism does not recognize how queer people of Color are particularly affected by classist institutional policies and practices, then leaves out significant numbers of our students. In the same vein, a race analysis with no critique as Crenshaw points out above also leaves out the particular ways that people at the intersections of racism with other forms of oppression experience the college environment or are pushed out from it altogether. This is not intersectional praxis.

If higher education and student affairs scholars and practitioners are going to promote social justice, then we must commit to an authentic practice of intersectionality. I have noted in previous research that perhaps the articulation of a truly intersectional perspective about one's self and lived experiences may be a matter of gaining increasing complexity (Stewart, 2010). It may be the same for the field and those studying and practicing within it. However, growing up into intersectionality must happen if we seek to transform institutional policy and practice to be equitable and just. Through addressing theory, research, and praxis, this text is a vital element in doing what Crenshaw recommends, "developing and protecting" intersectionality (Guobadia, 2018, para. 13).

D-L Stewart
Colorado State University
Fort Collins, Colorado

REFERENCES

Guobadia, O. (2018, August 31). Kimberlé Crenshaw and Lady Phyll talk intersectionality, solidarity, and self-care. *them.* Retrieved from https://www.them.us/story/kimberle-crenshaw-lady-phyll-intersectionality

Stewart, D. L. (2010). Researcher as instrument: Understanding "shifting" findings in constructivist research. *Journal of Student Affairs Research and Practice, 47*(3), 291–306.

Preface

DONALD "DJ" MITCHELL, JR.

For a majority of my life I thought I held anti-racist views, but unfortunately, I did not. I thought being an African American man who experiences racism the United States of America and who openly voices my concerns against racism was enough. It was not until I was introduced to the term *intersectionality*, coined by Kimberlé Crenshaw in 1989, that I began to realize the limitation of my views on race and racism and truly started to become equity-minded and an advocate for moving further towards social justice. Crenshaw, a legal, critical race, and Black feminist legal scholar, first used the term intersectionality to highlight the lived experiences of Black women who, because of the intersection of race and gender are exposed to overlapping forms of oppression and marginalization, and are often theoretically erased from single-axis anti-discrimination laws (e.g., anti-racist laws, anti-sexist laws).

Crenshaw (1989) noted that Black women are not oppressed by *just* racism or *just* sexism since their lived experiences cannot be captured by simply stating that they are Black *or* they are women. On one hand, speaking about Black women in terms of race and racism ignores gender and sexism. On the other hand, speaking about Black women in terms of gender and sexism ignores race and racism. For Black women in particular, by highlighting marginalization or oppression in single-axis ways, they are erased in the process because their experiences as Black women (not Black *and* woman) are not fully acknowledged; and more importantly, the overlapping nature of racism and sexism as oppressive forces marginalizes them in unique ways (Crenshaw, 2015). In addition to race and gender, Black women also face other forms of oppression such as classism, heterosexism, and transphobia which lead to further marginalization and erasures. What Crenshaw's work taught me is that I was not anti-racist because I was not as, or at all, invested in fights against sexism, classism, heterosexism, transphobia/genderism, and xenophobia among other forms of oppression; and ultimately, one has to be invested in the fight against all –isms to truly be anti-racist since people of Color are heterogeneous and are often oppressed in multiple ways beyond racism and those ways overlap for those from multiple marginalized identities.

As another example, I often reference Susan B. Anthony who is considered one of the greatest feminists in United States history. Anthony is infamously known for stating, "I will cut off this right arm of mine before I will ever work or demand the ballot for the Negro and not the woman." In her quote, Anthony uses a single-axis approach to combating sexism while erasing Black women in the process by noting she would cut off her hand before advocating for voting rights for "the Negro" (which meant Black men at the time). Ultimately, while Anthony fought against sexism against White women, she oppressed Black women in the process by speaking against "the Negro." While many argue Anthony was a feminist, as defined as advocating for equality among the sexes or for women's rights, I argue against that claim since she communicated racist views or did not use an intersectional approach to her feminism; this highlights the constant fight for Black women to be seen, heard, and acknowledged, and what is often articulated in Black feminist thought (see Collins, 2000 for more on Black feminist thought).

While Crenshaw's articulation of intersectionality was my primary introduction to recognizing overlapping systems of oppression, Black women in the United States have written and spoken about their experiences and the ways they have been uniquely oppressed since the 19th century. Anna Julia Cooper, Sojourner Truth, Audrey Lorde, bell hooks, Patricia Hill Collins, and Bonnie Thorton Dill are some of these pioneers, and while intersectionality as articulated by Crenshaw is the focus of this text, their works must be acknowledged as intersectionality is further theorized and applied in new ways. Failing to recognize intersectionality has some roots in Black feminist thought is exactly what intersectionality originally articulates—Black women's erasure.

Still, while intersectionality as articulated by Crenshaw has some roots in Black feminist thought, the concept is now used to discuss overlapping systems of oppression that influence populations beyond Black women and is used in diverse ways. Cho, Crenshaw, and McCall (2013) noted intersectionality is now engaged in three primary ways: (1) as a frame of analysis for research and teaching; (2) as a theory or methodology, which includes the ways in which intersectionality has been developed and adapted; and, (3) through intersectional praxis or interventions since intersectionality was never meant to be solely theoretical. Intersectionality has also been adopted "in disciplines such as history, sociology, literature, philosophy, and anthropology as well as in feminist studies, ethnic studies, queer studies, and legal studies" (Cho, Crenshaw, & McCall, 2013, p. 787), and more recently, the field of higher education (e.g., see Griffin & Museus, 2011; Mitchell, Simmons, & Greyerbiehl, 2014; Stewart, 2010, 2013). This second edition of *Intersectionality & Higher Education: Theory, Research, & Praxis* seeks to further document the uses of intersectionality specifically within higher education contexts.

I argue using Crenshaw's articulation of intersectionality might be the most appropriate ways to shape higher education contexts in the future, particularly given the ways in which higher education of all forms shape societies across the globe. Cho, Crenshaw, and McCall (2013) note that some scholars argue centering Black women or the origins of intersectionality limit the applicability intersectionality. I contend just the opposite since intersectionality is not solely about multiple, intersecting identities; intersectionality is about overlapping systems of oppression and how those with multiple marginalized identities are made vulnerable in the process (Crenshaw, 2015). Similarly, Jones (2014) notes,

> To only see intersectionality as being about identity is to ignore its historical and disciplinary origins and intent and thereby miss the mark of its full analytic power … intersectionality is only about identity when structures of inequality are foregrounded and identities considered in light of social issues and power dynamics. (p. xii)

Given this, intersectionality as a framework can, and I argue should, be used to articulate the experiences of people beyond Black women, and given this, my working definition for intersectionality is "the intersection of salient socially constructed identities and the extent to which individuals or groups are oppressed or marginalized as a result of interlocking, socially constructed systems of oppression associated with those identities" (Mitchell, 2014, para. 2) which highlights its capacity for broader use. I also recognize there are those who argue the intersections of race and gender must be present in intersectional analyses given Crenshaw's original use of the term.

Further, since using intersectionality as a framework requires centering those who are the most marginalized or oppressed, those who are "singularly disadvantaged" (Crenshaw, 1989, p. 167) also benefit from dismantling multiple oppressions. For example, in a blog I wrote about using intersectionality as a framework for student success, I asked the following to highlight various forms of marginalization for students attending U.S. higher education institutions:

> In what ways does having advising hours only during business hours marginalize some students?
> In what ways do requiring multiple books for a class and the prices of books marginalize some students?
> In what ways do limited or no gender-neutral restrooms marginalize some students?
> In what ways does closing housing during Christian religious holiday breaks marginalize some students? (Mitchell, 2016, para. 4)

I should have also asked, "What about the students who experience all of these marginalizations simultaneously?" By centering those students who deal with all of these oppressive policies and seeking to dismantle the various forms of institutional oppressions they face, it also benefits students who deal with one or some of these marginalizing practices. That is the potential power of using intersectionality to improve higher education across the globe.

Just as in the first edition of *Intersectionality & Higher Education*, this edition is organized in three sections: theory, research, and praxis. While some of the chapters from the first edition of the text are included in the present edition, this updated edition includes new pieces articulating and applying intersectionality while ensuring attention to the origins of intersectionality are aptly acknowledged and applied. Still, as Bowleg (2008), McCall (2005), and Stewart (2010) all note, conducting research and scholarship on intersectionality is not easy; "scholars and practitioners must view [scholarly works] as living documents that are fallible and open to correction and revision" (Stewart, 2010, p. 305). Perhaps echoing Stewart, I encourage readers to read these chapters, not just as intersectionally-focused and social justice-centered, but also as snapshots of where authors are in their current understandings and applications of intersectionality recognizing that their understandings and applications could shift later on. My understanding of intersectionality has definitely shifted since the first edition of this text and, as a result, my editorial approach to the second addition was much different; however, I am thankful for this shift, and as a result, I am able to co-present to readers, *Intersectionality & Higher Education: Theory, Research, and Praxis* (2nd ed.).

Crenshaw's articulation of intersectionality pushed me to grow and to acknowledge that systems of oppression overlap and not acknowledging these overlaps erases. Still, me changing as an individual is not enough since intersectionality is not about individuals; systemic and societal changes are the changes that are most important, and this is where I hope this text makes a contribution by using intersectionality as the frame of reference. Higher education institutions across the globe are becoming more diverse; nevertheless, those who inhabit higher education institutions are being erased by overlapping systems of oppression that are often operationalized through marginalizing and oppressive structures, policies, practices and campus cultures. The collection of chapters presented in this volume are presented to move us further from this erasure. As Crenshaw (2015) noted, "We simply do not have the luxury of building social movements that are not intersectional, nor can we believe we are doing intersectional work just by saying words" (para. 12). The purpose of this text is to move us as global citizens, educators, and change agents toward social justice using intersectionality as a guide.

REFERENCES

Bowleg, L. (2008). When Black + lesbian + woman ≠ Black lesbian woman: The methodological challenges of qualitative and quantitative intersectionality research. *Sex Roles: A Journal of Research, 59*(5–6), 312–325.

Cho, S., Crenshaw, K., & McCall, L. (2013). Toward a field of intersectionality studies: Theory, application, and praxis. *Signs: Journal of Women in Culture and Society, 38*(4), 785–810.

Collins, P. H. (2000). *Black feminist thought: Knowledge, consciousness and the politics of empowerment* (2nd ed.). New York, NY: Routledge.

Crenshaw, K. (1989). Demarginalizing the intersection of race and sex: A Black feminist critique of antidiscrimination doctrine, feminist theory, and antiracist politics. *University of Chicago Legal Forum, 1989*(8), 139–167.

Crenshaw, K. (2015, September 24). Why intersectionality can't wait. *Washington Post.* Retrieved from https://www.washingtonpost.com/news/in-theory/wp/2015/09/24/why-intersectionality-cant-wait/?utm_term=.55e1fa267f79

Jones, S. R. (2014). Foreword. In D. Mitchell, Jr., C. Y. Simmons, & L. A. Greyerbiehl (Eds.), *Intersectionality & higher education: Theory, research, & praxis* (pp. xi–xiv). New York, NY: Peter Lang.

McCall, L. (2005). The complexity of intersectionality. *Signs: Journal of Women in Culture & Society, 30*(3), 1771–1800.

Mitchell, D., Jr. (2014, November 21). Intersectionality to social justice = theory to practice [Web log post]. Available at https://www.naspa.org/constituent-groups/posts/projectintersections-post-1

Mitchell, D., Jr. (2016, May 31). How to start a revolution: Use intersectionality as a framework to promote student success [Web log post]. Available at http://videos.myacpa.org/how-to-start-a-revolution-by-donald-mitchell

Mitchell, D., Jr., Simmons, C., & Greyerbiehl, L. (Eds.). (2014). *Intersectionality & higher education: Theory, research, and praxis* (1st ed.). New York, NY: Peter Lang.

Museus, S. D., & Griffin, K. A. (2011). Mapping the margins in higher education: On the promise of intersectionality frameworks in research and discourse. In K. A. Griffin & S. D. Museus (Eds.), *Using mixed-method approaches to study intersectionality in higher education.* (New Directions for Institutional Research, No. 151, pp. 5–13). San Francisco, CA: Jossey-Bass.

Stewart, D. L. (2010). Researcher as instrument: Understanding "shifting" findings in constructivist research. *Journal of Student Affairs Research and Practice, 47*(3), 291–306.

Stewart, D. L. (2013). Complicating belief: Intersectionality and Black college students' spirituality. In T. L. Strayhorn (Ed.), *Living at the intersections: Social identities and Black collegians* (pp. 93–108). Charlotte, NC: Information Age.

Acknowledgments

We would like to thank those who made the publication of the second edition of *Intersectionality & Higher Education: Theory, Research, & Praxis* possible. First, we thank all of the chapter authors who helped shape this volume through their writings and blind peer reviews. Second, we thank Dr. D-L Stewart for contributing the Foreword. Third, we thank Patricia Mulrane, Monica Baum, and Jackie Pavlovic—at Peter Lang—for all that they brought to the production of this volume. Finally, we thank a host of family, friends, and colleagues, whose love and support keep us going each day.

PART ONE

Theory

CHAPTER ONE

Intersectionality, Identity, AND Systems OF Power AND Inequality

CHARMAINE L. WIJEYESINGHE AND SUSAN R. JONES

The concept of identity has received attention in many facets of higher education, including teaching (Adams, Bell, & Griffin, 2007; Goodman & Jackson, 2012; Jones & Wijeyesinghe, 2011), research (Cross, 1991; Helms, 1990/1993; Stewart, 2008, 2009; Torres, Jones, & Renn, 2009) and student affairs practice (Abes, 2016; Jones & Abes, 2013; Jones & Stewart, 2016; Wijeyesinghe, 2017). Knefelkamp, Widick, and Parker (1978) noted that the developmental orientation of the college student personnel field, in particular, emphasized "the importance of responding to the whole person, attending to individual differences, and working with the student at his or her developmental level" (p. viii). Over the years, the ways in which the "whole person" has been conceptualized has shifted, with varying emphases on the parts and the whole (Torres et al., 2009), and although the social world and its contexts have always been considered in identity theories, exactly what constitutes context has evolved to also include larger structures of inequality.

In this chapter, we focus on two areas increasingly linked in theory, research, and practice in higher education: models of social identity development (the parts) and the framework of intersectionality (the whole). We begin by exploring how intersectionality addresses themes often seen in the study and representations of identity. Next, we focus more specifically on the implications of applying an intersectional lens to models grounded in individual identity narratives. We conclude the chapter by identifying several issues and questions, referred to as tension points, that have arisen in our work and teaching related to identity and intersectionality.

INTERSECTIONALITY AND PSYCHOSOCIAL
PERSPECTIVES ON IDENTITY

The question of "Who Am I?" has been the bedrock of identity research and models for decades. The study of identity in higher education emerged primarily from the psychological tradition of Erik Erikson (1959/1994), who described the psychosocial nature of identity development. From this perspective, identity evolves through a complex pattern of interaction between internal stages of growth and external social forces. Reflecting the sociocultural norms of his time, Erikson's conceptualization of these social forces or contexts led to very narrow views of individuals from nondominant groups. This realization led subsequent scholars in student development, racial identity development, and other fields to investigate social identities as significant contributors to understanding the whole person.

The term *social identity* has its roots in social psychology and the work of Tajfel (1982), who highlighted the role of intergroup dynamics and perceptions of group membership in understanding identity. Tajfel defined social identity as "that part of the individual's self-concept which derives from their knowledge of their membership in a social group (or groups) together with the value and emotional significance attached to that membership" (p. 2). Understanding identities as socially constructed means that "their significance stems not from some 'natural' state, but from what they have become as the result of social and historical processes" (Andersen & Collins, 2007, p. 62). Contemporary understandings of psychosocial identity, or how individuals see and understand their experiences in relation to various groups or roles they inhabit, incorporate specific attention to socially constructed groups that are tied to larger systems of power, privilege, and inequality. As Weber (2010) noted, "[A]t the individual level, race, class, gender, and sexuality are fundamental sources of identity for all of us: how we see ourselves, who we think we are. They are, in fact, so fundamental that to be without them would be like being without an identity at all" (p. 119).

Intersectionality is gaining currency among higher education scholars and practitioners because it acknowledges an individual's multiple social identities, thus creating a more complete portrayal of the whole person. While Dill, McLaughlin, and Nieves (2007) noted that "to a large extent, intersectional work is about identity" (p. 630), it is not *only* about identity (Collins & Bilge, 2016; Jones & Abes, 2013). Although Nash (2008) referred to "intersectionality's theoretical dominance as a way of conceptualizing identity" (p. 3), the framework does not seek to unveil how each person within a marginalized group or many groups develops their own sense of self under systems of oppression. It also does not foreground individual identity narratives (Collins, 2015). Instead, intersectionality highlights how people—as members of multiple groups of individuals—experience marginalization and inequality, even in movements designed to further social justice and institutional change. Clearly, individual voices inform the understanding and analysis of how inequality as well as privilege are experienced. Honoring the day-to-day experiences of *each person*, however, is not a core function of intersectionality.

Intersectionality attends to identity by placing it within a macrolevel analysis that ties individual experience to a person's membership in social groups, during a particular social and historical period, and within larger, interlocking systems of advantage and access. This complex view of identity more fully describes how individuals, as members of social groups constructed and affected by larger systems, experience their lives, interactions, and various contexts (Dill & Zambrana, 2009; Holvino, 2012). In describing her model of "simultaneity," Holvino (2012) indicated that such an orientation toward identity

> attends to the ways in which race, gender, class, sexuality, and nation are not just about a personal and individual identity, but about the social and institutional processes that determine opportunities, which also produce and reproduce racial, gender, class, and other social differences. (p. 172)

An intersectional perspective also forms a foundation for understanding the interconnections between systems of power and privilege in which personal narratives related to identity develop, evolve, and are understood. Therefore, not only are the experiences of social groups complex and mutually constituted, so are the systems of power and privilege, such as classism, ageism, Christian hegemony, and racism, that so strongly shape personal and group experience. Extending the perspective that identity at the individual level embodies multiple social locations that interact and influence each other to larger social systems allows us to see how forms of oppression interface, support, and reinforce each other, as well as the experience of individual people based on their respective identities (Holvino, 2012). For example, Suzanne Pharr's (1988) classic book, *Homophobia: A Weapon of Sexism*, provides compelling analysis of how the interconnectedness of two systems of oppression, homophobia and sexism, combine with economic issues to create institutional heterosexism. In terms of interventions, Matsuda suggested a technique of "ask[ing] the other question" (as cited in Nash, 2008, p. 12). She wrote "When I see something that looks racist, I ask, 'where is the patriarchy in this?' When I see something that looks sexist, I ask, 'Where is the heterosexism in this?'" (Matsuda, as cited in Nash, 2008, p. 12). This strategy forces an analysis of how these systems reinforce one another and connects privilege and oppression in more complex ways.

INTERSECTIONALITY AND MODELS OF
IDENTITY DEVELOPMENT

Several insights are revealed when psychosocial approaches to identity development are examined in the context of intersectionality. First, psychosocial theories often focus on experiences and developmental tasks facing a person or the experience of a person based on one social axis, such as race. Intersectionality complicates identity (Collins & Bilge, 2016; Dill & Zambrana, 2009), because it highlights the intricacies of individuals' experiences when they embody multiple identities simultaneously. In addition, intersectionality acknowledges the diversity within social groups, often overlooked in earlier identity theories that described experiences based on a single social identity. Given this complexity and diversity, the question arises as to whether new identity models can legitimately attend to one "Black experience," or a single experience of gay or lesbian students, since individuals who share one common social identity (such as race, or gender, or faith identity) may differ across several others. Those differences often include multiple locations of privilege and subordination (Collins, 1991; Weber, 2010) that must be acknowledged and integrated into interventions that promote equity and social justice (Kendall & Wijeyesinghe, 2017). For example, if a campus organization sponsors a program on the lives of Latino/a students on campus, the event and the chosen speakers should address a range of experiences in addition to those attributed to race, ethnicity, and nationality.

Second, several identity models link an individual's multiple social group memberships and the salience that the individual attaches to each social identity at different life stages or in different contexts (Cross & Fhagen-Smith, 2001; Jones & Abes, 2013; Wijeyesinghe, 2012). While context and salience are reflected in how each person experiences identity in daily life, intersectionality does not directly and purposefully address the concept of salience at the level of each individual's experiences. As opposed to understanding social identities as discrete parts of an individual, each with its own level of personal significance, intersectionality encourages the consideration of multiple identities, notwithstanding the salience individuals attach to them personally. Core tenets of intersectionality addressing the unveiling of power, recognizing interconnected structures of inequality, and promoting social justice, may be helpful in expanding how we view the concept of salience. People may feel drawn to various movements for social change—such as women working to address sexism in the work place—based on the salience they attach to their various social identities. If such actions do not also recognize the interconnection among race, class, and other social memberships, interventions may address the needs of only some of the people within that entire social group, such as White women in the aforementioned example.

Last, linking personal identity narratives to larger systems of domination helps individuals understand the connection between the social groups they inhabit and their day-to-day experiences within society, as well as concepts of privileged and marginalized positions. People working in social justice education often encounter individuals who deny that they receive any social benefit from being, for example, White, male, heterosexual, or economically advantaged. Intersectionality is useful as an awareness building tool, in that through it, peoples' experiences transcend the lens of individual and personal, to that of a socially constructed group, differentially influenced by access to power and privilege. Increased recognition of the connection between personal identities and social systems that either support or confront oppression is an essential component in engaging people in social justice work (Bell, 1997; Goodman, 2011). Understanding how these systems shape opportunity and experience at the individual level is a cornerstone of anti-oppression work (Adams et al., 2007; Goodman, 2011) and can serve to motivate individuals to engage in actions toward a more just and equitable society, another cornerstone of intersectionality.

In light of the analysis thus far, one may begin to wonder: can models of psychosocial identity development capture core tenets of intersectionality, and are these models examples of intersectional practice? We believe that identity development models can integrate several themes drawn from intersectionality. Jones and Abes (2013) noted that "identity models *informed* [emphasis added] by intersectionality offer better ways of capturing the complexity of identity and portraying the full range of factors, contextual influences, social identities, lived experiences, and structures of power that contribute to a holistic interpretation of identity" (p. 154). Examples of such models include the Intersectional Model of Multiple Dimensions of Identity (Jones & Abes, 2013), the Intersectional Model of Multiracial Identity (Wijeyesinghe, 2012), and Simultaneity (Holvino, 2012). To varying degrees, these models acknowledge the interplay among multiple social group memberships (such as race, gender, class, age, sexual orientation) and the fluid nature of identity. In addition, they all specifically reference the impact of larger social, political, institutional, and historical contexts on how individuals develop and experience their identities. Authors of new models exploring individual narratives from an intersectional framework should continue to investigate several areas: how various social group memberships and identities interface and mutually constitute others, how a more universal and omnipresent conception of salience can exist alongside a sense of personal connection to various identities, and how to represent the influence and confluence of all identities in models that primarily focus on one (such as gender, sexual orientation, or race).

TENSION POINTS: ISSUES AND QUESTIONS RELATED TO THE INTERPLAY BETWEEN IDENTITY AND INTERSECTIONALITY

A number of questions emerged as we considered the relationship between identity and intersectionality, how each informs the other, and the issues that arise when we attend to individual narratives, identity, and larger structures of inequality. We use the term *tension points* to describe these questions and issues, and we explore some of the more pressing ones in this section of the chapter. Fundamentally, these tension points reflect, or are informed by such questions as the following: how can evolving conceptualization and application of intersectionality assist in understanding, mapping, rescarching, and teaching about social identity? Is intersectionality experienced at the individual as well as the social group level? And what, if anything, do psychosocial models that highlight the experiences of individuals offer intersectionality, and how can they inform the development of intersectional interventions in higher education practice?

Identity

As we noted throughout the chapter, an intersectional perspective of identity requires the connecting of individual lived experience to larger structures of privilege and oppression. Therefore, there may be limits to the extent and the ways that intersectionality can be applied to the experience of individuals, even when psychosocial models of identity development include references to larger social systems, power, and privilege. As theorists and practitioners, we are faced with the following question: can identity truly be an individual experience when people embody social identities that carry meaning in society and result in differential access to resources and control of various domains that fundamentally influence a person's life, regardless of whether the person acknowledges the existence or influence of those identities?

Psychosocial identity models that incorporate intersectional themes, like those examples mentioned in the previous section, can enhance our understanding of key concepts such as social group memberships and social location, institutional power and privilege, and oppression and liberation. This knowledge lays the groundwork for discussions that move beyond individual experiences to how systems of power and privilege support and intersect and the need to create interventions that reflect multiple social locations and concerns.

Tensions between managing the individual experience of identity and further reaching aspects of intersectionality should be considered when planning and implementing actions for social change. Dill et al. (2007) noted that "in the discussion surrounding identity, it is the tension between intersectionality as a tool for illuminating group identities that are not essentialist, and individual identities that are not so fragmented as to be meaningless" (p. 631). Attending to the mutually constituting nature of forms of oppression is not the same as treating them as the same or as so intertwined that the ways in which they differ become unrecognizable or disappear. Therefore, theories and change efforts must acknowledge common aspects and interconnections, while also attending to areas where experiences of identity and forms of inequality differ. Intersectionality, with its emphasis on individual and social location within multiple groups, pushes researchers, faculty, and practitioners to acknowledge the diversity within socially constructed groups, while avoiding the obscuring of real differences between manifestations of oppression by applying intersectionality uniformly (Luft, 2009).

Salience

In relation to identity, intersectionality illustrates how we embody all of our social identities and experience the world based on larger, interconnected systems that respond to these identities, at all times and in all circumstances. Weber (1998) pointed out the following:

> Race, class, gender, and sexuality simultaneously operate in every social situation. At the societal level, these systems of social hierarchies are connected to each other and are embedded in all social institutions. At the individual level, we each experience our lives and develop our identities based on our location along all dimensions, whether we are in dominant groups, subordinate groups, or both. (p. 24)

Tension may arise when individuals feel that their lived experience reflects one, or only some of their social identities, as when a gay, White man who is economically privileged feels that his identity is grounded primarily in his sexual orientation and resists considering how his race, economic position, and gender afford him social power and privilege. Intersectionality frames all identities as being mutually constituted, meaning that social identities are not discrete entities that are isolated from the influences of all others. Therefore, while the man described here may define himself and view the world primarily through the lens of sexual orientation, his class, race, emotional and physical ability, faith background, and other social groups also influence his particular experiences as a gay man. Thus, his experiences of being gay would be different if one or more of his other identities changed, for example, if he were Asian or economically disadvantaged. Scholars and practitioners may encounter challenges to operationalizing core tenets of intersectionality when there are the perceived gaps between the lived experience of identity salience by the individuals with whom they are working and the perspective that all identities are at play at all times.

Tension related to salience also occurs at the systems levels of analysis. At a broader social level, intersectionality highlights that it is not possible to grasp an understanding of the complex interplay of power, privilege, and social structures if we view forms of oppression as singular and separate units (like racism, ableism, sexism, classism), or if the focus is only on those forms of oppression that feel most salient to an individual, in a specific setting, or at a certain point in life. A more intersectional level of awareness recognizes

> that each of us simultaneously experiences all of these dimensions, even if one is fore-grounded in a particular situation, and can help us see the often obscured ways in which we benefit from existing race, class, gender, sexuality social arrangements, as well as the ways which we're disadvantaged. Such an awareness can be key in working together across different groups to achieve a more equitable distribution of society's valued resources. (Weber, 1998, p. 25)

Decades after Lorde (1983) so aptly highlighted that there is no hierarchy of oppressions, individuals may still feel that there is, based on how they live and experience their range of social identities.

Privileged and Oppressed Identities

Intersectionality centers the voices of people and groups previously overlooked or excluded, especially in the analysis of inequality and efforts to remedy specific social problems. An ongoing debate among intersectional scholars and observers of the popularity of the framework foregrounds the question of definition—what exactly is intersectionality and who is intersectional (Kendall & Wijeyesinghe, 2017; Nash, 2008; Warner & Shields, 2013)? Stated another way, is intersectionality a general theory of identities or a theory focused only on those people from multiple marginalized social groups? Nash (2008) argued, "In its emphasis on black women's experiences of subjectivity and oppression, intersectional theory has obscured the question of whether all identities are intersectional, or whether only multiply marginalized subjects have an intersectional identity" (p. 9). If intersectionality is applied as a general theory of identity, all people may locate themselves within its purview. However, if intersectionality is primarily grounded in the experiences of individuals with multiple marginalized identities, those people with privileged identities are outside of the framework. Of course, many individuals inhabit both privileged and oppressed identities, so these boundaries may not be so clearly drawn.

What seems critical to us is what Nash (2008) advocated for as "a nuanced conception of identity that recognizes the ways in which positions of dominance and subordination work in complex and intersecting ways to constitute subjects' experience of personhood" (p. 10). The question of whether intersectionality applies to everyone reinforces a point made earlier, that intersectionality is not simply about multiple identities, which we all have, but multiple identities connected to groups and structures of power, thus, paving the way for a "both/and" approach. Considering the application and relevance of intersectionality to people and groups who receive social advantages begins to draw some boundaries related to privileged and oppressed identities.

The purpose of intersectionality is not simply to locate individuals within a matrix of domination and privilege. Instead, intersectionality sheds light on the ways that some people within social groups receive benefit while others are disproportionately targeted and constrained by certain social-structural situations (this was Crenshaw's [1991] initial analysis of the inutility of a gender-only lens when investigating domestic violence against women). Yet, individuals who hold multiple privileged identities can use an intersectional analysis in ways that are productive and contribute to a more socially just society. The task then becomes less about locating oneself within an intersectional framework and more so about using intersectionality to understand the experiences of others and the social structures that perpetuate privilege and oppression.

From discussion, research, and application of intersectionality in various settings, we may develop a greater awareness of how intersectionality captures the lived experiences of people who hold multiple privileged identities or how experiences related to these identities are mediated by any targeted groups to which these individuals belong. Caution is advised, however, so that the core tenet of intersectionality related to foregrounding the experience of marginalized groups remains central to its understanding and application and to prevent it from becoming a lens that is co-opted to reinforce and re-center the experience of those people and groups with privileged identities.

CONCLUSION

In closing this chapter, we reaffirm that identity and intersectionality are relevant to each other and can be used to explore questions and areas unanswered by foundational theories within the fields of student, racial, and social identity development. As authors of two models that are informed by intersectionality, we see psychosocial models that incorporate aspects of the framework as tools to enhance our understanding of the experiences of individuals and groups on campus. Yet, as new theories and approaches evolve, we also pay homage to the context, goals, and contributions of existing theories, especially those models that paved the way in the early years and formed the foundation for research and theory building related to identity.

Intersectionality is a powerful tool for understanding, constructing, and deconstructing: the experience of identity, the complex and mutually constituting nature of social identities, the relationships between identity and larger social systems, and the interwoven nature of manifestations of social oppression. While centering the interconnections inherent in intersectional analysis, we also must honor the unique aspects of various social identities, systems of inequality, and efforts to enact social justice. The journey of writing this chapter has led us to see that in relation to identity and intersectionality, the situation is not one of "either/or" when it comes to the exploration of individual narratives or narratives of larger group experiences influenced by social systems. Instead, we appreciate how these two levels of analysis inform each other, contribute to our understanding of identity, stretch our thinking, drive model building, and guide our work. Thus, our efforts as theorists, researchers, and practitioners becomes less about "capturing" intersectionality via models and more about using the complexity and connections in the framework to more fully understand the lived experience of individuals within the context of their social groups, oppression and inequality, and interventions for social change.

REFERENCES

Abes, E. S. (2016). Situating paradigms in student development theory. In E. S. Abes (Ed.), *Critical perspectives in student development theory* (New Directions for Student Services, No. 154, pp. 9–16). San Francisco, CA: Jossey Bass.

Adams, M., Bell, L. A., & Griffin, P. (2007). *Teaching for diversity and social justice* (2nd ed.). New York, NY: Routledge.

Andersen, M. L., & Collins, P. H. (Eds.). (2007). *Race, class, & gender: An anthology* (7th ed.). Belmont, CA: Thomson/Wadsworth.

Bell, L. A. (1997). Theoretical foundations for social justice education. In M. Adams, L. A. Bell, & P. Griffin (Eds.), *Teaching for diversity and social justice: A sourcebook* (pp. 3–15). New York, NY: Routledge.

Collins, P. H. (1991). *Black feminist thought: Knowledge, consciousness, and the politics of empowerment.* New York, NY: Routledge.

Collins, P. H. (2007). Pushing the boundaries or business as usual? Race, class, and gender studies and sociological inquiry. In C. J. Calhoun (Ed.), *Sociology in America: A history* (pp. 572–604). Chicago, IL: University of Chicago Press.

Collins, P. H. (2015). Intersectionality's definitional dilemmas. *Annual Review of Sociology, 41,* 1–20.

Collins, P. H., & Bilge, S. (2016). *Intersectionality.* Malden, MA: Polity Press.

Crenshaw, K. (1991). Mapping the margins: Intersectionality, identity politics, and violence against women of Color. *Stanford Law Review, 43*(6), 1241–1299.

Cross, W. E. (1991). *Shades of black: Diversity in African-American identity.* Philadelphia, PA: Temple University Press.

Cross, W. E., & Fhagen-Smith, P. (2001). Patterns of African-American identity development: A life span perspective. In C. L. Wijeyesinghe & B. W. Jackson (Eds.), *New perspectives on racial identity development: A theoretical and practical anthology (pp. 243–270).* New York: New York University Press.

Dill, B. T., McLaughlin, A. E., & Nieves, A. D. (2007). Future directions of feminist research: Inter-sectionality. In S. N. Hesse-Biber (Ed.), *Handbook of feminist research* (pp. 629–637). Thousand Oaks, CA: Sage.

Dill, B. T., & Zambrana, R. E. (2009). Critical thinking about inequality: An emerging lens. In B. T. Dill & R. E. Zambrana (Eds.), *Emerging intersections: Race, class, and gender in theory, policy, and practice* (pp. 1–21). New Brunswick, NJ: Rutgers University Press.

Erikson, E. H. (1994). *Identity and the life cycle*. New York, NY: W. W. Norton. (Original work published 1959).

Goodman, D. J. (2011). *Promoting diversity and social justice: Educating people from privileged groups (2nd ed.)*. New York, NY: Routledge.

Goodman, D. J., & Jackson III, B. W. (2012). Pedagogical approaches to teaching about racial iden-tity from an intersectional perspective. In C. L. Wijeyesinghe & B. W. Jackson III (Eds.), *New perspectives on racial identity development* (2nd ed., pp. 216–239). New York: New York University Press.

Helms, J. E. (1993). *Black and White racial identity theory, research, and practice*. Westport, CT: Praeger. (Original work published 1990).

Holvino, E. (2012). The "simultaneity" of identities: Models and skills for the twenty-first century. In C. L. Wijeyesinghe & B. W. Jackson III (Eds.), *New perspectives on racial identity development* (2nd ed., pp. 161–191). New York: New York University Press.

Jones, S. R., & Abes, E. S. (2013). *Identity development of college students*. San Francisco, CA: Jossey-Bass.

Jones, S. R., & Stewart, D-L. (2016). Evolution of student development theory. In E. S. Abes (Ed.), *Critical perspectives in student development theory* (New Directions for Student Services, No. 154, pp. 17–28). San Francisco, CA: Jossey-Bass.

Jones, S. R., & Wijeyesinghe, C. L. (2011). The promises and challenges of teaching from an inter-sectional perspective: Core components and applied strategies. In M. L. Ouellett (Ed.), *An inte-grative analysis approach to diversity in the college classroom* (New Directions for Teaching and Learning, No. 125, pp. 11–20). San Francisco, CA: Jossey-Bass.

Kendall, F. E., & Wijeyesinghe, C. L. (2017). Advancing social justice work at the intersections of multiple privileged identities. In C. L. Wijeyesinghe (Ed.), *Enacting intersectionality in stu-dent affairs* (New Directions for Student Services, No. 157, pp. 91–100). San Francisco, CA: Jossey-Bass.

Knefelkamp, L., Widick, C., & Parker, C. (Eds.). (1978). *Applying new developmental findings*. (New Directions for Student Services, No. 4). San Francisco, CA: Jossey-Bass.

Lorde, A. (1983). *There is no hierarchy of oppressions*. New York, NY: Council on Interracial Books for Children.

Luft, R. E. (2009). Intersectionality and the risk of flattening difference: Gender and race logics, and the strategic use of antiracist singularity. In M. T. Berger & K. Guidroz (Eds.), *The intersectional approach: Transforming the academy through race, class, & gender* (pp. 100–117). Chapel Hill, NC: The University of North Carolina Press.

Nash, J. C. (2008). Re-thinking intersectionality. *Feminist Review, 89*(1), 1–15.

Pharr, S. (1988). *Homophobia: A weapon of sexism*. Inverness, CA: Chardon Press.

Stewart, D. L. (2008). Being all of me: Black students negotiating multiple identities. *Journal of Higher Education, 79*(2), 183–207.

Stewart, D. L. (2009). Perceptions of multiple identities among Black college students. *Journal of College Student Development, 50*(3), 253–270.

Tajfel, H. (Ed.). (1982). *Social identity and intergroup relations.* Cambridge, UK: Cambridge University Press.

Torres, V., Jones, S. R., & Renn, K. A. (2009). Identity development theories in student affairs: Origins, current status, and new approaches. *Journal of College Student Development, 50*(6), 577–596.

Warner, L. R., & Shields, S. A. (2013). The intersections of sexuality, gender, and race: Identity research at the crossroads. *Sex Roles, 68*(11–12), 803–810.

Weber, L. (1998). A conceptual framework for understanding race, class, gender, and sexuality. *Psychology of Women Quarterly, 22*(1), 13–22.

Weber, L. (2010). *Understanding race, class, gender, and sexuality: A conceptual framework* (2nd ed.). New York, NY: Oxford University Press.

Wijeyesinghe, C. L. (2012). The intersectional model of multiracial identity: Integrating multiracial identity theories and intersectional perspectives on social identity. In C. L. Wijeyesinghe & B. W. Jackson III (Eds.), *New perspectives on racial identity development* (2nd ed., pp. 81–107). New York: New York University Press.

Wijeyesinghe, C. L. (2017). Editor's notes. In C. L. Wijeyesinghe (Ed.), *Enacting intersectionality in student affairs* (New Directions for Student Services, No. 157, pp. 5–13). San Francisco, CA: Jossey-Bass.

CHAPTER TWO

Living Liminal

Conceptualizing Liminality for Undocumented Students of Color

ROSE ANN E. GUTIERREZ

Theoretical frameworks and conceptual models provide a frame in which to view, understand, and interpret the world. Frames, however, are filtered realities based on exposure to varying social and cultural contexts (Goffman, 1974). Thus, frames are social constructs that influence how people communicate their perceived or imagined realities. What if society does not have a frame to understand—better yet, *recognize* a fundamental reality—that exists regarding a specific student population within higher education institutions? This has been the case for undocumented students in higher education who have been living in the shadows until former President Barack Obama passed Deferred Action for Childhood Arrivals (DACA) in 2012 that provided a renewable two-year period of deferred action from deportation while also being able to apply for a work permit in the United States (Suárez-Orozco, Yoshikawa, Teranishi, & Suárez-Orozco, 2011; Teranishi, Suárez-Orozco, & Suárez-Orozco, 2015). Prior to DACA, the United States did not have a policy for undocumented individuals that made them feel unapologetic and unafraid to come out of the shadows. Policies such as DACA influenced a set of emerging research on the educational experiences of undocumented students beyond high school. Society, however, still possesses limited frames in understanding the nuanced experiences compounded by the layers of oppression that manifest in the daily realities for undocumented students in higher education.

Intersectionality, presented by Kimberlé Crenshaw (2016), acknowledges, examines, and dissects the intersecting layers of oppression that Black women face that have "slipped through [our societal] consciousness because there are no frames for us to see them." Crenshaw posits intersectionality to be used as a frame "[acknowledging] the ways multiple social realities, structured by the dominant norms and values of institutions, converge to produce distinct, overlapping moments and experiences of disadvantages that are often rendered invisible by the majority" (as cited in Nguyen & Nguyen, 2018, p. 150). This chapter uses intersectionality as an analytical tool to conceive the overlapping and intersecting layers of oppression, subordination, and subjugation of undocumented Students of Color in higher education. I intentionally capitalize Students of Color, Immigrants of Color, and People of Color to challenge and reject conventional grammatical norms and reclaim this population's sense of identity, knowledge, and agency. Within these overlapping states of oppression, I explore and conceptualize liminality and its positive, unintended consequences for these students.

This chapter focuses on how racism, nativism, and xenophobia manifest in the daily realities of undocumented Students of Color. I recognize that undocumented students who may not racially identify as White but phenotypically pass off as White—thus receiving advantages of Whiteness (Harris, 1993)—have challenges as well due to their undocumented status. My focus, however, is on Students of Color due to the layer of racism and racist nativism these students experience because of the historical social construction of race (Omi & Winant, 2015) in the United States. Immigrants of Color experience heightened anti-immigrant sentiments as immigrants and systemic racism as People of Color. These racist, nativist, and xenophobic attitudes are covertly expressed in practices and policies. Moreover, this chapter contributes to a new sociocultural frame—offering an additional lens to conceptualize liminality—that complicates an understanding of a population rendered invisible and oppressed by social structures. Overall, this conceptual model can untangle a complex social phenomenon like immigration, so researchers better understand educational trajectories and outcomes of undocumented youth.

This chapter is organized into four sections: (1) defining intersectionality and adapting its methodological approach within the context of developing this conceptual model; (2) providing an overview of the literature on liminality in social sciences and educational research; (3) introducing a conceptual model in examining racism, nativism, and xenophobia in the liminal status of undocumented Students of Color; and (4) discussing implications for future research in higher education.

DEFINING AND ADAPTING INTERSECTIONALITY

Intersectionality has foundational roots in Black feminist thought and pedagogy (Collins, 2009; Crenshaw, 1989). The concept provides a reference frame to examine overlapping forms of oppression and marginalization that is not captured from a single-axis analysis. Although I discuss the identities of undocumented Students of Color in regard to their race, ethnicity, immigrant identity, and citizenship status, intersectionality is not to be a "totalizing theory of identity" (Crenshaw, 1991, p. 1244). In other words, the theory is not about adding identities and comprehensively naming it intersectionality, but rather dissecting the overlaps and intersections of social categories that shape the life experiences of individuals (Núñez, 2014). Nguyen and Nguyen (2018) clarify how a single category conceals "institutional structure and culture" and these "[byproducts] of multiple social dominance" (p. 159). I adapt intersectionality to be used as an analytical tool to examine "the intersection of salient socially constructed identities and the extent to which individuals or groups are oppressed or marginalized as a result of interlocking, socially constructed systems of oppression associated with those identities" (Mitchell, 2014, para. 2).

I use Mitchell (2014), Núñez (2014), and Nguyen and Nguyen's (2018) analytical application of intersectionality in research to examine racism, nativism, and xenophobia for undocumented Students of Color as they experience liminal status. Intersectionality becomes a frame to acknowledge multiple social realities and overlapping, interlocking systems of oppression (Nguyen & Nguyen, 2018; Núñez, 2014) constructed by "dominant norms and values of institutions" (Nguyen & Nguyen, 2018, p. 150) to reproduce racial and social hierarchies. While enduring a state of liminality, this conceptual model argues for an asset-based reconceptualization of an ambiguous transitional and perpetual state of being as solely negative. Although interlocking systems of oppression in combination with socially constructed categories that have real or imagined consequences exist for undocumented Students of Color, these students, in their liminal status, develop ways of surviving and thriving in the midst of heightened anti-immigrant sentiments and public discourse (Muñoz & Espino, 2017; Muñoz & Maldonado, 2012) which change throughout the course of time in historical, political, economic, and social contexts.

LIMINALITY IN LITERATURE

In his research on tribal rituals of initiation and its processes of separation, transition, and incorporation, social anthropologist Victor Turner (1967) refers to a *liminal space* as "neither here nor there; [people] are betwixt and between the positions assigned and arrayed by law, custom, convention, and ceremony" (p. 95). Thus, liminality is a state of being in between worlds, spaces, and experiences which are often ambiguously defined. Ybema, Beech, and Ellis (2011) expound on Turner's premise by operationalizing liminality in two social contexts: (1) transitional liminality and (2) perpetual liminality. *Transitional liminality* refers to a transformational change from one identity to another. *Perpetual liminality* refers to an individual experiencing in-between occupying two identities for a prolonged time.

Due to *Plyler v. Doe* in 1982, the U.S. Supreme Court decided that K–12 public education cannot deny students access to education based on their immigration status. The court's decision has consequentially socialized undocumented students to be included socially, culturally, political, and legally. They are U.S. citizens in heart and mind (Pérez, 2012). Students' legal inclusion, however, changes when students transition into adulthood at 18 years old (*transitional liminality*) and decide to pursue higher education. Policies and practices, specifically financial aid regulations, contribute to inaccessibility and limited opportunities in higher education for undocumented students. Undocumented young adults reconcile with (social and cultural) inclusion and (political and legal) exclusion (Gonzales, 2016). Thus, they experience *perpetual liminality* in a continuous flux of belonging and not belonging. This proposed conceptual model aims to explore the liminal space—an in-between (Beech, 2011; Turner, 1969), ambiguous space where the intersection of salient socially constructed identities collide and how interlocking oppressive structures result in further marginalization of these groups (Mitchell, 2014).

Educational researchers have used the term liminality or liminal status to refer to an ambiguous transitional state for undocumented students (e.g., see Gonzales, 2016; Gonzales & Burciaga, 2018; Pérez, 2012; Suárez-Orozco et al., 2011; Teranishi et al., 2015; Torres & Wicks-Asbun, 2014). For undocumented students enrolled in higher education, liminality shows up in two ways: (1) educational institutions serving as a liminal, transitory state until they graduate and (2) their status as an undocumented student due to the ambiguity of their liminal identity. Liminality cannot be limited to solely referencing social identities and processes of transition. For undocumented Students of Color, liminality exposes interlocking systems of oppression they experience in higher education institutions that shape their life trajectory.

DISCOVERING LIGHT WITHIN DARK, COMPOUNDED FORMS OF OPPRESSION THROUGH LIMINALITY

Undocumented Students of Color are at the epicenter of this discussion due to their distinct ways in experiencing overlapping layers of oppression through racialization, criminalization, and demonization in public discourse. Intersectionality (Crenshaw, 1989, 1991) provides a tool to analyze their intersections that can unveil hidden mechanisms operating in the reproduction of inequities in society. An intersectional lens clarifies what has intentionally been obscured by those in power who want to stay in power. This proposed model recognizes the interlocking systems of oppression based on nativist, racist, and xenophobic ideologies which have material consequences that insidiously discriminate through institutional policies and practices. I draw on Pérez Huber and colleagues' (2008) theoretical framework on racist nativism, Kim and Sundstrom's (2014) conceptual analysis on xenophobia and racism, and Higham's (1955) work in nativism in conjunction with Sundstrom's (2013) philosophical analysis of xenophobia. While important to distinguish the differences between racism, nativism, and xenophobia, they cannot be understood in isolation (Kim & Sundstrom, 2014). At the intersection of their work is a frame to examine how xenophobia is rooted in racist nativist sentiments and disguises racism, anti-Black discourse, and Islamophobia through nationalism. Race is entangled and at the epicenter of this tripartite overlap due to its social construction in the United States.

Higham (1955) defines nativism as an "intense opposition to an internal minority on the grounds of its foreign connection" and "influence originating abroad threaten[s] the very life of the nation from within" (p. 4). Golash-Boza (2015) defines racism as having two parts: an ideology and its practices. Entrenched in the ideology is that "races are populations of people whose physical differences are linked to significant cultural and social differences and that these innate hierarchical differences can be measured and judged" (Golash-Boza, 2015, p. 131), and practices consist of micro- and macro-level "[subordination] of races believed to be inferior" (Golash-Boza, 2015, p. 131). Xenophobia derives from Greek origins; xenos meaning "stranger" or "foreigner," and phobos meaning "fear." Kim and Sundstrom (2014) expand upon this definition of fearing strangers or foreigners and define xenophobia as civic ostracism, an "idea associated with a distinct set of attitudes, beliefs, and affects that are about national inclusion and exclusion" (p. 30). All definitions encompass an ideology separating groups based on presumed inferiority, foreignness, and nativity in a society to justify practices that exclude, ostracize, and subordinate. When used separately or in pairs, these ideologies have the ability to shelter one form of oppression. For example, Islamophobia is a form of xenophobia but has been justified through nationalism (i.e., protecting a national identity). Therefore, prejudice against immigrants is disguised as patriotism, so if discrimination happens to Immigrants of Color who also identify as Arab, Muslim, or Sikh, ostracization through nativist and xenophobic reasoning are justified but conceals racism. Scholars have produced literature connecting concepts in pairs and analyzing their ideological weight and meaning, yet a conceptual model identifying the overlap and intersections between the three concepts remain nonexistent.

For undocumented Students of Color, intersectionality acts as a reference frame to acknowledge their multiple social realities reproduced by socially constructed categories and unveil overlapping systems of oppression in regard to racism, nativism, and xenophobia (see Figure 2.1). Their undocumented status adds a complicated layer in their reality within a liminal state of being.

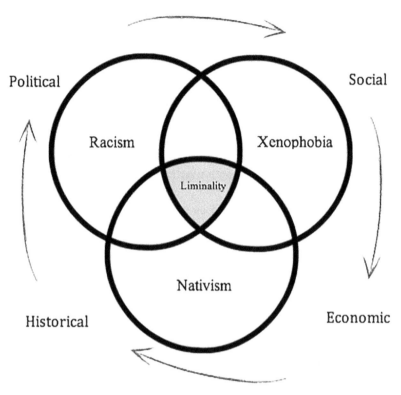

Figure 2.1. Conceiving a Frame of Liminality Interlaced in Racism, Nativism, and Xenophobia. Source: Author.

The concept of liminality requires reframing since it has been traditionally defined in literature as an ambiguous, in-between state and often perceived in negative terms due to an association with fear and uncertainty. The state of being liminal for undocumented Students of Color can also function as a source of growth, sustenance, and building block for resilience. Occupying and living in multiple worlds where an undefined, ambiguous space exists cultivates divergent thinking (Anzaldúa, 1999) to maneuver through and around systemic and systematic barriers in this liminal space. In experiencing liminality, undocumented Students of Color tap into a new consciousness (Anzaldúa, 1999) that enriches their creativity, nurtures their sustenance, and builds their resilience. For example, undocumented students can also be in mixed-status families where they develop and prepare a contingency plan if government authorities imprison or deport family members. This type of pedagogical strategy of survival is a part of parental racial-ethnic socialization of families with members with undocumented statuses (Suárez-Orozco, Abo-Zena, & Marks, 2015). In terms of educational institutions, a study by Pérez (2012) of undocumented Latinx students in higher education revealed that educational institutions serve as a means of hope and reason for them to survive despite barriers. Muñoz and Maldonano (2012) found that undocumented Mexicana students develop positive self-identities fueling their persistence through college despite oppressive discourses of race, gender, and class in the classroom and contemporary United States. According to Suárez-Orozco (2015), undocumented youth "actively attempt to construct an identity that empowers them to believe in their self-worth" (p. 26) rather than be confined and defined by their undocumented and liminal status. Liminality forces undocumented Students of Color to develop strategies of survival within oppressive structures, like higher education institutions, where their networks share resources with one another; sharpen their ability to assess people and situations (i.e., who to trust and disclose information); and learn ways to cope with stigma, frustration, fear, and anxiety (Suárez-Orozco, 2015).

In addition to experiencing race and racism due to phenotypical characteristics society attributed to a particular racial category, immigrants can be characterized by accent, generation status, and citizenship status. Through an intersectional lens, these characteristics offer a way for researchers to critically examine how Immigrants of Color continue to be racialized, criminalized, and demonized with a compounded layer of being undocumented.

IMPLICATIONS

Researchers need an analytical nexus to explicitly connect racism, immigration, and higher education. Historically, the literature on these topics exists in separate vacuums. Immigration literature has focused on assimilation theories and perspectives based on the experiences of White Europeans which neglect the racial impact for Immigrants of Color when they are encouraged to assimilate in the United States (Sáenz & Douglas, 2015). Moreover, immigration studies have traditionally focused on demographic aspects of immigration and has not incorporated social processes into the analysis (e.g., social construction of race and citizenship; Sanchez & Romero, 2010). The exclusion of race in immigration literature becomes problematic as Immigrants of Color experience overlapping layers of subordination and subjugation through their racialized and criminalized experiences in the United States. Thus, they become targets in institutionalized forms of violence (e.g., raids, midnight searches, city ordinances, and changes to social services legislation; Sanchez & Romero, 2010).

Institutionalized forms of discrimination are embedded within policies and practices of institutions and act as hidden mechanisms that maintain racial and social hierarchies. Johnson (2009) recommends scrutinizing immigration law and connecting it to race and immigration scholarship—as it has not been done enough—because historically, it has been designed and continues to operate to prevent poor and Noncitizens of Color from immigrating to and from the United States. There is a necessity in explicitly connecting racism, nativism, and xenophobia in educational research to illuminate the ways undocumented Students of Color experience systemic and systematic oppression in our educational structures (Fan, 1997; Garcia, 1995; Gordon & Lenhardt, 2007; Johnson, 2000, 2009, 2011; Martínez, 2012; Romero, 2006, 2008; Sáenz & Douglas, 2015; Sanchez & Romero, 2010). As the immigrant population in the United States continue to be non-Europeans and are primarily Immigrants of Color, intersectionality provides a promising reference frame to explore, analyze, and identify how historically marginalized groups continue to be oppressed in our institutional structures like higher education.

Future research should include exploring the experiences of Black immigrants, who continue to be an increasing population in the United States in recent years. Primarily, immigration research and discourse has focused on the experiences of Latinx and Asian populations, and these conversations need to expand to immigrants from African, Caribbean, and Middle Eastern countries. While the experiential knowledge of Immigrants of Color includes pedagogies of migration (Benavides Lopez, 2016), this research comes from Chicanx and Latinx immigrants. More research needs to be conducted to understand the nuanced ways undocumented Students of Color know and learn pedagogical strategies to survive and thrive in hostile sociopolitical contexts where they are racialized, criminalized, and demonized in addition to navigating higher educational spaces. This conceptual model leads back to the theoretical realm of research where researchers can continue to ask questions that have not yet been asked to shed light on the unique, nuanced experiences of undocumented Students of Color to provide them the necessary support in all facets of life.

Cherrie Moraga (2015) wrote, "It is in the nightmare that the dream is found" (p. 34) when interpreting one of Audre Lorde's poems. When using intersectionality to examine the interlocking systems of oppression for undocumented Students of Color and having a frame to conceive their liminal space, researchers can begin to untangle complex social phenomenon to understand educational trajectories and outcomes of immigrant youth situated within a continuum of historical, political, economic, and social contexts. Furthermore, frames can uncover what has been rendered invisible. Reframing concepts illuminate connections where frames intersect and align (Snow & Benford, 1988) to transform society and reimagine future possibilities. Researchers need to continue to theorize—even in the absence of information—by retooling traditional methodologies and reconceptualizing concepts in research to expand frames of reference. Given the recent sociopolitical climate in the United States, research needs to acknowledge historical and social connections—bounded by a common thread that sustains White supremacist ideology and practices. This chapter uses intersectionality to analyze interlocking systems of oppression for undocumented Students of Color that can unveil hidden mechanisms operating in the reproduction of inequities. In doing so, society can continue to untangle complex social phenomenon and contribute to an understanding of issues like immigration and globalization. Thus, society can transcend thinking beyond disciplinary boundaries to transform future research, policy, and practice in higher education for *all* students.

REFERENCES

Anzaldúa, G. (1999). *Borderlands: La frontera* (2nd ed.). San Francisco, CA: Aunt Lute.

Beech, N. (2011). Liminality and the practices of identity construction. *Human Relations, 64*(2), 285–302.

Benavides Lopez, C. (2016). Lessons from the educational borderlands: Documenting the pedagogies of migration of Chicana/o, Latina/o undocumented immigrant students and households. *Association of Mexican American Educators Journal, 10*(1), 80–106.

Collins, P. H. (2009). *Black feminist thought: Knowledge, consciousness, and the politics of empowerment.* New York, NY: Routledge.

Crenshaw, K. (1989). Demarginalizing the intersection of race and sex: A black feminist critique of antidiscrimination doctrine, feminist theory and antiracist politics. *University of Chicago Legal Forum, 1989*(8), 139–167.

Crenshaw, K. (1991). Mapping the margins: Intersectionality, identity politics, and violence against women of Color. *Stanford Law Review, 43*(6), 1241–1299.

Crenshaw, K. (2016, October). *The urgency of intersectionality* [video file]. Retrieved from https://www.ted.com/talks/kimberle_crenshaw_the_urgency_of_intersectionality

Dao, L. T. (2017). Out and Asian: How Undocu/DACAmented Asian Americans and Pacific Islander youth navigate dual liminality in the immigrant rights movement. *Societies, 7*(17), 1–15.

Fan, S. S.-W. (1997). Immigration law and the promise of critical race theory: Opening the academy to the voices of aliens and immigrants. *Columbia Law Review, 97*(4), 1202–1240.

Garcia, R. J. (1995). Critical race theory and proposition 187: The racial politics of immigration law. *Chicano-Latino Law Review, 17*(118), 118–154.

Goffman, E. (1974). *Frame analysis: An essay on the organization of experience.* New York, NY: Harper Torchbooks Year.

Golash-Boza, T. (2016). A critical and comprehensive sociological theory of race and racism. *Sociology of Race and Ethnicity, 2*(2), 129–141.

Gonzales, R. G. (2016). *Lives in limbo: Undocumented and coming of age in America.* Oakland: University of California Press.

Gonzales, R. G., & Burciaga, E. M. (2018). Segmented pathways of illegality: Reconciling the coexistence of master and auxiliary statuses in the experiences of 1.5-generation undocumented young adults. *Ethnicities, 18*(2), 178–191.

Gordon, J., & Lenhardt, R. A. (2007). Citizenship talk: Bridging the gap between immigration and the race perspectives. *Fordham Law Review, 75*(5), 2493–2519.

Harris, C. I. (1993). Whiteness as property. *Harvard Law Review, 106*(8), 1707–1791.

Higham, J. (1955). *Strangers in the land: Patterns of American nativism 1860–1925.* New Brunswick, NJ: Rutgers University Press.

Johnson, K. R. (2000). Race matters: Immigration law and policy scholarship, law in the ivory tower, and the legal indifference of the race critique. *University of Illinois Law Review, 2000*(2), 525–558.

Johnson, K. R. (2009). The intersection of race and class in U.S. immigration law and enforcement. *Law and Contemporary Problems, 72*(1), 1–35.

Johnson, K. R. (2011). Race and the immigration laws: The need for critical inquiry. In F. Valdes, J. M. Culp, & A. P. Harris (Eds.), *Crossroads, directions, and a new critical race theory* (pp. 187–198). Philadelphia, PA: Temple University Press.

Kim, D. H., & Sundstrom, R. R. (2014). Xenophobia and racism. *Critical Philosophy of Race, 2*(1), 20–45.

Martínez, G. A. (2012). Arizona, immigration, and Latinos: The epistemology of Whiteness, the geography of race, interest convergence, and the view from the perspective of critical theory. *Arizona State Law Journal, 44*, 175–211.

Mitchell, D., Jr. (2014, November 21). Intersectionality to social justice = theory to practice [Web log post]. Retrieved from https://www.naspa.org/constituent-groups/posts/projectintersections-post-1

Moraga, C. (2015). La güera. In C. Moraga & G. Anzaldúa (Eds.), *This bridge called my back: Writings by radical women of Color* (4th ed., pp. 22–29). Albany: State University of New York Press.

Muñoz, S. M., & Espino, M. M. (2017). The freedom to learn: The voices and experiences of undocumented students at Freedom University. *The Review of Higher Education, 40*(4), 533–555.

Muñoz, S. M., & Maldonado, M. M. (2012). Counterstories of college persistence for undocumented Mexicana students: Navigating race, class, gender, and legal status. *International Journal of Qualitative Studies in Education, 25*(3), 293–315.

Nguyen, T-H., & Nguyen, B. M. D. (2018). Is the "first-generation student" term useful for understanding inequality? The role of intersectionality in illuminating the implications of an accepted—yet unchallenged—term. *Review of Research in Education, 42*, 146–176.

Núñez, A. M. (2014). Employing multilevel intersectionality in educational research: Latino identities, contexts, and college access. *Educational Researcher, 43*(2), 85–92.

Omi, M., & Winant, H. (2015). *Racial formation in the United States* (3rd ed.). New York, NY: Routledge.

Pérez, W. (2012). *Americans by heart: Undocumented Latino students and the promise of higher education.* New York, NY: Teachers College Press.

Pérez Huber, L., Benavides Lopez, C., Malagon, M. C., Velez, V., & Solórzano, D. G. (2008). Getting beyond the "symptom," acknowledging the "disease": Theorizing racist nativism. *Contemporary Justice Review, 11*(1), 39–51.

Romero, M. (2006). Racial profiling and immigration law enforcement: Rounding up of usual suspects in the Latino community. *Critical Sociology, 32*(2–3), 447–473.

Romero, M. (2008). Crossing the immigration and race border: A critical race theory approach to immigration studies. *Contemporary Justice Review, 11*(1), 23–37.

Sáenz, R., & Douglas, K. M. (2015). A call for the racialization of immigration studies: On the transition of ethnic immigrants to racialized immigrants. *Sociology of Race and Ethnicity, 1*(1), 166–180.

Sanchez, G., & Romero, M. (2010). Critical race theory in the US sociology of immigration. *Sociology Compass, 4*(9), 779–788.

Snow, D. A., & Benford, R. D. (1988). Ideology, frame resonance, and participant mobilization. *International Social Movement Research, 1*(1), 197–217.

Suárez-Orozco, C., Abo-Zena, M. M., & Marks, A. K. (Eds.). (2015). *Transitions: The development of children of immigrants*. New York: New York University Press.

Suárez-Orozco, C., Yoshikawa, H., Teranishi, R. T., & Suárez-Orozco, M. M. (2011). Growing up in the shadows: The developmental implications of unauthorized status. *Harvard Educational Review, 81*(3), 438–472.

Sundstrom, R. R. (2013). Sheltering xenophobia. *Critical Philosophy of Race, 1*(1), 68–85.

Teranishi, R. T., Suárez-Orozco, C., & Suárez-Orozco, M. (2015). *In the shadows of the ivory tower: Undocumented undergraduates and the liminal state of immigration reform*. Los Angeles, CA: The Institute for Immigration, Globalization, and Education.

Torres, R. M., & Wicks-Asbun, M. (2014). Undocumented students' narratives of liminal citizenship: High aspirations, exclusion, and "in-between" identities. *The Professional Geographer, 66*(2), 195–204.

Turner, V. (1967). *The forest of symbols*. Ithaca, NY: Cornell University Press.

Ybema, S., Beech, N., & Ellis, N. (2011). Transitional and perpetual liminality: An identity practice perspective. *Anthropology Southern Africa, 23*(1–2), 21–29.

CHAPTER THREE

Intersectionality

A Legacy from Critical Legal Studies and Critical Race Theory

ALLISON DANIEL ANDERS AND JAMES M. DeVITA

Activists, scholars, and researchers in education studies (Bettie, 2003; Patel, 2013), higher education (Abes, Jones, & McEwen, 2007; Mitchell & Means, 2014; Strayhorn, Blakewood, & DeVita, 2008, 2010), human rights (Raj, Bunch, & Nazombe, 2002), political science (Berger, 2004), and women's studies (Collins, 2008; Davis, 1983; Lorde, 1984) have studied experience at the intersection of multiple identities and have argued for understandings and practices that acknowledge them. In this chapter, we argue that studying the legacies of critical legal studies, critical race theory, and, in particular, *intersectionality* (Crenshaw, 1991a, p. 58), a term first used by Kimberlé Crenshaw, can guide research about multiple targeted identities in productive ways. Crenshaw (1991b), an African American Woman, legal scholar, and critical race theorist, argued that dominant social patterns and systemic inequities affect the lived experience of groups and individuals who embody multiple targeted identities and that such patterns and inequities often produce "intersectional disempowerment" (p. 1245). Crenshaw's conceptions of intersectionality deepen opportunities for activists, scholars, and researchers in higher education who are committed to studying racial and social justice, to theorize about experience at the intersection of multiple targeted identities and to strategize against dominant social patterns and systemic inequity.

Not only because Crenshaw (1991a) emphasized the importance of "the experiences and concerns of Black women" (p. 58), but also because too often White scholars committed to racial and social justice "tokenize" (Thompson, 2003, p. 13) the work produced by scholars of Color, we trace intersectionality to its first use by Crenshaw and her applications.[1] Our aims are to situate the relevancy of intersectionality racially, historically, and politically, and to encourage White activists, scholars, and researchers interested in ideas produced by scholars of Color to study the context of the work produced by scholars of Color before applying it to their own. Thompson (2003) warned that, "taking the work of people of Color seriously requires studying their projects, not just quoting the occasional point that coincides with what we were going to say anyway" (p. 13). Personally, as White scholars, applying Crenshaw's ideas means, too, representing the historical and political context from which she worked and celebrating the lived experiences she and her colleagues endured as they confronted predominantly White law schools, White colleagues, and White, conventional legal scholarship.

This chapter begins with introductions to the history, politics, and context of critical legal studies (CLS). Specifically, we address Crenshaw's critique of neoconservative influence on antidiscrimination law and the ways her critique informed her ideas about intersectionality and the field of critical race theory (CRT). We follow these sections with Crenshaw's (1991b) work on structural, political, and representational intersectionality. Lastly, we offer as example our application of Crenshaw's ideas to DeVita's (2010) study of Black, gay men in higher education. Ultimately, we argue that the application of Crenshaw's concept of intersectionality requires understandings of its historical and political context and offers activists, scholars, and researchers ways to critique the reproduction of power in the everyday subjugation of multiple targeted identities (Anders, DeVita, & Oliver, 2012; DeVita & Anders, 2014). In doing so, we invite readers to discern between scholarship that reflects Crenshaw's conception of intersectionality and scholarship that represents intersections of identity.

The privilege that Whiteness provides in "white supremacist capitalist patriarchy" (hooks, 1992), precludes any claim we (Anders & DeVita) might make about intersectionality and our own identities. Although Crenshaw did not exclude the possible application of intersectionality to analyze intersections of targeted and privileged identities (for example, the lived experiences of White women in higher education or White gay men in higher education), we argue that multiple targeted identities must remain prominent and centered in applications of intersectionality. As White folks, using intersectionality to theorize about our own lives would mean altering Crenshaw's arguments about multiple subordinations in order to fit our own needs. Other language and concepts exist for us to refer to our experiences. For example, "intersections of identity" reflects the general concept without misappropriating or co-opting the history and politics of Crenshaw's conceptions or applications of her term. Our approach is not prescriptive, as we believe each individual scholar must face the burden of application (DeVita & Anders, 2014). For us, keeping multiple targeted identities prominent and centered in empirical studies that utilize Crenshaw's work is what is important. We do not suggest that scholars count the number of multiple targeted identities to evaluate the applicability of Crenshaw's work but instead clarify the ways that multiple targeted identities remain prominent and centered in their analyses.

CRITICAL LEGAL STUDIES

According to Crenshaw, Gotanda, Peller, and Thomas (1995), in the 1970s civil rights lawyers faced "attacks on the limited victories they had only just achieved in the prior decade, particularly with respect to affirmative action and legal requirements for the kinds of evidence required to prove illicit discrimination" (p. xvii). During the same time, in law schools across the United States, groups of predominantly White, neo-Marxist scholars began to organize with colleagues, teachers, and practitioners to challenge presuppositions of legal doctrine and critique the ways it legitimated and reproduced systemic inequities. Critical legal studies scholars argued that dominant ideologies affect the construction of legal doctrine. Specifically, critical legal studies scholars analyzed legal doctrine "to reveal both its internal inconsistencies (generally by exposing the incoherence of legal arguments) and its external consistencies (often by laying bare the inherently paradoxical and political worldviews embedded within legal doctrine)" (Crenshaw, 1995, p. 108). CLS scholars explicated the ideology and politics of court decisions rendered in the name of legal doctrine. Together with a network of "New Left activists, ex-counterculturalists and other varieties of oppositionists in law schools" (Crenshaw et al., 1995, p. xvii), critical legal studies scholars encouraged students and left-leaning faculty to produce scholarship that confronted the myths of apolitical legal doctrine and a neutral legal system. Such analyses provided opportunities for scholars to identify ways that the practice of law creates, legitimates, and reproduces "an unjust social order" (Crenshaw et al., 1995, p. xviii).

For many CLS scholars, Antonio Gramsci's (1992) work on hegemony elucidated the enduring power of the law, the limits of rights-based approaches in reform movements, and the dominance of an economic system that continued to exploit laborers. As do other institutions of the state, the legal system legitimates and reproduces hegemonic relationships of power. Belief in the myth of an apolitical and neutral system of law contributes to the system's reproduction (Crenshaw, 1995; Kairys, 1998). Both the dominant and the dominated reify the law's centrality and the order of the state by consenting to the power of the law and to their own subjugation to it. Critical legal scholars criticized "mainstream legal ideology for its tendency to portray American society as basically fair, and thereby to legitimate the oppressive policies that have been directed toward racial minorities" (Crenshaw, 1995, p. 110). They established the Conference on Critical Legal Studies and challenged the rising neoconservative rhetoric of equal opportunity in the 1970s.

Neoconservative agendas touted equal process and equality of opportunity arguments. Then and now, neoconservatives and many neoliberals argue that equal process, or access to equal protection under the law, addresses the axis of economic and racial inequity in the United States. Neoconservatives maintain that equal process is a sufficient doctrine; moreover, they contend that, "equal process is completely unrelated to equal results" (Crenshaw, 1995, p. 105). Decoupling equal process from equal process outcomes allows neoconservatives to ignore evidence of disparity along economic and racial axes, to reproduce the myth of color blindness, and to de-legitimate claims of discrimination based on race.

Crenshaw (1995) confronted the neoconservative rhetoric and argued that if color-blind policies were "the only legitimate and effective means of ensuring a racially equitable society, one would have to assume not only that there is only one 'proper role' for law but also that such a racially equitable society already exists" (p. 105). As the United States fails to reflect such histories, Crenshaw critiqued both the de-coupling of equal process from equal process outcomes and the myth of color blindness:

> Society's adoption of the ambivalent rhetoric of equal opportunity law has made it that much more difficult for black people to name their reality. There is no longer a perpetrator, a clearly identifiable discriminator. Company Z can be an equal opportunity employer even though Company Z has no blacks or any other minorities in its employ. Practically speaking, all companies can now be equal opportunity employers by proclamation alone. Society has embraced the rhetoric of equal opportunity without fulfilling its promise. (pp. 106–107)

According to Crenshaw "only in such a society, where all other social functions operate in a nondiscriminatory way, would equality of process constitute equality of opportunity" (p. 106). In a society where groups of people have been treated differently, as is the case of the United States, advocates for the idea of color blindness deny the histories of exploitation, oppression, and disenfranchisement and their effects. Moreover, they silence interpretations of the world that center the relationship of ontology to epistemology. That is to say, the ways one is located and positioned in the world and the ways one is classed, gendered, and raced, affect one's way of experiencing and knowing the world (Butler, 1999; Crenshaw, 1991b; Collins, 2008; Freire, 2000; hooks, 1992; Noblit, 1999; Noddings, 1992; Scott, 1999). Crenshaw signified Black experience as a meaningful and tactical response to neoconservative strategies designed to disrupt advocacy for economic and racial justice:

> The lasting harm must be measured by the extent to which limited gains hamper efforts of African-Americans to name their reality and to remain capable of engaging in collective action in the future ... If the civil rights constituency allows its own political consciousness to be completely replaced by the ambiguous discourse of antidiscrimination law, it will be difficult for this constituency to defend its genuine interests against those whose interests

are supported by opposing visions that also employ the same discourse. The struggle, it seems, is to maintain a contextualized, specified worldview that reflects the experience of blacks. The question remains whether engaging in legal reform precludes this possibility. (p. 107)

Crenshaw urged African Americans to name their own realities in order to remain "capable of engaging in collective action" (p. 107). The challenge, she wrote, would be "to maintain a contextualized, specified worldview that reflects the experience of blacks" (p. 107). Crenshaw's critiques of neoconservative influence on interpretations of antidiscrimination law and her advocacy for the centrality of Black experiences in political action historicize her work on intersectionality. Ultimately, both the critiques she provides and the emphasis she places on experiences and identities in African American communities inform the development of CRT.

CRITICAL RACE THEORY

According to Crenshaw et al. (1995), although CLS scholars disrupted conventional thought and teaching in many law schools through analyses of hegemony in legal doctrine, questions of racial power were not part of the dominant discourse in CLS. The absence of analysis regarding institutionalized racism and experiences of coercion and threat by targeted groups and individuals remained unexamined (Crenshaw, 1995; Delgado & Stefancic, 2001). In the 1970s, "race crits" (Crenshaw et al., 1995, p. xxii) began discussing racial power within CLS and the historic dismissal of rights-based arguments in CLS. Although race crits agreed that rights discourse was indeterminate, many believed that a "rights discourse held a social and transformative value in the context of racial subordination that transcended the narrower question of whether reliance on rights could alone bring about any determinate results" (Crenshaw et al., 1995, p. xxiii). As analyses of racial power expanded in CLS the differences between CLS and analyses emphasizing contexts of race and racism eventually produced a body of scholarship that reflected what scholars think of now as critical race theory.

CRT was named such in order to specifically locate it at the intersection of critical theory, race, racism, and the law. Activists and scholars in the CRT movement sought

> to understand how a regime of white supremacy and its subordination of people of Color have been created and maintained in America, and, in particular, to examine the relationship between that social structure and the professed ideals such as "the rule of law" and "equal protection." (Crenshaw et al., 1995, p. xiii)

They sought not merely to "understand the vexed bond between law and racial power but to *change* it" (Crenshaw et al., 1995, p. xiii). In contrast to positions in the civil rights movement, many of which embraced incrementalism, critical race theorists questioned "the very foundations of the liberal order, including equality theory, legal reasoning, Enlightenment rationalism, and neutral principles of constitutional law" (Delgado & Stefancic, 2001, p. 3).

According to Delgado and Stefancic (2001), CRT scholars argue that, "racism is ordinary, not aberrational" (p. 7) and the history of White supremacy and White dominance in the United States creates a racial hierarchy that serves the social and material purposes of Whites. CRT scholars argue that White elites acquiesce to change for racial justice only when the change produces benefit for them. CRT scholars studying this process named the response of White elites to targeted groups: interest convergence.

In an ongoing debate among CRT scholars, racial realists argue that racism is permanent; racial idealists do not. Many racial realists analyze issues of structural determinism. Some study the reproduction of legal precedent, others the diversity and at times conflict of Black interests in civil rights cases. Others analyze relationships of power always already present in everyday and judiciary contexts and critique the notion that empathy will generate equity amongst competing narratives of reality. Still others study the relationship between court decisions and the maintenance of the racial hierarchy in the status quo. Many CRT scholars critique liberalism, because neoconservative and neoliberal agendas that perpetuate the rhetoric of color blindness limit redress, and therefore, allow condemnation of only the most "egregious racial harms" (Delgado & Stefancic, 2001, p. 22). Relatedly, CRT scholars critique the ways rights-based tactics failed to produce substantive change. Other CRT scholars analyze the way "society invents, manipulates, or retires when convenient" (Delgado & Stefancic, 2001, p. 7) particular constructions of race. Many CRT scholars study ways race is socially constructed and deployed and differential racialization, or the ways "dominant society racializes different minority groups at different times in response to shifting needs such as the labor market" (Delgado & Stefancic, 2001, p. 8).

Related to differential racialization is Crenshaw's (1991a, 1991b) concept of intersectionality. Crenshaw's commitment to strategies for collective action amidst neoconservative and often neoliberal policymaking underscores the importance of analyses at the intersections of lived experience, identity politics, and context. The analysis and representation of lived experience of targeted groups and individuals generate evidence against a majoritarian history of the United States. CRT scholars, many of whom are racial realists, reexamine "America's historical record," in order to confront and replace "comforting majoritarian interpretations of events with ones that square more accurately with minorities' experiences" (Delgado and Stefancic, 2001, p. 30). Celebrating and encouraging ontological and epistemological understandings of race and racism from the perspectives of targeted people, many CRT scholars pursue the production of counternarratives and legal storytelling. Analyzing the ways dominant groups, in this case elite Whites in the United States, position groups of people racially, culturally, and economically for their own purposes allows targeted groups to build collective action and deploy tactics against the prevailing economic and social order.

INTERSECTIONALITY

Kimberlé Crenshaw (1991a, 1991b) is recognized as the first scholar to name and theorize the term *intersectionality*. She used intersectionality to conceptualize the intersections of race and gender in her analyses of antidiscrimination in legal cases, for example, cases where Black women and non-English-speaking immigrant women of Color were plaintiffs. Crenshaw criticized the courts for forcing Black women and non-English-speaking immigrant women of Color to articulate discrimination along only one category of identity. Crenshaw argued that "the intersectional experience is greater than the sum of racism and sexism" and that "any analysis that does not take intersectionality into account cannot sufficiently address the particular manner in which Black women are subordinated" (p. 58). The experience of racism and sexism is neither discrete nor summative for women of Color. Women of Color do not experience racism in the same ways that men of Color do, nor do they experience sexism in the same ways that White women do. Procedurally, the courts denied the existence of everyday lived experience at the intersection of multiple targeted identities. Antidiscrimination law failed to account for the experiences of women of Color.

In *Mapping the Margins*, Crenshaw (1991b) conceptualized structural intersectionality, political intersectionality, and representational intersectionality. To illustrate structural intersectionality, Crenshaw represented the issue of domestic violence and analyzed the issues of gender and race at the intersections of employment and housing, access and relationships to court advocates, and English as the language of the court in domestic violence cases. She examined the qualitative differences between women who have racial, economic, and linguistic privilege, and those who do not.

Crenshaw's (1991b) work on political intersectionality assessed the ways identity politics affect experiences of and participation by women of Color in collective action. Crenshaw demonstrated political intersectionality by analyzing the ways dominant political agendas and social movements separate the politics of women of Color into two (minimally) different subordinated groups: people of Color in pursuit of racial equity and women in pursuit of gender equity. Because collective action for antiracist practice and policy is central to Crenshaw's work, finding ways to analyze and navigate productively identity politics across multiple targeted identities is paramount.

As an analytical tool, representational intersectionality demands the inclusion of multiple targeted identities and the discourses produced around and through them when the representation occurs of a single targeted identity. Crenshaw (1991b) warned: "when one discourse fails to acknowledge the significance of the other, the power relations each attempts to challenge are strengthened" (p. 1282). Representational intersectionality offers scholars a way to analyze the absences between the everyday experience of multiple targeted identities and the ways media produce representations of women of Color for consumption.

Structural Intersectionality and LGBTQ Populations in Higher Education

Crenshaw's (1991b) structural intersectionality emphasized the ways that the everyday discourses, policies, and practices of an institution target the experiences of women of Color and immigrant women differently than those of a dominant group, in this case, White women. In higher education, ideally LGBTQ (Lesbian, gay, bisexual, transgender, and queer) individuals of Color will encounter systems of support that celebrate their identities. However, too often these institutions fail to support students holistically. For example, according to Strayhorn, Blakewood, and DeVita (2008, 2010), many college campuses develop cultural centers to provide support for targeted students. Typically, these centers reflect only one axis of identity (e.g., Black cultural centers and LGBTQ centers). Even on campuses where collaboration is encouraged, supported, and realized, these centers represent the ways campuses have been structured to recognize the issues faced by students from specific targeted groups at the expense of individuals who must navigate multiple targeted identities. The resources, though important, are inadequate when students who embody and enact multiple targeted identities must negotiate everyday campus politics and potential discrimination.

Indeed, research on the experiences of Black gay males at predominantly White institutions (PWI) conducted by Strayhorn et al. (2008, 2010) found that Black gay males seldom felt comfortable in either of the spaces established to support their identity affiliations: a Black cultural center and a LGBTQ center. Black gay male undergraduates at PWIs frequently experienced homophobia in the Black cultural center and racism in the LGBTQ center. Experiences with discrimination in both places forced them to choose the least oppressive space. The development of separate resource centers is directly linked to tensions associated with a lack of systemic support for a particular group (i.e., Black or LGBTQ), thus it should not be surprising that the distance established between physical spaces produced equally disparate social and political climates (Bentley Historical Society, 2007). Individuals who identify as non-White and LGBTQ are forced to endure targeting of their identities by institutional structures in ways individuals who identify as White and LGBTQ or non-White and straight do not.

On many campuses, it is not feasible to alter the physical spaces (i.e., distinct cultural centers) that have been established. Thus, programming and other initiatives must provide support to address structural intersectionality. Educational programming focused on LGBTQ topics (e.g., safe zones, safe spaces) should be inclusive of discussions that examine the intersections of LGBTQ identities with other targeted identities (e.g., race/ethnicity, socioeconomic status). The failure to include other axes of identity reifies the whitewashing of LGBTQ identities and further marginalizes racial identities.

Additionally, a common feature of educational programs is the issuance of a card or sign, which indicates that the individual has completed the training and is a "safe resource" for LGBTQ people (Consortium, 2013). This sign becomes a public proclamation that an individual is an LGBTQ ally, presumably with the ability to support all LGBTQ individuals, including those with multiple targeted identities. However, programs that reflect the neoconservative myth of color blindness ignore the explicit experiences and needs of non-White LGBTQ individuals and affirm a White normative view of LGBTQ topics on campus. Such programs re-center White privilege and limit the potential support for LGBTQ individuals of Color.

Political Intersectionality and LGBTQ Populations in Higher Education

Paying close attention to political intersectionality may improve communication and resources in higher education and open new spaces for collective action. For example, the policies and initiatives supported by LGBTQ groups are whitewashed often by a lack of attention to the experiences and needs of non-White LGBTQ individuals (Teunis, 2007; Ward, 2008). Ward's (2008) research on an LGBTQ community center revealed numerous practices that aligned with White normative culture. The center "was sustained by its mainstream and corporate approach to diversity" (p. 582). Similarly, Teunis (2007) characterized various LGBTQ organizations' foci on marriage equality and military service as political agenda items that primarily privileged White, gay individuals. Teunis described the absence of attention to the intersections of identity in the pursuit of marriage equality this way:

> In the struggle for marriage equality, spokespersons are very generally white women and men who display little or no concern for critical political issues that face gays and Lesbians of colour. That these struggles promote whiteness is not due to the inherent nature of the issues, but rather due to the manner in which they are promoted and in which they usurp all other concerns that drive the community. (p. 268)

Similar tensions face LGBTQ cultural centers on college campuses. First, although centers exist on over 200 campuses across the United States and Canada

(Consortium, 2013), only three such centers exist at Historically Black Colleges and Universities (HBCUs; Human Rights Campaign, 2013). The prevalence of centers at PWIs suggests that services and support for LGBTQ individuals, educational programming for heterosexual individuals, and LGBTQ-inclusive programs for all individuals are more likely to be present at PWIs, and therefore, more likely to reflect policy and practice generated in and reproduced by White normative culture.

While a meaningful campus resource, the creation of a center based along a single axis of identity at a PWI likely primes White potential L, G, B, T, or Q identified-students for leadership roles. As Teunis' (2007) and Ward's (2008) findings suggest, White LGBTQ leadership must actively center experiences of LGBTQ people of Color in order to produce an inclusive platform in agenda setting. Institutional inclusion and inclusive organizing are paramount as Crenshaw (1995) wrote:

> The struggle for blacks, like that of all subordinated groups, is a struggle for inclusion, an attempt to manipulate the elements of the dominant ideology in order to transform the experience of domination. It is a struggle to create a new status quo through the ideological and political tools that are available. (p. 119)

An intersectional approach to support individuals with multiple, targeted identities would include an examination of the ways in which different identity groups could align resources and energies to benefit from a common goal. "Alliance means action" is one theme that we (Anders & DeVita) have produced from in vivo coding and pattern coding (Saldaña, 2011) from an interview study with LGTQ-identified faculty, staff, and students in higher education. Participants articulated a distinction between heterosexual individuals, who only identify as an "ally" through the posting of a safe zone or safe space placard, and those who engage in activities, events, and policy changes that support LGBTQ communities. One participant, a White male faculty member who identified as gay, discussed his frustration with passive "allies," arguing that shared ideology and active political engagement was the tactic LGBTQ communities and their allies needed to use. As he explained: "We need to join in what is called ideology politics. Joining with people of like minds, of like visions of the world, from different identity groups." He and other participants discussed the need to work toward equal rights that demonstrate support for LGBTQ individuals on campus, such as partner benefits, gender neutral bathrooms, and inclusive policies and practices across all parts of higher education.

Relatedly, racial inequity persists on college campuses (Liptak, 2013). One such initiative is the development of an "anti-racism" working group as part of the Consortium of Higher Education LGBT Resource Professionals (Consortium, 2013). The consortium is an international organization comprised of administrators who work at institutions of higher education. The inclusion of an "anti-racism" working group centered issues of antiracism within the consortium. Such inclusion is one example of how individuals and professional entities can begin to diversify political agendas and collective action.

Representational Intersectionality and LGBTQ Populations in Higher Education

Often in higher education, faculty and staff fraction into separate spaces in acknowledgement of LGBTQ individuals of Color. Consider the following examples: (a) end of year recognition ceremonies that honor students of Color (e.g., Black graduation ceremony) and LGBTQ students (e.g., Lavender graduation); (b) separate commissions or committees that give voice to faculty, staff, and students of Color, and LGBTQ faculty, staff; and (c) educational programming and events (e.g., film series, speaker series) that invite individuals to discuss issues of race/ethnicity *or* LGBTQ topics—and that may or may not be cosponsored by multiple offices or student organizations. In each of these examples, the representation of a single axis of identity is reified. Institutional structure, campus organization, and professional practice reinforce monolithic conceptions of identity. Unfortunately, everyday practice rarely includes critical consideration of individuals. Often targeted individuals are supported partially but never holistically.

Consider the additional example of center hiring practices and the diverse populations of individuals that center directors and staff must represent. At LGBTQ centers, student affairs professionals and students assume that the leadership must identify as Lesbian, gay, bisexual, transgender, or queer. Often the LGBTQ center leadership then becomes *the* people who represent all LGBTQ issues for the campus. Similarly, student affairs professionals and students assume that the leadership at a Black cultural center must identify as Black or African American. The Black leadership becomes, too, *the* people who represent all Black issues for the campus. Certainly, targeted group experiences inform practice in campus centers. Here we are not arguing that the recruitment and retention of LGBTQ-identified staff and staff members of Color is not important; it is important. Rather, we are emphasizing Crenshaw's (1991a, 1991b) point that individuals with multiple targeted identities must work against multiple systems of oppression. Critiquing contemporary analyses of representation, Crenshaw (1991b) argued that

> [D]ebates over representation continually elide the intersection of race and gender in the popular culture's construction of images of women of Color. Accordingly, an analysis of what may be termed "representational intersectionality" would include both the ways in which these images are produced through a confluence of prevalent narratives of race and gender, as well as a recognition of how contemporary critiques of racist and sexist representation marginalize women of Color. (p. 1283)

Administrators and student affairs professionals need to work against monolithic representations of targeted groups and complicate their understandings of how multiple systems of oppression affect students, faculty, and staff who embody multiple targeted identities.

CONCLUDING THOUGHTS ON CRENSHAW'S INTERSECTIONALITY

In this chapter, we introduced brief histories of critical legal studies and critical race theory. Crenshaw's (1991a, 1991b) work on intersectionality stemmed from a rich history of neo-Marxist work on hegemony and the law, oppositional debate between neoconservatives and critical scholars on antidiscrimination law and equal process, the subsequent creation of color blindness by neoconservatives as a political tool, and the CLS critique of it as a myth. Centering the importance of ontology and its relationship to epistemology and in particular African American experience in her own work in CRT, Crenshaw reminded us to theorize carefully as well as tactically when we engage in racial justice work. Applying her concept of "intersectionality" means working with not only the legacies of CLS and CRT and the theoretical sophistication of political, structural, and representational intersectionality but also with the lived experiences Crenshaw and her colleagues endured as they confronted predominantly White law schools, White colleagues, and White, conventional legal scholarship. We invite readers to work with memory and care as they apply Crenshaw's work to their own.

NOTE

1. For a different interpretation of Crenshaw's emphasis on the lived experiences of women living at the intersection of multiple targeted identities see McCall (2005) and Nash (2008). For a conceptual critique of the binary position between poststructuralism and essentialism, as represented in McCall (2005) and Nash (2008), see Moi (1999).

REFERENCES

Abes, E. S., Jones, S. R., & McEwen, M. K. (2007). Reconceptualizing the model of multiple dimensions of identity: The role of meaning-making capacity in the construction of multiple identities. *Journal of College Student Development, 48*, 1–22.

Anders, A. D., DeVita, J. M., & Oliver, S. T. (2012). Southern predominantly White institutions, targeted students, and the intersectionality of identity: Two case studies. In C. Clark, K. J. Fasching-Varner, & M. Brimhall-Vargas (Eds.), *Occupying the academy: Just how important is diversity work in higher education?* (pp. 71–82). Lanham, MD: Rowman & Littlefield.

Bentley Historical Library, University of Michigan. (2007, October 17). *Gay, Lesbian, bisexual, and transgender collections.* Retrieved from http://bentley.umich.edu/research/guides/gaylesbian/

Bettie, J. (2003). *Women without class: Girls, race, and identity.* Berkeley: University of California Press.

Berger, M. (2004). *Workable sisterhood: The political journey of stigmatized women with HIV/AIDS.* Princeton, NJ: Princeton University Press.

Butler, J. (1999). *Gender trouble: Feminism and the subversion of identity.* New York, NY: Routledge.

Collins, P. H. (2008). *Black feminist thought: Knowledge, consciousness, and the politics of empowerment.* New York, NY: Routledge.

Consortium of Higher Education LGBT Resource Professionals. (2013). Retrieved from http://www.lgbtcampus.org

Crenshaw, K. (1991a). De-marginalizing the intersection of race and sex: A black feminist critique of antidiscrimination doctrine, feminist theory, and antiracist politics. In K. Bartlett & R. Kennedy (Eds.), *Feminist legal theory: Readings in law and gender* (pp. 57–80). Boulder, CO: Westview.

Crenshaw, K. (1991b). Mapping the margins: Intersectionality, identity politics, and violence against women of Color. *Stanford Law Review, 43,* 1241–1299.

Crenshaw, K. (1995). Race, reform, and retrenchment: Transformation, and legitimation in anti-discrimination law. In K. Crenshaw, N. Gotanda, G. Peller, & K. Thomas (Eds.), *Critical race theory: The key writings that formed the movement* (pp. 103–122). New York, NY: The New Press.

Crenshaw, K., Gotanda, N., Peller, G., & Thomas, K. (1995). Introduction. In K. Crenshaw, N. Gotanda, G. Peller, & K. Thomas (Eds.), *Critical race theory: The key writings that formed the movement* (pp. xiii–xxxii). New York, NY: The New Press.

Davis, A. Y. (1983). *Women, race and class.* New York, NY: Vintage Books.

Delgado, R., & Stefancic, J. (2001). *Critical race theory: An introduction.* New York: New York University Press.

DeVita, J. M. (2010). *Gay male identity in the context of college: Implications for development, support, and campus climate* (Unpublished doctoral dissertation). University of Tennessee, Knoxville.

DeVita, J. M., & Anders, A. D. (2014). Intersectionality and the performances of identities: Experiences of Black gay male undergraduates at predominantly White institutions. In E. Meyer & D. Carlson (Eds.), *Gender and sexuality in education: A reader* (pp. 464–478). New York, NY: Peter Lang.

Freire, P. (2000). *Pedagogy of the oppressed.* New York, NY: Bloomsbury.

Gramsci, A. (1992). *Prison notebooks.* New York, NY: Columbia University Press.

hooks, b. (1992). *Black looks: Race and representation.* Boston, MA: South End.

Human Rights Campaign Staff. (2013, October 3). Fayetteville State University becomes third historically black college to open LGBT resource center. *HRC Blog.* Retrieved from http://www.hrc.org/blog/entry/fayetteville-state-university-becomes-third-historically-black-college-to-o

Kairys, D. (1998). Introduction. In D. Kairys (3rd ed.). *The politics of law: a progressive critique* (pp. 1–20). New York, NY: Basic.

Liptak, A. (2013, October 15). Justices weigh Michigan law and race in college admissions. *The New York Times.* Retrieved from http://www.nytimes.com/2013/10/16/us/justices-weigh-michigan-law-and-race-in-college-admissions.html?pagewanted=all&_r=0

Lorde, A. (1984). *Sister outsider: Essays and speeches by Audre Lorde.* Berkeley, CA: The Crossing Press.

McCall, L. (2005). The complexity of intersectionality. *Signs, 30,* 1771–1800.

Mitchell, D., Jr., & Means, D. R. (2014). "Quadruple consciousness": A literature review and new theoretical consideration for understanding the experiences of Black gay and bisexual college men at predominantly white institutions. *Journal of African American Males in Education, 5,* 1–13.

Moi, T. (1999). *What is a Woman? And other essays.* Oxford, UK: Oxford University Press.

Nash, J. C. (2008). Re-thinking intersectionality. *Feminist Review, 89*, 1–15.

Noblit, G. W. (1999). *Particularities: Collected essays on ethnography and education.* New York, NY: Peter Lang.

Noddings, N. (1992). *The challenge to care in schools: An alternative approach to education.* New York, NY: Teacher's College Press.

Patel, L. (2013). *Youth held at the border: Immigration, education, and the politics of inclusion.* New York, NY: Teacher's College Press.

Raj, R. Bunch, C. & Nazombe, E. (2002). *Women at the intersection: Indivisible rights, identities, and oppressions.* New Brunswick, NJ: Rutgers, the State University of New Jersey, Center for Women's Global Leadership.

Saldaña, J. (2011). *The coding manual for qualitative researchers* (2nd ed.). Los Angeles, CA: Sage.

Scott, J. (1999). *Seeing like a state: How certain schemes to improve the human condition have failed.* New Haven, CT: Yale University Press.

Strayhorn, T. L., Blakewood, A. M., & DeVita, J. M. (2008). Factors affecting the college choice of African American gay male undergraduates: Implications for retention. *NASAP Journal, 11*, 88–108.

Strayhorn, T. L., Blakewood, A. M., & DeVita, J. M. (2010). Triple threat: Challenges and supports of black gay men at predominantly white campuses. In T. L. Strayhorn & M. C. Terrell (Eds.), *The experiences of black college students: Enduring challenges, necessary supports* (pp. 111–134). Herndon, VA: Stylus.

Teunis, N. (2007). Sexual objectification and the construction of whiteness in the gay male community. *Culture, Health, & Sexuality, 9*, 263–275.

Thompson, A. (2003). Tiffany, friend of people of Color: White investments in antiracism. *Qualitative Studies in Education, 16*, 7–29.

Ward, J. (2008). White normativity: The cultural dimensions of whiteness in a racially diverse LGBT organization. *Sociological Perspectives, 51*, 563–586

CHAPTER FOUR

Thinking Theoretically

WITH AND BEYOND

Intersectionality

Frameworks to Center Queer and Trans People of Color Experiences

ANTONIO DURAN AND ROMEO JACKSON

The misuse of intersectionality (Crenshaw, 1989, 1991) remains a key site for a critical intervention within the epistemological landscape of higher education. That is, the intellectual labor of Black women continues to be erased through the lack of intentionality to, what Ahmed (2017) might call, a citation policy. In other words, higher education scholars have failed to trace a genealogy of intersectionality to its roots within a radical Black feminist tradition. Though the framework has traveled across a number of disciplines (Cho, Crenshaw & McCall, 2013; Collins, 2015; Crenshaw, 2011; Hancock, 2007a, 2007b, 2016; McCall, 2005; Nash, 2008), intersectionality has both activist and scholarly historical origins that must be recognized. As intersectionality has gained prominence in the field of higher education, the questions become: how do we call attention to its history in Black feminist scholarship and activism? (Davis, 2016); moreover, when is it appropriate to employ other frameworks that accomplish complementary, yet different aims? As scholars who study the lives of queer and trans people of Color (QTPOC) on college campuses, we focus this chapter on the complexity that exists when choosing to utilize intersectionality *or* other frameworks to center QTPOC.

This chapter invites readers to envision a future of intersectional research that honors the contribution of Black feminist work while also critically pondering the usefulness of intersectionality to study the experiences of queer and trans people of Color. For the purposes of this chapter, we utilize the term *intersectional* to refer to analyses that examine how overlapping structures of power and oppression affect individuals with multiple marginalized identities. In particular, numerous modes of analysis other than intersectionality exist that articulate the specific experiences of queer and trans communities of Color, including queer of Color critique (QOCC; Ferguson, 2004) and two spirit critique (TSC; Driskill, 2016). Intersectionality is not useless in understanding queer and trans people of Color experiences in higher education, but this chapter explores how QOCC and TSC may be more useful for researchers and practitioners working with QTPOC on college campuses. To provide scholars the tools to choose between these three frameworks, this chapter is organized in three sections: (1) a brief overview of QTPOC research in higher education, (2) the historical origins of intersectionality and its applicability to QTPOC, and (3) the unique features of QOCC and TSC that can inform QTPOC studies, including the similarities/differences to intersectionality. Ultimately, this theoretical exploration of frameworks that center QTPOC challenges higher education professionals to critically engage their use of intersectionality, thinking theoretically within its genealogy and possibly thinking beyond it.

OVERVIEW OF QTPOC RESEARCH IN HIGHER EDUCATION

To situate this chapter within the broader higher education landscape, we offer a brief overview of research that studies the experiences of queer and trans collegians of Color. In his systematic literature review on QTPOC research in higher education, Duran (2018) noted that despite the increase in research on queer students broadly, a lack of scholarship on queer and trans students of Color still exists. Of the existing research, Duran (2018) identified sixty-eight scholarly texts (books, peer-reviewed articles, book/monograph chapters, and dissertations) that specifically focus on queer collegians of Color, in addition to noting two existing pieces that center transgender students of Color (i.e., Jourian, 2017; Nicolazzo, 2016).

Duran (2018) found that the following themes emerge in the extant literature on QTPOC in higher education: "coming out and finding sources of support, campus climate and navigating singular identity spaces, acknowledging the complex individuality of QPOC students, and the lack of resources/representation for these collegians" (p. 5). This scholarship, for example, has underscored how QTPOC make different decisions in living out their sexuality and gender compared to their White queer and trans peers (e.g., Eaton & Rios, 2017; Garvey, Mobley, Summerville, & Moore, 2018; Goode-Cross & Good, 2008; Narui, 2014; Nicolazzo, 2016; Patton, 2011; Patton & Simmons, 2008); additionally, queer and trans students of Color must contend with racism, heterosexism, genderism, and other oppressive systems within their collegiate environments (Blockett, 2017; Harris, 2003; Jourian, 2017; Mitchell & Means,

2014). Because queer and trans students of Color experience their time at colleges and universities differently from their White queer and trans peers, it is integral to comprehend and center their lives within higher education research. To understand the multiple axes of oppression that queer and trans students of Color encounter, scholars have opted to utilize intersectional frameworks in their research, such as the ones discussed below.

PAYING HOMAGE TO THE GENEALOGY OF INTERSECTIONALITY

Theories come with rich intellectual and activist histories that scholars must engage with in order to appropriately apply them to their work. As such, at the center of this section on intersectionality, we place Sojourner Truth's iconic speech "Ain't I a Woman," the Combahee River Collective Statement (1983), and, of course, the texts of Kimberlé Crenshaw (1989, 1991) who coined the term intersectionality within the academy and critical legal scholarship. By engaging the work above, we attempt to counter the epistemological erasure that furthers an anti-Black project within higher education scholarship. Importantly, this expunction typically targets Black women's work, rendering it to an epistemological death. For example, we argue the erasure of Kimberlé Crenshaw's texts when referencing intersectionality is a form of gendered anti-Blackness that, in turn, institutionalizes a Black feminist home theory (Nash, 2011). In the following section, we counter this institutionalization by highlighting the origins of intersectionality within Black women's work. Though not intended to be an intensive genealogy (see Hancock, 2016 for a more extensive historical exploration), we use two examples of Black women's intellectual production that laid the groundwork for Crenshaw's (1989, 1991) coining of intersectionality.

Though Crenshaw (1989, 1991) is often cited as the originator of the framework within the academy, intersectional arguments have existed as a tradition within Black feminist thought and women of Color feminism far before Crenshaw's pathbreaking work (Cho et al., 2013; Collins, 2015; Hancock, 2007a, 2016; Nash, 2008). Theorists have referenced examples of abolitionists such as Maria Stewart (Hancock, 2016) and Sojourner Truth (Crenshaw, 1989) to demonstrate the origins of intersectional thought outside of the academy. Of note, Sojourner Truth's (1851) "Aint I a Woman?" speech famously exposed how race and racism mediates access to womanhood, pointing to the hypocrisy of White femininity by stating, "Nobody ever helps me into carriages, or over mud-puddles, or gives me any best place! And ain't I a woman?" (para. 2). In calling attention to the category of women, Truth laid bare to the ways in which anti-Black racism and chattel slavery does not give Black women the "protection" of womanhood. That is, White women and Black women experience social oppression differently. Future movements echoed Truth's words as seen in the example of the Combahee River Collective (1983), a Black feminist lesbian organization, that wrote "it [is] difficult to separate race from class from sex oppression because in our lives they are most often experienced simultaneously" (p. 267). In this period of Black feminist mobilizing, the Combahee River Collective once again emphasized how White feminism obscured the lives of Black women. The Combahee River Collective Statement and "Aint I a Woman?" are two of the many ways that activists have engaged intersectional theorizing in the past, leading to the coining of the term by Crenshaw.

In her seminal work, Kimberlé Crenshaw (1989, 1991) mapped the systemic and legal barriers that renders Black women invisible to antidiscrimination laws, drawing attention to the fact that Black women were experiencing the effects of gender and race discrimination simultaneously. Crenshaw (1989) made visible the experiences of Black women in legal contexts, and in her later essay, the ways in which anti-racist and feminist movements render Black women invisible (Crenshaw, 1991). Previously, those enforcing antidiscrimination policies framed racial and gender marginalization separately, which overlooked the unique forms of oppression lived by Black women. Crenshaw gave activists and academics language to name intersectional erasures that fail to approach social justice beyond a single axis of analysis. That is, intersectionality is not about individual identity (e.g., race, sex, and class); it is a mode of systemic and structural analysis of multiple forms of oppression (e.g., racism, sexism, and classism; Collins, 2000/2009; Crenshaw, 1989, 1991).

Intersectionality thus allows scholars and practitioners in higher education to understand how intersecting systems of racism, genderism, classism, and heterosexism affect queer and transgender students of Color. For example, this framework illuminates how structures of domination can lead to heightened discrimination of QTPOC on college campuses and also contributes to their marginalization in spaces that only center one oppressed identity (e.g., those that focus on race *or* sexuality). Still, though some higher education researchers studying QTPOC have utilized intersectionality (e.g., see Blockett, 2017; Cisneros, 2015; Hughes, 2015; Miller & Vaccaro, 2016; Russell, 2012; Tillman-Kelly, 2015), other scholars have opted for different theoretical frameworks, such as quare theory (e.g., see Johnson, 2001) or queer of Color critique (e.g., see Ferguson, 2004). Important to note, the work of Black (queer) feminists (e.g., see Beal, 1970; Davis, 1981; hooks, 1981; Hull, Bell-Scott, & Smith 1982; Lorde, 1984) is foundational to any intersectional analysis that reaches far beyond the term intersectionality. As we demonstrate in the ensuing section, queer of Color critique and two-spirit critique are indebted to women of Color, Black, and Native feminist theories for laying the groundwork to address the specificity of oppression for queer and trans people of Color.

ADDITIONAL POTENTIAL FRAMEWORKS TO CENTER QTPOC EXPERIENCES

Although intersectionality remains a key theoretical insight into the study of oppressive systems that impact individuals with multiple marginalized identities, other intersectional frameworks exist that may better serve higher education researchers when exploring the experiences of QTPOC. For example, queer of Color critique (Ferguson, 2004) and two spirit critique (Driskill, 2016) both identify different discourses that lend themselves to study queer and trans students of Color. Therefore, this section will detail the various histories and potentials for application that these frameworks have for QTPOC individuals, including their focus on colonial histories or materialist systems. Though these theories align with intersectionality in some notable ways, it is their departures that warrant attention from scholars and practitioners alike.

Queer of Color Critique

Queer of Color critique is one framework that has started to emerge in QTPOC studies in higher education. Similar to intersectionality, queer of Color critique stems from a history of women of Color feminism and seeks to analyze the intersections of gender, race, sexuality, and nationhood. Notably, Roderick Ferguson (2004) is often credited for queer of Color critique, advancing this lens in order to refute the whiteness and heteronormativity that undergirded the discipline of sociology. As Ferguson contends, canonical sociology "becomes an epistemological counterpart to the state's enforcement of universality as the state suppresses nonheteronormative racial difference" (p. 21). In challenging canonical sociology, queer of Color critique deconstructs and opposes the ways that the nation-state has regulated queer of Color bodies and realities. To this point, Ferguson argued that social and cultural structures, in what is currently referred to as the United States, disproportionately disenfranchise queer communities of Color through social policy and economic discrimination. Differing from intersectionality's origins in critical legal studies, Ferguson constructed an argument rooted in materialism, interrogating how the nation-state's system of liberal capitalism reinforces the normalization of heterosexuality and exclusion of racial groups. The way that the nation-state utilizes capital, in Ferguson's perspective, results in policies that regulate queer of Color communities, and specifically Black queer individuals. For example, though people of Color are frequently utilized for their labor in what is currently known as the United States, they are systematically denied access to social and material resources. In an attempt to navigate the larger capitalist system, communities of Color are forced to align themselves with normalized modes of expressing gender and sexuality (e.g., through respectability politics) that then marginalizes queers of Color.

Though queer of Color critique began as a sociological project, scholars have started to imagine its potential for educational research. Describing the ways that researchers can deploy queer of Color critique in education, Brockenbrough (2013) observed that "institutional policies, classroom cultures, identity politics, and interpersonal practices that produce the marginalized racial, gender, and sexual subjectivities of queer youth of [C]olor" (pp. 429–430) are rich topics for exploration. Queer of Color critique is an intersectional mode of analysis that interrogates the ways that policies and structures of educational institutions oppress queer and trans collegians of Color. In particular, this theoretical tradition's focus on materialist systems creates the possibility for scholars to critically interrogate how queer and trans collegians of Color experience differential fiscal and political realities on campus. For example, how does the distribution of identity center funds towards certain programming further marginalize queer and transgender students of Color, causing a campus culture that obscures QTPOC realities? Higher education researchers, such as Means and Jaeger (2013), have noted the analytical power that queer of Color critique can provide to QTPOC studies but have not fully elaborated on its potential. Scholars outside of education and sociology like cultural studies scholar, Andrea Smith (2010), have also extended queer of Color critique, interrogating the ways that settler colonialism shapes identities. This leads us to highlight another theoretical framework that takes up a similar aim of identifying and resisting settler colonialism, which may consequently lend itself to QTPOC studies in higher education.

Two Spirit Critique

Drawing on and expanding Native feminist theories, Qwo-Li Driskill (2016) offered a two-spirit critique (TSC) in the hopes of building a coalition between Native and queer studies. TSC makes the relationship between the regulation of gender, sexuality and settler colonialism central to understanding trans, queer, gender, and Native oppression. Intersectionality and TSC both seek to understand overlapping systems of oppression. However, TSC centers two-spirit people's resistance to colonialism, a depart from intersectionality's concern and theoretical origins with the experiences of Black women.

TSC asserts the need for an ongoing analysis of the relationship between settler-colonialism and heteropatriarchy. The need for such an analysis expands outside of research on Indigenous peoples, for oppression happens "on occupied Indigenous lands and both over and through Indigenous bodies and peoples" (Driskill, 2016, p. 22). TSC is useful in understanding non-native QTPOC oppression within higher education because QTPOC oppression is not removed from settler colonialism. TSC resists the settler revisionist history of what is currently called the United States which suggests Native genocide and removal was predestined (Dunbar-Ortiz, 2014). Higher education scholars and practitioners can more accurately address contemporary issues facing QTPOC by understanding this truer history.

Making clear that there is no one TSC, Driskill (2016) suggested that there are seven practices of a TSC. For the purposes of this chapter, we highlight two practices as they may be the most helpful for higher education research. TSC: (1) sees two-spirit people and traditions as both integral to and a challenge to nationalist and decolonial struggles, and, (2) is woven into Native feminisms by seeing sexism, homophobia and transphobia as colonial tools.

These practices can inform research in three ways. First, Driskill (2016) saw TSC as an intervention into queer of Color research that centers two-spirit memory. TSC allows scholars to understand the colonial tools at play that limit the possibilities of queer and trans people of Color. For example, two-spirit memory shows fluid gender identity and expression was common and integrated into Native nations with no need for formal documentation (Driskill, 2016). The need for formal documentation for students to change their name and gender markers thus functions as a colonial tool of gender at work within higher education. In remembering two-spirit people, we then know of a time before administrative processes regulated gender, opening possibilities for a future where gender identity is not regulated by the state nor universities and colleges.

Secondly, by centering two-spirit resistance, researchers who seek to study queer and trans students of Color can be in solidarity with a decolonial project by gleaning lessons from two-spirit art and activism that furthers liberation for all QTPOC. Being aligned with a decolonial project starts with evoking Native feminist theories as a valued starting and ending place for theorizing race, gender, and nation (see Arvin, Tuck, & Morrill, 2013). Native theories also require engaging the material cost of decolonization (Tuck & Yang, 2012). Lastly, as Wilder (2013) showed, higher education continues to be deeply invested in a settler colonial and anti-Black project of what is currently called the United States. Every researcher and practitioner should be interested in naming, understanding, and dismantling settler logics within higher education because it is only by dismantling settler logics that we can truly begin to honor the theoretical contributions of Black feminist thinking and start to imagine new liberatory possibilities for queer and trans people of Color in higher education. TSC offers researchers an entry point to understand how current epistemological and ontological norms further settler colonialism and Native oppression. At the time of this writing, TSC has not been used in higher education research, reflecting the ongoing erasure of Nativeness within educational research (Waterman & Lindley, 2013) beyond deficit models (Tuck, 2009).

CONCLUSION

Ultimately, this chapter encourages scholars and practitioners to reflect on their use of intersectionality and other theoretical frameworks when studying QTPOC in college. Though intersectionality can serve as a powerful tool to illuminate systems of oppression that are embedded within university environments, individuals in higher education and student affairs have frequently misused and misappropriated this theory, obscuring its origins in Black feminist activism (Lange, 2017; Nuñez, 2014). For this reason, we echo Collins' (2015) words when she wrote, "Scholars and practitioners think they know intersectionality when they see it. More importantly, they conceptualize intersectionality in dramatically different ways when they use it" (p. 3). This chapter's theoretical exploration ensures that professionals practice good stewardship of Black feminist thought (Davis, 2016), honoring the contributions of Black women when evoking intersectionality as a framework in their praxis. It is only then that we can start to return the labor of Black women from an epistemological death. Moreover, in analyzing the academic genealogies of intersectionality, queer of Color critique, and two spirit critique, this piece better equips those in higher education to select appropriate frameworks to guide their scholarship. Whether scholars think with or beyond intersectionality, it is imperative that they recognize the histories behind these theories in order to envision equitable futures for queer and trans people of Color in higher education.

REFERENCES

Ahmed, S. (2017). *Living a feminist life*. Durham, NC: Duke University Press.

Arvin, M., Tuck, E., & Morrill, A. (2013). Decolonizing feminism: Challenging connections between settler colonialism and heteropatriarchy. *Feminist Formations, 25*(1), 8–34.

Beal, F. M. (1970). Double jeopardy: To be Black and female. In T. Cade Bambara (Ed.), *The Black woman: An anthology* (pp. 90–100). New York, NY: New American Library.

Blockett, R. A. (2017). 'I think it's very much placed on us': Black queer men laboring to forge community at a predominantly White and (hetero)cisnormative research institution. *International Journal of Qualitative Studies in Education, 30*(8), 800–816.

Brockenbrough, E. (2013). Introduction to the special issue: Queers of Color and anti-oppressive knowledge production. *Curriculum Inquiry, 43*(4), 426–440.

Cho, S., Crenshaw, K. W., & McCall, L. (2013). Toward a field of intersectionality studies: Theory, applications, and praxis. *Signs: Journal of Women in Culture and Society, 38*(4), 785–810.

Cisneros, J. (2015). *Undocuqueer: Interacting and working with the intersection of LGBTQ and undocumented* (Doctoral dissertation). Retrieved from https://repository.asu.edu/items/34804

Collins, P. H. (2009). *Black feminist thought: Knowledge, consciousness, and the politics of empowerment*. New York, NY: Routledge. (Original work published 2000)

Collins, P. H. (2015). Intersectionality's definitional dilemmas. *Annual Review of Sociology, 41*(1), 1–20.

Combahee River Collective (1983). The Combahee River collective statement. In B. Smith (Ed.), *Home girls: A Black feminist anthology* (pp. 264–275). New Brunswick, NJ: Rutgers University Press.

Crenshaw, K. (1989). Demarginalizing the intersection of race and sex: A Black feminist critique of antidiscrimination doctrine, feminist theory, and antiracist politics. *University of Chicago Legal Forum, 1989*(8), 139–167.

Crenshaw, K. (1991). Mapping the margins: Intersectionality, identity politics, and violence against women of Color. *Stanford Law Review, 43*(6), 1241–1299.

Crenshaw, K. (2011). Postscript. In H. Lutz, M. T. H. Vivar, & L. Supik (Eds.), *Framing intersectionality: Debates on a multi-faceted concept in gender studies* (pp. 221–234). Burlington, VT: Ashgate.

Davis, A. (1981). *Women, race, and class.* New York, NY: Random House.

Davis, A. (2016). *Freedom is a constant struggle: Ferguson, Palestine, and the foundations of a movement.* Chicago, IL: Haymarket Books.

Driskill, Q.-L. (2016). *Asegi stories: Cherokee queer and two-spirit memory.* Tucson, AZ: The University of Arizona Press.

Dunbar-Ortiz, R. (2014). *An indigenous peoples' history of the United States.* Boston, MA: Beacon.

Duran, A. (2018). Queer *and* of Color: A systematic literature review on queer students of Color in higher education. *Journal of Diversity in Higher Education.* Advance online publication. doi: 10.1037/dhe0000084

Eaton, A., & Rios, D. (2017). Social challenges faced by queer Latino college men: Navigating negative responses to coming out in a double minority sample of emerging adults. *Cultural Diversity and Ethnic Minority Psychology, 23*(4), 457–467.

Ferguson, R. A. (2004). *Aberrations in Black: Toward a queer of Color critique.* Minneapolis, MN: University of Minnesota Press.

Goode-Cross, D. T., & Good, G. E. (2008). African American men who have sex with men: Creating safe spaces through relationships. *Psychology of Men & Masculinity, 9*(4), 221–234.

Hancock, A.-M. (2007a). Intersectionality as a normative and empirical paradigm. *Politics & Gender, 3*(2), 248–254.

Hancock, A.-M. (2007b). When multiplication doesn't equal quick addition: Examining intersectionality as a research paradigm. *Perspectives on Politics, 5*(1), 63–79.

Hancock, A.-M. (2016). *Intersectionality: An intellectual history.* Oxford, UK: Oxford University Press.

Harris, W. G. (2003). African American homosexual males on predominantly White college and university campuses. *Journal of African American Studies, 7*(1), 47–56.

hooks, b. (1981). *Ain't I a woman: Black women and feminism.* Brooklyn, New York: South End.

Hughes, K. L. (2015). *The experiences queer college women of Color have of friendship* (Doctoral dissertation). Retrieved from http://athenaeum.libs.uga.edu/

Hull, G. T., Bell Scott, P., & Smith, B. (Eds.). (1982). *But some of us are brave: Black women's studies.* Old Westbury, NY: Feminist.

Johnson, E. P. (2001). "Quare" studies, or (almost) everything I know about queer studies I learned from my grandmother. *Text and Performance Quarterly, 21*(1), 1–25.

Jourian, T. J. (2017). "Fun and carefree like my polka dot bowtie": Disidentifications of trans*masculine students of Color. In J. M. Johnson & G. C. Javier (Eds.), *Queer people of Color in higher education* (pp. 123–144). Charlotte, NC: Information Age.

Lange, A. (2017, October 15). The (mis)use of intersectionality in student affairs: A call to practitioners & researchers [Web log post]. Retrieved from http://www.itsalexcl.com/blog/2017/10/15/the-misuse-of-intersectionality-a-call-to-student-affairs-researchers-practitioners

Lorde, A. (1984). *Sister outsider: essays and speeches.* Berkeley, CA: Crossing.

McCall, L. (2005). The complexity of intersectionality. *Signs: Journal of Women in Culture & Society, 30*(3), 1771–1800.

Means, D. R., & Jaeger, A. J. (2013). Black in the rainbow: "Quaring" the Black gay male student experience at historically Black universities. *Journal of African American Males in Education, 4*(2), 124–140.

Miller, R. A., & Vaccaro, A. (2016). Queer student leaders of Color: Leadership as authentic, collaborative, culturally competent. *Journal of Student Affairs Research and Practice, 53*(1), 39–50.

Mitchell, D., Jr., & Means, D. R. (2014). "Quadruple consciousness": A literature review and new theoretical consideration for understanding the experiences of Black gay and bisexual college men at predominantly White institutions. *Journal of African American Males in Education, 5*(1), 23–35.

Garvey, J. C., Mobley, S. D., Jr., Summerville, K. S., & Moore, G. T. (2018). Queer and trans* students of Color: Navigating identity disclosure and college contexts. *The Journal of Higher Education.* Advance online publication. doi: https://doi.org/10.1080/00221546.2018.1449081

Narui, M. (2014). Hidden populations and intersectionality: When race and sexual orientation collide. In D. Mitchell Jr., C Y. Simmons, & L. A. Greyerbiehl (Eds.), *Intersectionality & higher education: Theory, research, and praxis* (pp. 185–200). New York, NY: Peter Lang.

Nash, J. C. (2008). Re-thinking intersectionality. *Feminist Review, 89*(1), 1–15.

Nash, J. C. (2011). "Home truths" on intersectionality. *Yale Journal of Law and Feminism, 23*(2), 445–470.

Nicolazzo, Z. (2016). "It's a hard line to walk": Black non-binary trans* collegians' perspectives on passing, realness, and trans*-normativity. *International Journal of Qualitative Studies in Education, 29*(9), 1173–1188.

Nuñez, A-M. (2014). Employing multilevel intersectionality in educational research: Latino identities, contexts, and college access. *Educational Researcher, 43*(2), 85–92.

Patton, L. D. (2011). Perspectives on identity, disclosure, and the campus environment among African American gay and bisexual college men at one historically Black college. *Journal of College Student Development, 52*(1), 77–100.

Patton, L. D., & Simmons, S. L. (2008). Exploring complexities of multiple identities of lesbians in a Black college environment. *Negro Educational Review, 59*(3–4), 197–215.

Russell, E. I. A. (2012). *Voices unheard: Using intersectionality to understand identity among sexually marginalized undergraduate college students of Color* (Doctoral dissertation). Retrieved from https://etd.ohiolink.edu/

Smith, A. (2010). Queer theory and native studies: The heteronormativity of settler colonialism. *GLQ: A Journal of Gay and Lesbian Studies, 16*(1–2), 42–68.

Tillman-Kelly, D. L. (2015). *Sexual identity label adoption and disclosure narratives of gay, lesbian, bisexual, and queer (GLBQ) college students of Color: An intersectional grounded theory study* (Doctoral dissertation). Retrieved from https://etd.ohiolink.edu/

Truth, S. (1851). Ain't I a woman? Retrieved from https://www.sojournertruth.com/p/aint-i-woman.html

Tuck, E. (2009). Suspending damage: A letter to communities. *Harvard Educational Review, 79*(3), 409–427.

Tuck, E., & Yang, K. W. (2012). Decolonization is not a metaphor. *Decolonization: Indigeneity, Education & Society, 1*(1), 1–40.

Waterman, S. J., & Lindley, L. S. (2013). Cultural strengths to persevere: Native American women in higher education. *NASPA Journal About Women in Higher Education, 6*(2), 139–165.

CHAPTER FIVE

Intersectionality WITHIN THE South Asian American Student Population

Breaking Down the "Asian Box"

SHADAB FATIMA HUSSAIN

When evaluating a scholarship or fellowship application, what assumptions are made by the reviewer when someone checks Asian[1] as their ethnic group? Does it mean the respondent's heritage is from East Asian countries such as China, South Korea, and Japan? Does it help us understand if the respondent immigrated to the United States? Does it provide an idea of the parents' educational background and social status? Put simply, this answer cannot convey more than that the respondent's heritage is from the Asian continent which holds 60% of the world's population.

In the context of higher education, when a respondent checks the "Asian box," there is often an assumption by administrators that the student may not need as much academic support as a student from another underrepresented minority group. Perhaps because Asians, as an aggregate group in the United States, have high degree attainment, household income, and employment rates when compared to the national average (U.S. Census Bureau, 2015), they are not typically targeted as in need of additional academic and financial support (Museus & Kiang, 2009). The federal government does not require all states to collect detailed data on Asians. However, when disaggregating the Asian group, the U.S. Census reports three major groups (i.e., East Asian, Southeast Asian, and South Asian) and over 30 sub-ethnic groups with diverse educational outcomes. While Malaysian, Indian, and Taiwanese groups may report above average educational attainment, Bhutanese, Cambodian, and Vietnamese populations perform below the national average (U.S. Census Bureau, 2015). These statistics suggest the need for a more nuanced approach to understanding Asian American (AA) experiences, particularly through the lens of intersectionality.

Kimberlé Crenshaw's (1991) intersectionality theory posits that identity categories such as race, gender, social class, and religion, and associated oppressions (e.g., racism, sexism, classism), do not operate exclusively. Rather, these different entities act as "reciprocally constructing phenomena that in turn shape complex social inequalities" (Collins, 2015, p. 2). Although AA experiences contain many intersections, AA students are typically left out of the conversation of intersectionality in higher education settings. This exclusion may be due to the group's association with the model minority stereotype which claims that AAs are universally successful in education, wealth, and well-being (Gupta, Szymanski, & Leong, 2011; Museus & Kiang, 2009). However, as asserted by intersectionality theory and past research, it is important to understand the variety of identities represented within the Asian group beyond these stereotypes and how these systems of identities intersect and contribute to social and educational inequalities for AAs (Museus & Griffin, 2011). This understanding will better enable higher education researchers and administrators to support inclusion for Asian American groups in the discussion of equity in higher education.

Thus, utilizing an intersectionality framework, this chapter aims to disaggregate the "Asian box" by emphasizing the diversity of identities within it and highlight how interlocking systems of oppression marginalize AA students. As this racial group encompasses those from a variety of ethnic, religious, and class backgrounds, I will highlight the experiences of South Asians in the United States (i.e., those with heritage from India, Pakistan, Bangladesh, Sri Lanka, Bhutan, Nepal, and the Maldives)—who were born or have lived in the United States at a young age—as mechanisms of oppression may differ for international students who were not raised in the United States from a young age. South Asian American (SAA) college students are currently at high risk of racial and religious discrimination due to hostile attitudes towards Muslims that even impact non-Muslims. So, their experiences are especially relevant in the context of intersectionality (Ahluwalia & Pellettiere, 2010; Khan, 2012). I will then analyze how intersectionality informs the narratives of SAAs through discussion of the model minority stereotype and traditional cultural and community values, and then discuss the psychological literature on biculturalism and how two theories of biculturalism can provide an understanding of South Asian students' experiences with intersectionality (LaFromboise, Coleman, & Gerton, 1993; West, Zhang, Yampolsky, & Sasaki, 2017). Lastly, based on this review of psychological, educational, and sociological research, I will provide recommendations to higher education administrators and counselors on how to promote positive academic outcomes for SAA students. These recommendations will broadly emphasize institutional valuing and support and will address the impact that interlocking systems of oppression can have on South Asian students' academic and personal success.

THE MODEL IMMIGRANT GROUP

South Asians are the fastest growing Asian group in the United States with about 4.3 million currently living in the United States, just over 30% of the AA population (U.S. Census, 2015). Despite these growing numbers, research on SAA college students is relatively scarce; Inman, Devdas, Spektor, and Pendse (2014) estimate that just 10% of research on SAA identity focuses on college students.

Before delving into the multiplicity of identities among SAA college students, a discussion of the model minority stereotype and its historical underpinnings is warranted. The negative psychological and societal impacts of this stereotype are widespread amongst AAs and impact AAs across identity categories of race, class, gender, and religion (Yu, 2006). Considering this sphere of influence, this review will also include research focusing on other AA groups.

Broadly, the model minority myth is a "positive stereotype" which states that AAs, as a group, obtain relatively high educational attainment and occupational prestige (Yu, 2006). The myth was perpetrated in the 1960s around the Civil Rights movement when publication outlets like the *New York Times* reported on the relative success of Japanese immigrant populations and attributed this success to cultural factors that place an emphasis on hard work and family connections (Pettersen, 1966). Following the publication of this article, several articles continued to be released through the 1980s spreading similar messages. The group's success implied that if other minority groups are not able to succeed, it is due to their own shortcomings— a statement directed particularly towards African Americans to impose the anti-Black, racist agenda of those in power and maintain White dominance (Poon et al., 2016). AAs are evidence of the meritocratic "American dream" which asserts that hard work always leads to success and are the minority group other groups should aspire to become. While it may seem beneficial to be part of a group associated with this positive stereotype, this generalization is concerning due to its educational and psychological ramifications on AA individuals (Czopp, Kay, & Cheryan, 2015).

As mentioned previously, the model minority stereotype does not account for the diversity within the Asian group and may lead university administrators, counselors, or faculty to believe that AAs do not require as much academic, personal, and programmatic support. For example, Kim, Chang, and Park (2009) revealed that AA college students are less likely to academically engage with faculty than other minority groups, possibly due to incorrect perceptions faculty may have about these students' academic performance. Additionally, there are negative psychological ramifications of feeling pressure to live up to a model minority stereotype. In a study of 291 AAs from various ethnic groups (e.g., Chinese, Indian, Korean, Japanese, Filipino), Gupta et al. (2011) revealed that students who endorsed the model minority stereotype but felt they did not meet its expectations reported psychological distress and less engagement in help-seeking behaviors. A similar result was found in a study comparing help-seeking behaviors in White American and South Asian American college students, who not only believed in a personal stigma against mental health (e.g., "something is wrong with me if I seek mental health care"), but believed they were personally at fault for their distresses because they could not live up to the expectations of the model minority stereotype (Loya, Reddy, & Hinshaw, 2010).

This body of research highlights the internalization (i.e., unconscious incorporation of a subject into attitudes and behavior) AA students experience because of the model minority stereotype. AA students who are underprivileged are particularly negatively impacted, as this internalization of the stereotype coupled with economic and academic stress can result in more academic and psychological difficulties (Ngo & Lee, 2007). Despite financial hardship, these students do not receive relevant support by their schools because of societal expectations of their behavior as part of the aggregated Asian group. For example, Bhutanese students are largely underrepresented within the academy, but because of their categorization as AA, they may not qualify for scholarships or services typically provided for underrepresented minority students (U.S. Census Bureau, 2015). This lack of institutional support demonstrates Crenshaw's (1991) assertion that it is not enough to create policies or solutions based on one generalized depiction of a group. In order to promote academic success for all students who are negatively impacted by the model minority stereotype, we must understand intragroup experiences and address the limitations of current federal, state, and institutional policies that perpetuate educational inequalities for AA students (Teranishi, Nguyen, & Alcantar, 2014; Yu, 2006).

CULTURAL VALUES AND COMMUNITIES

Identity development of SAA students is differentially impacted by multiple identities (e.g., ethnic group, religion, gender, and sexual orientation). According to Ibrahim, Ohnishi, and Sandhu (1997), each of these aspects must be considered in understanding SAA students' experiences. Many studies exist that detail specific experiences of SAA students who are female (Hermansen & Khan, 2009), LGBTQ (Sandil, Robinson, Brewster, Wong, & Geiger, 2015), and Muslim (Khan, 2012). This work helps establish the importance of approaching the study of SAA identity development with an intersectional lens. Individuals in these studies report challenging experiences such as difficulty navigating between different settings, feeling isolated by peers within and outside the SAA community, and losing outward expressions of their identity for fear of discrimination—all of which can contribute to psychological distress. Thus, it is important to address concerns about these populations through an understanding of their specific experiences and acknowledge the interlocking systems of oppression that contribute to discrimination against SAA students.

Many current SAA college students immigrated to the United States at an early age or are the children of immigrants, suggesting that these students may inherit traditional and collectivistic values of their family's culture (e.g., strong family and community ties, religious involvement, accordance with traditional norms of respect and gender roles; Ibrahim et al., 1997). Sometimes, students may feel conflicted about the values of their heritage culture and the values of the larger culture they primarily grew up in, an experience called cultural values conflict; such conflict is more frequently experienced by SAA women than men (Rahman & Witenstein, 2014). Yet, conflict is not the only outcome of experiencing multiple, different value systems. Many SAAs endorse collectivistic orientations and value connections among people along with individualistic notions of success—perhaps as a result of their experiences of negotiating the traditional cultural setting(s) of their upbringing and the mainstream American cultural setting (Hermansen & Khan, 2009; Inman et al., 2014). These dual values suggest their implicit identification as bicultural.

BICULTURALISM THEORY AND TRANSFORMATIVE THEORY OF BICULTURALISM

When considering the experiences of SAA students in higher education settings, the collectivistic orientation of their heritage culture may conflict with the typically individualistic culture constructed by universities. Previous research has highlighted that students who experience these conflicts have lower academic performance than students who do not, suggesting that a mismatch between the university culture and the student's culture may be detrimental for students' identity development and academic achievement (Stephens, Fryberg, Markus, Johnson, & Covarrubias, 2012). In order to counter this mismatch, universities can construct environments that value both individualistic and collectivistic orientations and value the intersecting identities of their students.

One avenue to reduce this mismatch is to encourage university administrators to understand students' *bicultural* identity. Bicultural people[2] are those who have internalized values from two or more different cultures (Hong, Morris, Chiu, & Benet-Martínez, 2000). In the case of SAA students, many are immigrants or children of immigrants who are frequently transitioning between, and operating within, two or more cultural settings. While some research and media portrayals of immigration focus on the challenges and conflicts that can come with being bicultural (e.g., pressure to assimilate), biculturalism theory focuses on the positive benefits of biculturalism (LaFromboise et al., 1993).

Building on the additive model of biculturalism theory, the transformative theory of biculturalism posits that one's bicultural identity is more than simply a sum of their two cultures. Rather, bicultural individuals' negotiation of their cultures influences them in ways that are different than the relative contribution of each culture alone, including the process of how they negotiate their two cultural identities (West, Zhang, Yampolsky, & Sasaki, 2017). This transformative theory highlights the heterogeneity among bicultural people by encouraging an understanding of individual experiences.

Both of these theories suggest that identity development is influenced by the strategies bicultural individuals use to negotiate between cultural settings. For example, one student may feel at ease transitioning between cultural settings by playing up and down particular parts of their identity depending on the context while another student may feel more comfortable operating in one cultural setting and not adjusting aspects of their identity in the other.

This facility of transitioning between different cultural settings is called bicultural competence (LaFromboise et al., 1993). A student with high bicultural competence will find it relatively easy to adjust their behavior depending on the cultural setting. Previous research has supported this assertion with college students and has found that bicultural competence is positively associated with psychological well-being and identity integration (seeing two cultures as complementary rather than conflicting); it can also act as a protective factor against the negative effects of minority stressors (e.g., perceived discrimination, feeling isolated; David, Okazaki, & Saw, 2009; Hussain, 2018a; Wei et al., 2010). Overall, promoting students' bicultural competence is beneficial to their mental health.

Biculturalism and intersectionality have different foci; the former highlights the benefits of bicultural identities and the latter highlights the structures that oppress individuals with intersecting marginalized identities. However, connecting the positive psychological impact of biculturalism with the knowledge that oppressive systems impact those with intersecting marginalized identities, these theories together highlight that institutions can be structured to actively dismantle the structures of oppression that often leave students invisible through positively recognizing students who have multiple, intersecting marginalized identities, and implementing initiatives to value and support these identities.

CULTURAL COMMUNITIES IN COLLEGE

How can higher education settings support their students' bicultural identities and subsequently provide relief for these students who may be experiencing stress as a result of systemic discrimination and marginalization? Museus's (2014) culturally engaging campus environments model posits that students who believe that the university values their culture, and see that value communicated through faculty, courses, and physical spaces, will ultimately experience an increase in their sense of belongingness, academic self-efficacy, and academic achievement. Thus, in order to best support these students who are often overlooked by institutions due to marginalization as a result of interlocking oppressive systems such as racism, classism, sexism and religious discrimination, among other oppressive systems, students must feel that all aspects of their identities are valued and understood by the university.

One way to implement such an inclusive environment for SAA students is to create a space, such as a dedicated community center on campus. Patton (2010) illustrates the beneficial effects of university cultural centers on student success, academic persistence, social involvement and support, and overall sense of belongingness. As evidenced by previous research, SAA students receive relatively little attention in research and in university services compared to East Asian students (Inman et al., 2014; Ngo, 2006). SAA students also do not feel a sense of belongingness in spaces which purportedly designed to support all Asian students but which are evidently geared towards East Asian students (Hussain, 2018b). A physical space for SAA students with relatable and supportive staff is one method to restructure institutions to support those who are marginalized and often overlooked by university administrators. This action will be a productive first step towards integrating the university environment with the students' cultures and supporting their bicultural identity.

Another step is to provide more institutional support for SAA students through: (1) offering courses focused on understanding their histories and identities and (2) employing staff and counselors who are sensitive to students' experiences. For example, prioritizing the recruitment of counselors with an expertise on coping with the psychological ramifications of the model minority stereotype and who understand how to promote help-seeking behaviors in SAA students may address students' mental health concerns. These services would be especially helpful for SAA students who identify as Muslim, given the increased discrimination and current hostile political climate in the United States against this religious group (Khan, 2012). Building supportive communities among students is essential as well. Sexism, colorism, and discrimination based on religion traditionally exist in South Asian culture (Ibrahim et al., 1997). Students have also reported feelings of discrimination from fellow South Asians due to low language competency in their heritage language and because of their LGBTQ identification (Hussain, 2018b). Providing community building activities or workshops which focus on intersecting identities, particularly intersecting marginalized identities, and celebrate differences among gender, sexuality, religion and class will promote an inclusive environment among students and help to dismantle current oppressive structures. Drawing from both the transformative theory of biculturalism and intersectionality theory, this purposeful cultivation of inclusive attitudes can reduce intragroup discrimination.

Lastly, institutions should assess current services that are provided for SAA students and determine whether these services are equitably addressing students' needs. While Asians—as a collective—are not an underrepresented minority group by federal standards, some South Asian groups are underrepresented (e.g., Bhutanese), and there are lower numbers of SAA students in the fields of humanities and social sciences as compared to the STEM fields (U.S. Census, 2015). By not defining Asian students as underrepresented minorities, it limits opportunities for SAA students who demonstrate low educational attainment and are underrepresented in the academy (Museus & Kiang, 2009). Administrators should carry a more nuanced understanding of the intersecting marginalized identities and experiences of SAA students, rather than relying on broad generalizations of the aggregated Asian group such as the model minority myth. Enacting change at these multiple levels (e.g., individual, community, policy) will be most effective in addressing the societal and educational inequalities enforced upon SAA students.

CONCLUSION: WHO IS ASIAN?

Who is the individual checking the "Asian box?" I approach this question by challenging the definition of the Asian category and analyzing the South Asian American (SAA) college student experience through the lens of intersectionality. SAA students are a unique population of interest in terms of values, identities, and experiences. However, their distinctiveness and intersectional experiences are erased in the context of higher education due to the model minority stereotype. This stereotype holds many psychological and societal ramifications that contribute to individual psychological distress, and also plays a role in the lack of policies to support SAA college students, contributing to educational inequalities. Given their collectivistic orientation and the importance of developing their bicultural identity, universities can structure environments and develop programming in ways that highlight the intersecting marginalized identities of SAA students, acknowledge and actively respond to the oppressive systems working against these students, and promote an environment of collaboration and inclusion among community members. Furthermore, policies should be implemented with consideration of SAA students so that those students who are currently trapped within the generalizations of the "Asian box" can break free and be fully supported by their university to thrive socially and academically.

NOTES

1. In this chapter, "Asian" will refer to the aggregate racial demographic group and "Asian Americans" will refer to those of Asian descent who are citizens of or live permanently in the United States.
2. "Bicultural" will also include those that are considered "multicultural."

REFERENCES

Ahluwalia, M. K., & Pellettiere, L. (2010). Sikh men post-9/11: Misidentification, discrimination, and coping. *Asian American Journal of Psychology, 1*(4), 303–314.

Collins, P. H. (2015). Intersectionality's definitional dilemmas. *Annual Review of Sociology, 41*, 1–20.

Crenshaw, K. (1991). Mapping the margins: Intersectionality, identity politics, and violence against women of Color. *Stanford Law Review, 43*(6), 1241–1299.

Czopp, A. M., Kay, A. C., & Cheryan, S. (2015). Positive stereotypes are pervasive and powerful. *Perspectives on Psychological Science, 10*(4), 451–463.

David, E. J. R., Okazaki, S., & Saw, A. (2009). Bicultural self-efficacy among college students: Initial scale development and mental health correlates. *Journal of Counseling Psychology, 56*(2), 211–226.

Gupta, A., Szymanski, D. M., & Leong, F. T. (2011). The "model minority myth": Internalized racialism of positive stereotypes as correlates of psychological distress, and attitudes toward help-seeking. *Asian American Journal of Psychology, 2*(2), 101–114.

Hermansen, M., & Khan, M. F. (2009). South Asian Muslim American girl power: Structures and symbols of control and self-expression. *Journal of International Women's Studies, 11*(1), 86–105.

Hong, Y., Morris, M. W., Chiu, C., & Benet-Martínez, V. (2000). Multicultural minds: A dynamic constructivist approach to culture and cognition. *American Psychologist, 55*(7), 709–720.

Hussain, S. F. (2018a). Examining relations between bicultural efficacy, the big five personality traits, and psychological well-being in bicultural college students. *Psi Chi Journal of Psychological Research, 23*(1), 16–27.

Hussain, S. F. (2018b, August). *Conceptualizations of biculturalism in female South Asian American college students.* Paper presented at the Asian American Psychological Association National Convention, San Francisco, CA.

Ibrahim, F., Ohnishi, H., & Sandhu, D. S. (1997). Asian American identity development: A culture specific model for South Asian Americans. *Journal of Multicultural Counseling and Development, 25*(1), 34–50.

Inman, A. G., Devdas, L., Spektor, V., & Pendse, A. (2014). Psychological research on South Asian Americans: A three-decade content analysis. *Asian American Journal of Psychology, 5*(4), 364–372.

Khan, M. E. (2012). Attitudes toward Muslim Americans post-9/11. *Journal of Muslim Mental Health, 7*(1), 1–16.

Kim, Y. K., Chang, M. J., & Park, J. J. (2009). Engaging with faculty: Examining rates, predictors, and educational effects for Asian American undergraduates. *Journal of Diversity in Higher Education, 2*(4), 206–218.

LaFromboise, T., Coleman, H. L., & Gerton, J. (1993). Psychological impact of biculturalism: Evidence and theory. *Psychological Bulletin, 114*(3), 395–412.

Loya, F., Reddy, R., & Hinshaw, S. P. (2010). Mental illness stigma as a mediator of differences in Caucasian and South Asian college students' attitudes toward psychological counseling. *Journal of Counseling Psychology, 57*(4), 484–490.

Museus, S. D. (2014). The culturally engaging campus environments (CECE) model: A new theory of success among racially diverse college student populations. In M. B. Paulsen (Ed.), *Higher education: Handbook of theory and research* (pp. 189–227). New York, NY: Springer.

Museus, S. D., & Griffin, K. A. (2011). Mapping the margins in higher education: On the promise of intersectionality frameworks in research and discourse. In K. A. Griffin & S. D. Museus (Eds.), *Using mixed methods to study intersectionality in higher education*. (New Directions in Institutional Research, No. 151, pp. 5–13). San Francisco, CA: Jossey-Bass.

Museus, S. D., & Kiang, P. N. (2009). The model minority myth and how it contributes to the invisible minority reality in higher education research. In S. D. Museus (Ed.), *Conducting research on Asian Americans in higher education* (New Directions in Institutional Research, No. 142, pp. 5–15). San Francisco, CA: Jossey-Bass.

Ngo, B. (2006). Learning from the margins: the education of Southeast and South Asian Americans in context. *Race, Ethnicity and Education, 9*(1), 51–65.

Ngo, B., & Lee, S. J. (2007). Complicating the image of model minority success: A review of Southeast Asian American education. *Review of Educational Research, 77*(4), 415–453.

Patton, L. D. (Ed.). (2010). *Culture centers in higher education: Perspectives on identity, theory, and practice.* Sterling, VA: Stylus.

Pettersen, W. (1966, January 9). Success story: Japanese-American style. *The New York Times*, pp. 20–34. https://www.nytimes.com/1966/01/09/archives/success-story-japaneseamerican-style-success-story-japaneseamerican.html

Poon, O., Squire, D., Kodama, C., Byrd, A., Chan, J., Manzano, L., ... Bishundat, D. (2016). A critical review of the model minority myth in selected literature on Asian Americans and Pacific Islanders in higher education. *Review of Educational Research, 86*(2), 469–502.

Rahman, Z., & Witenstein, M. A. (2014). A quantitative study of cultural conflict and gender differences in South Asian American college students. *Ethnic and Racial Studies, 37*(6), 1121–1137.

Sandil, R., Robinson, M., Brewster, M. E., Wong, S., & Geiger, E. (2015). Negotiating multiple marginalizations: Experiences of South Asian LGBQ individuals. *Cultural Diversity and Ethnic Minority Psychology, 21*(1), 76–88.

Stephens, N. M., Fryberg, S. A., Markus, H. R., Johnson, C. S., & Covarrubias, R. (2012). Unseen disadvantage: How American universities' focus on independence undermines the academic performance of first-generation college students. *Journal of Personality and Social Psychology, 102*(6), 1178–1197.

Teranishi, R. T., Nguyen, B. M. D., & Alcantar, C. M. (2014). The Asian American and Pacific Islander data disaggregation movement: The convergence of community activism and policy reform. *Asian American Policy Review, 25*, 26–36.

U.S. Census Bureau. (2015). *American FactFinder: 2015 American community survey 1-year estimates.* Retrieved from https://factfinder.census.gov/faces/nav/jsf/pages/searchresults.xhtml?refresh=t

Wei, M., Liao, K. Y.-H., Chao, R. C.-L., Mallinckrodt, B., Tsai, P.-C., & Botello-Zamarron, R. (2010). Minority stress, perceived bicultural competence, and depressive symptoms among ethnic minority college students. *Journal of Counseling Psychology, 57*(4), 411–422.

West, A. L., Zhang, R., Yampolsky, M., & Sasaki, J. Y. (2017). More than the sum of its parts: A transformative theory of biculturalism. *Journal of Cross-Cultural Psychology, 48*(7), 963–990.

Yu, T. (2006). Challenging the politics of the "model minority" stereotype: A case for educational equality. *Equity & Excellence in Education, 39*(4), 325–333.

CHAPTER SIX

Realizing THE Power OF Intersectionality Research IN Higher Education

SAMUEL D. MUSEUS AND NATASHA A. SAELUA

As postsecondary institutions have become more diverse, higher education scholarship has increasingly focused on diversity-related topics. For example, higher education research on the benefits of diversity, campus racial climates, and racialized campus cultures has become more common (e.g., Harper & Hurtado, 2007; Museus & Jayakumar, 2012). It is important to acknowledge, however, that this research can simultaneously contribute to a common diversity and equity agenda, while rendering particular identity groups voiceless within that narrative. If higher education research aims to increase understanding of all students in higher education and inform ways to maximize the likelihood that they will thrive, it is important for postsecondary education scholars to seek to excavate the voices of all marginalized populations and generate authentic understandings of these groups. In this chapter, we highlight intersectionality as a valuable conceptual lens and analytical tool for achieving these ends (Museus & Griffin, 2011).

Intersectionality has been described as an "analytic sensibility ... a way of thinking about the problem of sameness and difference and its relation to power" (Cho, Crenshaw, & McCall, 2013, p. 795). Intersectionality was first introduced in the legal field but has been adopted and has informed discourse in multiple disciplines—including gender studies, ethnic studies, sociology, and education— allowing researchers to excavate many voices and experiences marginalized by dominant narratives (e.g., Cole, 2009; Museus & Griffin, 2011). As a concept, intersectionality suggests that the confluence of systems of subordination shape individual experiences in distinct ways (Crenshaw, 1991). As a method, intersectionality allows researchers to move beyond simplistic one-dimensional analyses to ensure that particular groups are not excluded or marginalized from discussions of diversity and equity in higher education and ensures that the voices of these populations are integrated into this discourse (Museus & Griffin, 2011). Therefore, intersectionality constitutes both a valuable tool for deconstructing complex dominant systems of oppression while also serving as a salient theoretical lens for pursuing new lines of inquiry and illuminating new voices in higher education research.

Still, while scholars have employed intersectionality in higher education research, many of those studies examine the intersections among identities without centering the role of systems of power and privilege in the discussion or providing in-depth analyses of the ways in which multiple systems of subordination shape experiences within higher education. Consequently, we believe that intersectionality, as both a concept and method, is an underutilized tool in higher education scholarship. In this chapter, we make an effort to advance higher education discourse by underscoring the importance of scholars applying intersectionality as a tool to gain deeper and more complex understandings of how systems of oppression intersect to shape the experiences of people within higher education. Specifically, we demonstrate the utility of intersectionality as an analytical tool for examining sexual violence targeted toward Asian American and Pacific Islander (AAPI) women in postsecondary education.

The experiences of AAPI women offer a valuable example of the ways in which intersectionality shapes experiences with sexual violence. AAPI women are stereotyped as model minorities who achieve universal academic and occupational success, but existing evidence suggests that this population faces significant challenges in higher education (Chen & Hune, 2011; Espiritu, 2007; Hune, 1998; Museus & Kiang, 2009; Museus & Truong, 2013; Yeung, 2013). First, the model minority stereotype fuels misconceptions that AAPI women do not encounter challenges or need support. Second, AAPI women are underrepresented in certain spheres of postsecondary education, such as in faculty and executive administrative ranks. Third, AAPI women are frequently ignored or marginalized in the academy, often rendering them voiceless and invisible in higher education. Finally, in addition to the model minority myth, several other racialized and gendered stereotypes plague the experiences of AAPI women. These stereotypes include assumptions that all AAPI women are passive, exotic, and hypersexual, which we discuss in more detail later.

First, we provide a brief discussion of the concept of intersectionality, paying particular attention to the advantages of using the framework in higher education research. Second, we analyze the experiences of AAPI women who have experienced sexual violence, including sexual harassment and sexual assault, to provide an example of how intersectionality can be employed to generate a deeper understanding of specific marginalized populations in higher education. Finally, we call on higher education researchers to utilize intersectionality to examine issues in a richer, more in-depth way to advance research and discourse.

OVERVIEW OF INTERSECTIONALITY

In her seminal work, *Mapping the Margins*, Crenshaw (1991) introduced the term *intersectionality* through an analysis of the ways in which social structures, politics, and identities converge to shape the lives of women of Color. She emphasized three types of intersectionality. Representational intersectionality illuminates how the social production of images of individuals living at the intersections of systems of subordination can function to subordinate them while ignoring their interests. Structural intersectionality refers to ways in which the location of people at the intersections of systems of oppression makes their experiences qualitatively unique. And, political intersectionality illuminates how people can belong to multiple identity groups (e.g., women and communities of Color) with different and sometimes conflicting political agendas, which can lead to the silencing of their voices. Through her analysis, Crenshaw called attention to the importance of looking at systemic intersections and how they shape and manifest in individual experiences.

Since Crenshaw (1989) introduced the concept of intersectionality, it has been used to combat overreliance on singular conceptions of identity in multiple disciplines. It also has been used to understand the multiplicity of social systems and how those systems intersect to create a unique experience for identity groups that occupy the corresponding intersections. Intersectionality is not employed as a method of arguing who is more or less oppressed but to illuminate the unique influence of intersecting identities.

Intersectionality has also been critiqued as well. As a conceptual and analytical instrument, for example, intersectionality has been critiqued for its "excessive specificity" or "the complexity that arises when the subject of analysis expands to include multiple dimensions of social life and categories of analysis" (McCall, 2005, p. 1772). Intersectionality also has been critiqued because it multiplies lines of distinction among populations, creating boundaries that preclude generalization and diminish shared experiences within identity groups. Still, proponents of intersectionality have asserted that a truly intersectional analysis does not simply add variables (MacKinnon, 2013). That is, intersectionality is not an additive practice, whereby forms of subordination increase or decrease the amount of oppression experienced. Instead, intersectionality reveals and can create new possibilities for alliances across identity groups, because the specificity employed by intersectional researchers acknowledges, engages, validates, and empowers communities whose identities and experiences have otherwise been suppressed or ignored because of overreliance on a singular identity as the dominant analytical mode (Carastathis, 2013). Indeed, Crenshaw (1991) paid particular attention to the collaborative potential of intersectionality, pointing out how the framework can provide a basis for the building of coalitions against racism and other forms of oppression.

In the current discussion, we consider intersectional analysis a discursive exercise, allowing us to develop a discussion that magnifies intersections to develop a more nuanced understanding of social structures, politics, and individual experiences (Crenshaw 1989; MacKinnon 2013; Museus & Griffin, 2011). Employed in this way, intersectionality can enable higher education researchers to develop a more complex and multidimensional understanding of the confluence of race, gender, socioeconomic status, citizenship, and sexuality in the lives of administrators, faculty, staff, and students. In the following section, we present an example, specific to the AAPI community that disrupts dominant conversations about the community and generates new lines of inquiry and discourse.

RACIALIZED SEXUAL VIOLENCE AND ASSAULT
IN THE ACADEMY

In this section, we utilize intersectionality as a conceptual lens to illuminate the ways in which it can be used to generate a more intricate understanding of higher education phenomena. More specifically, we employ Crenshaw's (1991) concepts of representational, structural, and political intersectionality to analyze sexual violence toward AAPI women in higher education.

Sexual harassment and assault is a persisting problem within the academy. For example, approximately 1 in 5 women in college will experience an attempted or completed rape (Centers for Disease Control and Prevention, 2012). Moreover, while all women can experience sexual harassment and assault in higher education, statistics suggest that women of Color are both overrepresented among sexual harassment and assault victims and underreport such incidents compared to their White female counterparts (Hernandez, 2000). And, scholars have argued that the overrepresentation of women of Color among victims and their underreporting can be better understood using intersectional lenses that help understand how the confluence of gender, race, and other factors shape the experiences of this population (e.g., Cho, 1997; Crenshaw, 1991).

Representational Intersectionality

For centuries, the dominant White majority in the West has racialized Asian and Asian American women as sexually desirable, submissive, hypersexual, and subordinate beings (Cho, 1997; Espiritu, 2007; Museus & Truong, 2013; Prasso,

2005). Congruent with this stereotype, a plethora of objectifying stereotypical images of Asian American women as prostitutes and sexual commodities have pervaded the Western media throughout history. For example, in the 1987 film *Full Metal Jacket,* which depicts the experiences of American soldiers during the Vietnam War, a Vietnamese prostitute approaches a group of soldiers and repeats the phrases "Me so horny" and "Me love you long time" in broken English, which have endured as phrases that are still used to subordinate and objectify Asian American women in the present day. Similarly, in a 2005 episode of the sitcom *Two and a Half Men,* Charlie Sheen's character is watching his brother's chiropractic office when an Asian American Woman comes in looking for work, is hired by Sheen, and is shown charging a customer for implied sex acts. Shortly thereafter, Sheen's character turns the office into a brothel. And, in 2013, the band *Day Above Ground* released a video called *Asian Girlz.* The video portrayed an Asian American model undressing for the band members, who were standing in a cage, and included lyrics filled with comments about engaging in sex acts, slanted eyes, private body parts, and other stereotypical words and phrases. These are just a few examples of images that permeate the media and reflect the exoticization of women of Asian descent.

Similarly, for centuries, the White majority in Western nations has historically racialiezd and currently racializes Pacific Islander women as flower-adorned, exotic, and lacking in sexual inhibitions (Johnston, 2003; Tiffany, 2005). Indeed, while many people in the continental United States are exposed to very few images of Pacific Islander women, the representations that they do encounter frequently take on the form of uninhibited dancing hula girls who exist for the pleasure of (often White) men. A simple Google images search for *women in Hawaii,* for instance, generates a plethora of provocative pictures depicting half-dressed women in Hawaii lying in sand, wearing coconut bras, and sporting grass skirts. This objectification is different than, but parallel to, the hypersexual and submissive portrayals of Asian American women.

Such constructions of AAPI women as prostitutes or sexual commodities both inform the dominant majority's views of this population and contribute to the frequency with which these women might experience sexual harassment and assault in higher education specifically (Cho, 1997; Hernandez, 2000; Museus & Truong, 2013). Museus and Truong (2013), for example, demonstrated how Internet discussion boards illuminate college students' racialized and sexually objectifying views of Asian American women, and race-themed parties of White students dressed as geishas periodically illuminate these perspectives on college and university campuses around the country. Moreover, evidence suggests that these stereotypes shape the environmental conditions that AAPIs in postsecondary education must navigate. Cho (1997), for instance, detailed how the impact of race and gender converged to generate stereotypes of Asian American female faculty members and contributed to the sexist, hostile, and demeaning work environments that they were forced to negotiate within the academy.

Structural Intersectionality

As mentioned, structural intersectionality refers to the ways in which the location of women of Color at the intersection of racism, sexism, and other systems of oppression shape the experiences of these women in unique ways (Crenshaw, 1991). In the case of sexual harassment and assault in higher education, structural intersectionality can shed light on the challenges that AAPI women face in their efforts to report and fight these encounters. Indeed, both societal structures and structures within higher education might contribute to challenges that AAPI women face in reporting and challenging their encounters with sexual harassment and assault.

Regarding societal structures, it is important to note that racism and sexism can intersect with other systems of subordination, such as classism and heterosexism, to shape the experiences of women of Color in higher education (Crenshaw, 1991). For example, women who are burdened by poverty—including female students and pre-tenured faculty members—often must risk being put in vulnerable financial positions in order to report sexual harassment or assault from administrators and faculty. Specifically, they might risk jeopardizing their academic standing, employment prospects, or reputations at their institutions (which could influence promotion and tenure decisions for women faculty). In addition, international and undocumented AAPI women might not report incidents of sexual harassment or assault because of fear of deportation (Ontiveros, 2010).

Within institutions of higher education, there are environmental conditions that also pose challenges for female victims of sexual harassment and assault. For example, both women and AAPIs are underrepresented in leadership positions in institutions of higher education (Cobb-Roberts & Agosto, 2011–2012; Neilson & Suyemoto, 2010). While it is not impossible for men and non-AAPIs to be sympathetic or empathetic to the situation of victims, it is reasonable to suspect that they are less likely to fully understand the AAPI women's situations and support them. At the programmatic level, there is often an absence of racially, culturally, and linguistically relevant support services for AAPIs on college campuses (e.g., Suzuki, 2002), making it a challenge for AAPI women to locate such supports.

Political Intersectionality

In the previous section, we noted that political intersectionality underscores the reality that individuals can be situated within multiple subordinated groups that have incongruent and sometimes conflicting political agendas and that this intersection can work to silence their voices. In the case of AAPI women who experience sexual harassment and assault on college campuses, political intersectionality can also manifest in barriers to navigating these experiences. We highlight two of these barriers, including how political agendas can function to protect AAPI men and the adverse impact of cultural norms that work against disclosure.

AAPI women who experience sexual harassment or assault can encounter pressures not to report such experiences from within their own communities. Indeed, scholars have written about how women of Color can face pressures to suppress such experiences because disclosure could reflect poorly on their racial or ethnic community (e.g., Crenshaw, 1991; Donovan & Williams, 2002). Thus, AAPI women in higher education can feel pressures to conceal their experiences with sexual harassment and assault in higher education. Moreover, systems of racism and sexism also function to emasculate and subordinate Asian American men in the United States through the construction of polarized images that frame these individuals as asexual and socially awkward or threatening hypersexual deviants (Eng, 2001; Museus & Truong, 2013; Shek, 2006), while those same systems racialize Pacific Islander men as savages (Jolly, 1997; Thomas, 1987). Therefore, when AAPI women pursue reporting of sexual harassment and assault incidents *within* the AAPI community, they run the risk of divulging information that can reinforce these racial stereotypes of their male counterparts of Color as deviant. In this way, politics of race and gender can intersect to oppress Asian Americans in general but further subordinate the perspectives and needs of AAPI women.

Finally, researchers have written that racism and sexism intersect to silence women of Color through patriarchal norms (Ontiveros, 2010). Culture is often multidimensional, intersecting, complex, and changing. Thus, it is difficult to make culture-based generalizations. However, some have asserted that many AAPI cultures are more often based on collectivism, familial interest, self-control, shame, and interpersonal harmony than Western cultures (McEwen Kodama, Alvarez, Lee, & Liang, 2002; Ontiveros, 2010). While AAPIs come from communities that differ along all of these dimensions and adopt these characteristics to varying degrees, conceptualization of AAPI cultures in this way has led to White men racializing AAPI women as people who will not report sexual crimes because they do not want to shame their families and targeting them in sexual assault activities (Museus, 2013). In addition, while the aforementioned traits might not characterize all AAPI cultures uniformly, it is possible that some of these communities do perpetuate such norms in ways that make it more difficult for AAPI women to report incidents of sexual harassment and assault (Olive, 2012).

The analysis of sexual harassment and assault experienced by AAPI women in higher education through the analytic lenses of representational, structural, and political intersectionality yields valuable insights. The preceding analysis provides one salient example of how intersectionality can be used to shed light on AAPIs in higher education. It can also inform policymakers and practitioners about how they can construct and revise policies to better support AAPIs, especially AAPI women, in their efforts to navigate university policies and procedures around sexual harassment and assault. For example, the racially specific experiences illuminated in the preceding analysis underscore the reality that postsecondary educators should ensure that their AAPI students are educated about the ways in which racism and sexism can contribute to the incidents of sexual harassment and assault on their campuses. It demonstrates the value of educators creating space to deconstruct racialized sexual constructions of AAPI men and women. The examination also highlights the importance of increasing the representation of women and AAPIs in leadership positions in postsecondary education institutions and having culturally and linguistically relevant support services for AAPI women on college and university campuses.

CONCLUSION

We conclude this chapter by calling on higher education researchers to engage in intersectional analyses that complicate and deepen existing understandings of the issues and experiences faced by marginalized populations in higher education. Intersectionality offers the potential of a paradigm shift in higher education—the centering of systems of oppression and marginalized identities in discourse around postsecondary systems and institutions. The framework also offers a way for researchers to be critical of what they bring to the table, intellectually, when they conduct higher education research. It behooves researchers employing intersectionality as an analytical tool to ask whether their work advances efforts to shed light on intersecting systems of oppression and power and informs efforts that might be aimed at dismantling these organizations. Thus, herein, we argue that researchers should pursue intersectional analyses in higher education that are embedded in a critique of systemic power.

While intersectionality is about research, it is also about the researcher. Therefore, it is valuable to underscore the communal aspect of intersectionality (Cho et al., 2013). As researchers, intersectionality can be about generating a community of higher education scholars who are concerned with knowledge production, as well as the struggle against systems of oppression and power. If one chooses this path, the community becomes a vital source of courage, constructive dialogue, and critical hope for the deconstruction of systems of oppression.

REFERENCES

Carastathis, A. (2013). Identity categories as potential coalitions. *Signs: Journal of Women in Culture and Society, 38,* 941–965.

Centers for Disease Control and Prevention. (2012). *Sexual violence: Facts at a glance.* Washington, DC: Author.

Chen, E. W., & Hune, S. (2011). Asian American Pacific Islander women from Ph.D. to campus president: Gains and leaks in the pipeline. In G. Jean-Marie & B. Lloyd-Jones (Eds.), *Women of Color in higher education: Changing directions and new perspectives* (pp. 163–190). Bingley, England: Emerald.

Cho, S. (1997). Converging stereotypes in racialized sexual harassment: Where the model minority meets Suzie Wong. *Gender Race & Just, 7,* 177–185.

Cho, S., Crenshaw, K., & McCall, L. (2013). Toward a field of intersectionality studies: Theory, application, and praxis. *Signs: Journal of Women in Culture and Society, 38,* 785–810.

Cobb-Roberts, D., & Agosto, V. (2011–2012). Underrepresented women in higher education: An overview. *Negro Educational Review, 62–63*(1–4), 7–11

Cole, E. (2009). Intersectionality and research in psychology. *American Psychologist, 64,* 170–180.

Crenshaw, K. (1989). Demarginalizing the intersection of race and sex: A Black feminist critique of antidiscrimination doctrine, feminist theory, and antiracist politics. *University of Chicago Legal Forum, 139,* 139–167.

Crenshaw, K. (1991). Mapping the margins: Intersectionality, identity politics, and the violence against women of Color. *Stanford Law Review, 43,* 1241–1299.

Donovan, R., & Williams, M. (2002). Living at the intersection: The effects of racism and sexism on Black rape survivors. *Women and Therapy, 25,* 95–105.

Eng, D. L. (2001). *Racial castration: Managing masculinity in Asian America.* Durham, NC: Duke University Press.

Espiritu, Y. L. (2007). *Asian American women and men: Labor, laws, and love* (2nd ed.). Lanham, MD: Rowman & Littlefield.

Harper, S. R., & Hurtado, S. (2007). Nine themes in campus racial climates and implications for institutional transformation. In S. R. Harper & L. D. Patton (Eds.), *Responding to the realities of race on campus: New directions for student services* (No. 120, pp. 7–24). San Francisco, CA: Jossey-Bass.

Hernandez, T. K. (2000). Sexual harassment and racial disparity: The mutual construction of gender and race. *Gender, Race, and Justice, 4,* 183–224.

Hune, S. (1998). *Asian Pacific American women in higher education: Claiming visibility and voice.* New York, NY: Association of American Colleges and Universities.

Johnston, A. (2003). *Missionary writing and empire, 1800–1860.* Cambridge, UK: Cambridge University Press.

Jolly, M. (1997). From Point Venus to Bali Hai: Eroticism and exoticism in representations of the Pacific. In L. Manderson & M. Jolly (Eds.), *Sites of desire, economics of pleasure: Sexualities in Asian and the Pacific* (pp. 99–122). Chicago, IL: University of Chicago Press.

MacKinnon, C. (2013). Intersectionality as a method: A note. *Signs: Journal of Women in Culture and Society, 38,* 1019–1039.

McCall, L. (2005). The complexity of intersectionality. *Journal of Women in Culture and Society, 30,* 1771–1800.

McEwen, M. K., Kodama, C. M., Alvarez, A. N., Lee, S., & Liang, C. T. H. (Eds.). (2002). *Working with Asian American college students: New directions for student services* (No. 97). San Francisco, CA: Jossey-Bass.

Museus, S. D. (2013). *Asian American students in higher education*. New York, NY: Routledge.

Museus, S. D., & Griffin, K. A. (2011). Mapping the margins in higher education: On the promise of intersectionality frameworks in research and discourse. In K. A. Griffin & S. D. Museus (Eds.), *Using mixed-methods approaches to study intersectionality in higher education: New directions for institutional research* (No. 151, pp. 15–26). San Francisco, CA: Jossey-Bass.

Museus, S. D., & Kiang, P. N. (2009). The model minority myth and how it contributes to the invisible minority reality in higher education research. In S. D. Museus (Ed.), *Conducting research on Asian Americans in higher education: New directions for institutional research* (No. 142, pp. 5–15). San Francisco, CA: Jossey-Bass.

Museus, S. D., & Jayakumar, U. M. (2012). *Creating campus cultures: Fostering success among racially diverse student populations*. New York, NY: Routledge.

Museus, S. D., & Truong, K. A. (2013). Racism and sexism in cyberspace: Engaging stereotypes of Asian American women and men to facilitate student learning and development. *About Campus, 18*, 14–21.

Neilson, P. A., & Suyemoto, K. L. (2010). Using culturally sensitive frameworks to study Asian American leaders in higher education. In S. D. Museus (Ed.), *Conducting research on Asian Americans in higher education* (pp. 83–94). San Francisco, CA: Jossey-Bass.

Olive, V. C. (2012). Sexual assault against women of Color. *Journal of Student Research, 1*, 1–9.

Ontiveros, L. (2010). Three perspectives on workplace harassment of women of Color. *Women's Law Forum, 23*, 817–828.

Prasso, S. (2005). *The Asian mystique: Dragon ladies, geisha girls, and our fantasies of the exotic orient*. New York, NY: Perseus.

Shek, Y. L. (2006). Asian American masculinity: A review of literature. *The Journal of Men's Studies, 14*, 379–391.

Suzuki, B. H. (2002). Revisiting the model minority stereotype: Implications for student affairs practice and higher education. In M. K. McEwen, C. M. Kodama, A. N. Alvarez, S. Lee, & C. T. H. Liang (Eds.), *Working with Asian American college students: New directions for student services* (No. 97, pp. 21–32). San Francisco, CA: Jossey-Bass.

Tiffany, S. W. (2005). Contesting the erotic zone: Margaret Mead's fieldwork photographs of Samoa. *Pacific Studies, 28*, 19–45.

Thomas, N. (1987). Complementary and history: Misrecognizing gender in the Pacific. *Oceania, 57*, 261–270.

Yeung, F. P. F. (2013). Struggles for professional and intellectual legitimacy: Experiences of Asian and Asian American female faculty. In S. D. Museus, D. C. Maramba, & R. T. Teranishi (Eds.), *The misrepresented minority: New insights on Asian Americans and Pacific Islanders, and their implications for higher education* (pp. 281–293). Sterling, VA: Stylus.

CHAPTER SEVEN

Living Intersectionality
IN THE Academy

LEAH J. REINERT AND GABRIEL R. SERNA

From its establishment, higher education has operated within a patriarchal system. Institutions of higher education are still overwhelmingly led and run by White men (Bystydzienski & Bird, 2006). Indeed, the reward system in the academy is heavily influenced by a historical legacy that decidedly values Whiteness, maleness, and heterosexuality over other identities (Cress & Hart, 2009). The literature indicates that the academy continues to operate within a distinctly patriarchal and androcentric structure (e.g., Acker, 2006; Cress & Hart, 2009; Dill & Kohlman, 2012; Hirshfield & Joseph, 2011; Mason & Goulden, 2004). Encompassed in the patriarchal and androcentric structure is the assumption of the normative "straight, White, and male" that supports and sustains heteronormativity within the climate and culture of academia (Bilimoria & Stewart, 2009; Danby, 2007; Rankin, 2005). Within the academic culture and climate, identities socially marked as subordinate to the dominant norm are often pressured to exist on the periphery, to be within the culture but to make invisible certain identities in particular contexts, in order to enable achievement and success (Carbado, 2013; Dill, 2009). For those in academia who are already on the periphery, the academic environment can serve to further marginalize those multiple identities that inform their research and teaching. It also can mediate the way policies in the academy, especially around these two areas, are experienced and understood. Within academia, often, the more intersecting minority identities one experiences, the more opportunities for marginalization and exclusion exist.

Within some minority communities, specific hierarchies exist, causing further oppression of those who have minority identities that intersect (MacKinnon, 2013; Patil, 2013). It is safe to establish that White and male continues to hold dominance and affect policy and procedure within the dominant community as well as within certain minority communities (Carbado, 2013; Choo & Ferree, 2010; Crenshaw, 1989). To this end, intersectionality can aid in understanding why a White female who identifies as a Lesbian experiences marginalization within the LGBT community and why those experiences in the academy will differ from that of a Hispanic male who identifies as gay. The dynamics and interplay of intersecting identities within different contexts and communities—with specific reference to academia—are important to highlight in the discussion of intersectionality and higher education.

Acknowledging that established social hierarchy and norms create and determine the identity categories that are defined as oppressed or privileged (Crenshaw, 1989; MacKinnon, 2013), this chapter employs intersectionality to explore how we experience academia through our intersecting identities and discuss how higher education and institutional policy affect those experiences. Further, through multiple identities that intersect race, ethnicity, gender, sexual orientation, social class, ability, first-generation status, and experiencing academia as students, employees, and faculty, this chapter discusses the ways in which we experience academia in relation to our intersecting identities. Additionally, we outline how intersectionality informs and affects academic policy and structure and how policy and structure both can serve as a mechanism for continued oppression.

Our guiding mission in this chapter is to further the understanding of how intersecting identities affect experiences in academia and how policy often furthers marginalization of individuals with multiple intersecting minority identities through exclusion or overt notions of what constitutes "good policy, research, and teaching" in higher education. To this end, we begin by discussing our individual experiences in academia through the lens of our intersecting identities, representing both privilege and oppression. We follow this with an exploration of the ways in which policy in the academy attends to and is informed by notions of intersectionality and conclude with recommendations on how higher education can better attend to the multiple intersections of identity to provide the best culture and climate for all individuals.

INTERSECTIONALITY AND ACADEMIA

Crenshaw (1991) noted that failing to think in intersectional terms often furthers the continuation of oppression and discrimination against those with multiple intersecting marginalized identities. Acker (2006) further noted that focusing on just one category of identity prohibits understanding of the complexity of the inequalities and realities facing those with oppressed or marginalized identities. For both Crenshaw and Acker, thinking about intersectionality is vital to understanding the experiences of those within academia with intersecting identities. Still, it is often difficult for those within academia to operate within an intersectional perspective, because society operates heavily within a binary system (e.g., male or female, man or Woman, Black or White, heterosexual or nonheterosexual).

Lived experiences frame our individual understandings of identity, context, opportunities, and perceptions (Cole, 2009; Ropers-Huilman & Winters, 2010), and how we experience life within the complexities of identity provides the lens within which we operate in the larger social world (Dill & Kohlman, 2012). Therefore, it is important to understand how our own intersecting identities shape our experiences and how we operate within academia. In the following sections, we each discuss how we have experienced and continue to experience academia within the lens of our intersecting identities.

Leah

The majority of my (LR) experiences in higher education have been as a student, both in the classroom and as a student leader. While I also have held the roles of employee and teacher, my role as a college student is the lens from which I write in this section. The identities that I carry with me into the classroom include, but are not limited to, Lesbian, feminist, researcher, female, atheist, and White. These are the identities that most often intersect in my academic world, and some are easier than others to label and identify publicly. Yet, they all play a large role in the triumphs and struggles that I have encountered in academia. In my experience, academia struggles with intersectionality and approaching individuals as having multiple, layered, complex, and intersecting identities.

Navigating academia with multiple intersecting identities, many of which are "invisible," identities not easily visible or recognizable, has taught me many lessons. When considering my experiences within academia as a student in relation to my identities, I think of the following quote from Audre Lorde (1984):

> Those of us who stand outside the circle of this society's definition of acceptable women; those of us who have been forged in the crucibles of difference—those of us who are poor, who are Lesbians, who are Black, who are older—know that survival is not an academic skill. It is learning how to stand alone, unpopular and sometimes reviled, and how to make common cause with those others identified as outside the structures in order to define and seek a world in which we can all flourish. (p. 112)

In my student role, I have often found myself standing alone and feeling unpopular due to my minority or marginalized identities while seeking out that "common cause" or understanding to which Lorde refers. I have often encountered occasions in which I become the representative educator for those "different" identity categories individually. These occasions have been numerous and not always unwelcome. As anyone who has been that token voice in the classroom knows, being that voice can become tiresome and can feel so repetitive that you feel that it is the only identity you reveal or discuss within the classroom, and the obligation to be that voice always remains.

While my minority or marginalized identities have been prominent in my experiences within the classroom, it is important to note that my White identity and growing up middle class afforded me the opportunity and privilege to be in the classroom in the first place. Within the frame of those identities, my access and ability to succeed in higher education are privileges that have afforded me opportunity and mobility. It is easy to lose sight of the privileges and privileged identities one holds, because as the identities pile up and the minority or marginalized identities grow in number, the dominant identities are easily lost or forgotten. The few years in my adult life outside of academia taught me about the privilege of not only access to higher education but also in growing up with the cultural capital to know that I had the access at all. These experiences led me to be careful in my graduate career, lest I forget those identities that afford me great privilege. However, I acknowledge that this is often difficult, while also fighting on behalf of the identities that bring forth bias, discrimination, and oppression.

As my classroom time as a student comes to a close, my researcher role grows. Within my doctoral experience thus far, I have made very careful choices on the topics I will research and those that I will stray from until I establish a career. Gaining employment since graduating with my baccalaureate degree has been difficult, because the majority of my experiences in leadership and skill development occurred within my role as student leader of the campus Lesbian, gay, bisexual, and transgender (LGBT) student group. The skills I gained made me career ready, but many, if not most, employers could not look beyond the LGBT heading. This obstacle and the experience with my master's thesis, which focused on Lesbian academics, led me to realize that doing any further work explicitly with LGBT groups or entities or research on LGBT topics would likely label me as a queer/Lesbian/gay academic. Career success in academia relies on my ability to showcase all of my identities, not just my identity as a Lesbian. The inability of academia and larger society to think in intersectional terms leads to this overshadowing of one identity and presents a barrier to success and being able to exist within an always evolving and intertwined list of identities.

Gabriel

As a relatively new faculty member, my (GS) experience in the academy also has been primarily as a student. Yet, because the demands on a new professor quickly require a realigning of one's identities, I will focus on my experiences with the job market and through my short time as a faculty member.

I grew up in a very poor, Hispanic, Catholic family in a small town in New Mexico. While I was unaware of our poverty until I was a bit older, I realized that it informed our family's day-to-day perspectives and choices. With regard to education, college was not presented as an option; indeed, finishing high school barely was. In a family of five siblings, only one (my brother) obtained a high school diploma. Those without a diploma in my family included both parents, who incidentally divorced before I could walk. Growing up poor, many would argue, is already sufficiently difficult, but add to this a burgeoning awareness of my sexuality and the religiosity of my family, and the situation becomes more complex. Still, for the most part, I was surrounded by others with similar cultural capital endowments, that is, other than being gay. Since I had also dropped out of high school, I earned a GED and went to work. When I decided to continue my education at the community college, and transfer to the main campus of the local four-year university, I became keenly aware of a difference between my classmates and me, although I would have been hard-pressed to identify it at that time.

Ten years later, I found myself at the end of my PhD program, searching the job market, and seeking to start my career as a full-fledged member of the academy. Because much of my graduate education heavily emphasized social justice, I was completing my degree with a broad set of ideas, theories, and vocabularies that allowed me to identify that which eluded me earlier in life—that race, class, ethnicity, gender, and sexual orientation mattered. While looking for a job, I became intensely aware of the ways in which others perceived my identities and how being gay, Hispanic, male, poor, first-generation, both all at once and individually (Warner & Shields, 2013), influenced what others thought I should be doing and how I interpreted my experiences. The education I received helped me to understand that, in a very fundamental way, my identities had shifted. There were now more of them, namely, researcher and scholar, and some were, as Parent, DeBlaere, and Moradi (2013) explained, endowed with greater relative power and privilege.

In the job market, it became resoundingly clear that if I was to succeed, many of my marginalized identities would have to be set aside, lost, or replaced. It also was clear that if this were to occur, it would require a sort of balancing act. For example, during an on-campus interview, I was presenting some of my dissertation research. The audience was composed of both search committee members and a large group from the college and around campus. As I reached my conclusions, a number of individuals asked pertinent questions around the things many scholars would expect when presenting research, questions like, "How did you choose your method?" or "What are some implications of your research for practice?" At the end of my presentation, one search committee member raised his hand. With a perplexed look on his face he asked, "So you've done a really good job here, but I just don't understand why you didn't take it further." Perplexed, I asked for clarification. His response was, "Well you didn't really talk about poor students, Hispanics, or first-generation students; isn't that your focus?"

Around the room there were many hushed glances, and a sense of unease had set in. I responded that while my identities certainly informed my interest in the subject, my research agenda was focused on the interplay of state fiscal policies and higher education finance. This experience, coupled with other similar occurrences over the next few months, suggested that at least two things were taking place with regard to my experience in the academy. First, I had to validate my positionality in terms of the appropriateness of asking questions that are typically within the domain of White, heterosexual men, many of whom had come from advantaged backgrounds. Second, if I did not confine myself to questions relating to the intersecting identities that were most visibly identifiable, my work in academia would have to stand up to the highest levels of academic rigor, whereas the work of some of my colleagues, who shared dominant identities, might simply be assumed to be of high quality.

Upon reflection, I came to the conclusion that questions like those posed while seeking a job were asked because the individual posing them felt they had a right, or rather the privilege, to ask me to validate the very right that I had to ask such questions or to even exist within the academy, for that matter. This is not to suggest that valid questions regarding research are not in order. Rather, these examples are intended to highlight the notion that intersecting identities, and intersectionality as a construct, indicate a need for those in the academy to reexamine their notions of who is allowed to ask questions that pertain to areas considered to be in the sphere of actors from the dominant culture. It also underscores the power differentials that remain among those from dominant and marginalized groups, even in a field whose values are ostensibly closely tied to social justice.

Now I wish to discuss living intersectionality in the academy from the perspective of a teaching faculty member. As a new faculty member, the whirlwind of duties and pressures can often seem overwhelming. Adding to the already stressful transition, I also was confronted with another reality of the academy—that students can exert an oppressive power over faculty with marginalized identities, especially when many of those identities are visible externally and the majority of students are from the dominant culture. As mentioned previously, I had formed new identities and was aware that some were seen as more valuable than others.

In the classroom, it became evident that my intersecting identities would play a role in both the way I taught and how students perceived my teaching. For example, during a class session, an individual asked me why I preferred to go by Dr. Serna, rather than Gabriel, or for that matter, Gabe. His sense was that I was disconnecting myself from the class because the rest of the faculty went by their first names. Incidentally, the other faculty at this time shared a similar sociocultural background, although they were not privy to this exchange until much later. I explained that my cultural upbringing requires a certain level of formality when speaking to teachers, clergy, and other individuals who are in a position of authority or at a social distance as a sign of respect. I had to explain that my cultural capital differed from his, and that as a result, two interlocking identities were at play. That is to say, I was navigating a system where at least one of my intersecting identities conformed to the norms of the dominant culture and was valued (being a scholar/academic) and the other went against it to some extent (Hispanic notions of respect and social distance). This experience created a sense of marginalization on my part, although it is necessary to say that my privileged position as a male in academia probably made it easier for me to have this conversation and be taken more seriously by this particular student. Still, I had to explain that my cultural capital was just as valid and that my identities intersected in ways that were foreign to this individual, which reminded me of the extra burden placed on marginalized groups in the academy. It also highlighted for me how a number of salient, intersecting identities can inform the teaching and research one undertakes based on these same notions.

As mentioned previously, the academy remains a largely White, male, heterosexual institution. Hence, the reflection of the sociocultural norms of this group in the academy is not unexpected. Nonetheless, by providing these two experiences as examples of living intersectionality in the academy, my hope is that as an institution, we become more aware of the ways in which we attend to marginalized voices and the marginalized experience. Finally, while many a respected colleague has suggested that these experiences could serve as teaching moments, let us again be reminded that these moments place both a psychic and in some cases material burden on those with intersecting, nondominant identities.

ACADEMIA, POLICY, AND INTERSECTIONALITY

Within the frame of the patriarchal and androcentric environment of higher education, those with intersecting minority or marginalized identities must engage in a complex navigation of social norms and academic policy, especially if policy is linked to norms that privilege certain identities over others in implicit ways. This navigation includes undercurrents and occasional blatant messages (Schaefer Riley, 2012) of what is acceptable or "valid" research or research topics. Identity-related research—research on gender, sexuality, and race—is often discounted in academia. We have both provided examples of our own navigation of research and research topics, but it is important to note that these undercurrents give rise to the idea that certain individuals do not have the "right" to question the dominant culture or even to ask questions that are considered within the purview of those from the dominant culture.

As pointed out in the narratives, focusing on academic policy and structure through an intersectional lens is more important than ever before, as the demographics within institutions of higher education change and become exceedingly more diverse. When considering policy, in higher education intersectionality is important because it "suggests that we are composite, whole individuals whose membership in group matters, but is not definitive. All individuals within a group do not have the same 'essence'" (Ropers-Huilman & Winters, 2010, p. 40). While commonalities exist between intergroup identities, due to every individual having multiple, intertwined, and complex identities, no two individuals can be treated exactly the same. Creating policy that attends to the complexity of identity is difficult, as can be seen in the increasingly long list of identity categories offered in antidiscrimination policies.

For example, in my (GS) experience, it was clear to me that the social distance that was called for based on my less dominant sociocultural capital might be seen as bad teaching. Or my research, as evidenced by the exchanges I had seeking a job, might be seen as less valid or rigorous based on implicit assumptions about my visible identities.

In my (LR) case, I became aware that my research agenda was being interpreted in specific ways based on the assumptions surrounding my topic as understood by an androcentric and primarily heterosexual structure.

Therefore, we argue, that as policy makers and decision makers in higher education begin to understand the complex layers of identity, conversations and attempts to attend to intersecting identities in policy and the very structure of the academy itself must increase.

Although it is the ideal for academia to approach policy in an intersectional frame, both academia and the broader society continue to operate in a highly stratified structure. Cole (2009) noted, "[I]ntersectionality makes plain that gender, race, class, and sexuality simultaneously affect the perceptions, experiences, and opportunities of everyone living in a society stratified along these dimensions" (p. 179). Attempts by higher education institutions to protect individual identity categories from discrimination through policy only provide a "Band-Aid" over the problems of bias and oppression that exist within institutions, because policy must be met with broader societal or institutional change to be most effective. Additionally, discrimination policies often very carefully state which identities have fallen within the "protected class" and by omission those that are not worthy of protection. This also exemplifies which identities are considered marginalized, highlighting for all those identities that lie outside of the "norm" the fact that they are clearly seen as less important or possibly simply undeserving of consideration.

An example of policy marginalizing identity includes the reality that many institutions can decide whether to recognize LGBT couples in their benefits policies. The lack of recognition sets LGBT faculty, staff, and students apart.

Policies that make explicit the division between identities often do more harm than good in furthering marginalization by perpetuating the stratification of identity. Scholars have underscored the important symbolism and framing that policy narratives and policies themselves can have (e.g., Baumgartner & Jones, 1993; Jones & Baumgartner, 2005; Rosen, 2009). The nature of policy as both a symbolic mechanism by which marginalization is first understood and then accentuated, and as a framing device to understand what marginal identities should be protected, create a space where intersectionality can add to the policy dialogue. Beyond policies, the unwritten rules within academic culture in relation to scholarship and faculty roles prove problematic in the often overwhelming focus on one marginalized identity over any other identity, characteristic, or skill.

CONCLUSIONS AND RECOMMENDATIONS

In this chapter, we have discussed our own paths and experiences in higher education with reference to our intersecting identities and how policy attends to, disrupts, and negotiates the complexity of identities that exist within higher education. Through our experiences, we have discovered how intertwined and evolving identities can be and how our continuous exploration of our identities within higher education sometimes requires strategic negotiation. We also have learned and note that our strategic negotiation cannot always rely on or be supported effectively by policy. Considering intersectionality when creating and implementing policy is highly difficult, but Dill and Kohlman (2012) highlighted the following:

> In the discourse surrounding identity, it is the tension between intersectionality as a tool for illuminating group identities that are not essentialist and individual identities that are not so fragmentary as to be meaningless that provides the energy to move the concept forward to the future. (p. 164)

Future development of policy should consider intersectionality and avoid leaning on normative or binary ideas of identities. Instead of identifying what identity categories are protected or served in specific policies, policy makers might consider leaving the categories open for interpretation. In family leave policies, for instance, consideration of the multiple ways that individuals form and make meaning of "family" could allow for individuals to utilize the policy more toward their specific needs. In antidiscrimination policies, making clear that any and all identities are included in being protected from oppression or bias might make those policies more applicable to the diversity of individuals that exist within higher education today. Policies cannot perfectly attend to the complexities of identity; they can, however, make a better effort at adapting or evolving to the current needs of the stakeholders within higher education.

REFERENCES

Acker, J. (2006). Inequality regimes: Gender, class, and race in organizations. *Gender & Society, 20,* 441–469.

Baumgartner, F., & Jones, B. (1993). *Agendas and instability in American politics.* Chicago, IL: University of Chicago Press.

Bilimoria, D., & Stewart, A. J. (2009). "Don't ask, don't tell": The academic climate for Lesbian, gay, bisexual, and transgender faculty in science and engineering. *NWSA Journal, 21,* 85–104.

Bystydzienski, J. M., & Bird, S. R. (Eds.). (2006). *Removing barriers: Women in academic science, technology, engineering, and mathematics.* Bloomington: Indiana University Press.

Carbado, D. W. (2013). Colorblind intersectionality. *Signs, 38,* 811–845.

Choo, H. Y., & Ferree, M. M. (2010). Practicing intersectionality in sociological research: A critical analysis of inclusions, interactions, and institutions in the study of inequalities. *Sociological Theory, 28,* 129–149.

Cole, E. R. (2009). Intersectionality and research in psychology. *American Psychologist, 64,* 170–180.

Crenshaw, K. W. (1989). Demarginalizing the intersection of race and sex: A black feminist critique of antidiscrimination doctrine, feminist theory and antiracist politics. *University of Chicago Legal Forum, 139,* 139–167.

Crenshaw, K. (1991). Mapping the margins: Intersectionality, identity politics, and violence against women of Color. *Stanford Law Review, 43,* 1241–1299.

Cress, C. M., & Hart, J. (2009). Playing soccer on the football field: The persistence of gender inequalities for women faculty. *Equity & Excellence in Education, 42,* 473–488.

Danby, C. (2007). Political economy and the closet: Heteronormativity in feminist economics. *Feminist Economics, 13,* 29–53.

Dill, B. T. (2009). Intersections, identities, and inequalities in higher education. In B. T. Dill & R. E. Zambrana (Eds.), *Emerging intersections: Race, class, and gender in theory, policy, and practice* (pp. 229–252). New Brunswick, NJ: Rutgers University Press.

Dill, B. T., & Kohlman, M. H. (2012). Intersectionality: A transformative paradigm in feminist theory and social justice. In S. N. Hesse-Biber (Ed.), *The handbook of feminist research: Theory and praxis* (pp. 154–174). Thousand Oaks, CA: Sage.

Hirshfield, L. E., & Joseph, T. D. (2011). "We need a Woman, we need a black Woman": Gender, race, and identity taxation in the academy. *Gender and Education, 24,* 213–227.

Jones, B., & Baumgartner, F. (2005). *The politics of attention: How government prioritizes problems.* Chicago, IL: The University of Chicago Press.

Lorde, A. (1984). *Sister outsider: Essays and speeches by Audre Lorde.* Berkeley, CA: The Crossing.

MacKinnon, C. A. (2013). Intersectionality as method: A note. *Signs, 38,* 1019–1030.

Mason, M. A., & Goulden, M. (2004). Marriage and baby blues: Redefining gender equity in the academy. *The Annals of the American Academy of Political and Social Science, 596,* 86–103.

Parent, M., DeBlaere, C., & Moradi, B. (2013). Approaches to research on intersectionality: Perspectives on gender, LGBT, and racial/ethnic identities. *Sex Roles: A Journal of Research, 68,* 639–645.

Patil, V. (2013). From Patriarchy to Intersectionality: A Transnational Feminist Assessment of How Far We've Really Come. *Signs, 38*(4), 847–867.

Rankin, S. (2005). Campus climate for sexual minorities. In R. Sanlo (Ed.), *Gender identity and sexual orientation: Research, policy, and personal: New directions for student services* (No. 111, 17–23). San Francisco, CA: Jossey-Bass.

Ropers-Huilman, R., & Winters, K. T. (2010). Imagining intersectionality and the spaces in between: Theories and processes of socially transformative knowing. In M. Savin-Baden & C. H. Major (Eds.), *New approaches to qualitative research: Wisdom and uncertainty* (pp. 37–48). New York, NY: Routledge.

Rosen, L. (2009). Rhetoric and symbolic action in the policy process. In G. Skyes, B. Schneider, & D. Plank (Eds.), *The AERA handbook of education policy research* (pp. 267–285). New York, NY: American Educational Research Association.

Schaefer Riley, N. (2012, April 30). The most persuasive case for eliminating black studies? Just read the dissertations. *The Chronicle of Higher Education.* Retrieved from http://chronicle. com/blogs/brainstorm/the-most-persuasive-case-for-eliminating-black-studies-just-read-the-dissertations/46346

Warner, L. R., & Shields, S. A. (2013). The intersections of sexuality, gender, and race: Identity research at the crossroads. *Sex Roles, 68,* 803–810.

PART TWO

Research

CHAPTER EIGHT

Backward Thinking

Exploring the Relationship among Intersectionality, Epistemology, and Research Design

DANIEL TILLAPAUGH AND Z NICOLAZZO

Scholarship on intersectionality, particularly in educational research, often focuses on the intersecting identities of participants (e.g., Jones & Abes, 2013; Tillapaugh, 2012). Despite this focus, Renn (2010) argued that some scholars' use of intersectionality inadvertently created "some slippage of the term among educational researchers" (p. 7). The lack of exploration regarding the interrogation of power implicit in intersectionality, how it influences one's multiple identities and how it mediates one's interactions with others, troubles us as scholars. Informed by Bowleg's (2008) foundational work on the complex challenges of intersectionality research, we believe intersectional thinking that begins and ends with research participants' identities misses an important step, which is how intersectionality is implicated in, and thus influences, the research design. We argue that one's epistemological grounding, how one conceptualizes truth and power and the ways in which scholars influence each other's thinking about their research projects, has a direct impact on the fecundity of the research content. These are the topics around which we frame our analysis within this chapter. In doing so, we find it important to engage in *backward thinking*, or the idea that one not only needs to leverage intersectionality with participants and in data analysis but also prior to seeking participants, specifically in terms of one's epistemology, reflexivity, and overall research design.

In this chapter, we pose the following questions, which serve as a guide to our backward thinking:

1. What happens when one thinks about intersectionality as a concept influencing study design and the research process itself?
2. How might thinking about intersectionality as affecting what happens before data collection and analysis be an important lens for better addressing the multifaceted political aspects of research?
3. What could an investigation of intersectionality of researchers' epistemological groundings offer the field of educational research, particularly for higher education?

In asking these questions, we seek to expand our collective thinking about the concept of intersectionality by reflecting on how it impacts the design of research studies as well as how one thinks about the research one does. By doing so, we argue that not only do researchers and participants benefit, but the potential effect(s) of one's research may be positively influenced as well. In other words, by engaging in backward thinking regarding intersectional research, we allow for greater visibility for highly marginalized student populations, thus increasing our visibility of their (and our) lives.

EPISTEMOLOGY DEFINED

Epistemology, or the theory of knowledge, comprises "the relationship between what we know and what we see [and] the truths we seek and believe as researchers" (Lincoln, Lynham, & Guba, 2011, p. 103). Seen in this way, a researcher's epistemological grounding is always already embedded in a relationship between oneself (e.g., one's social identities) and something or someone else. Although concerns about truth, power, values, and knowledge are central to one's epistemology, these are understood not solely through internal thought but as a result of didactic interactions between an individual and others in one's social context, including between researcher(s) and participant(s). For higher education researchers, this means one comes to one's own epistemic beliefs as a result of interacting with research participants as well as other scholars.

Epistemes may range from positivism—the belief in absolute and objective truths that can be established through scientific inquiry—to poststructuralism—the belief that categories of identification are constantly in flux and do little to convey specific meaning about that which is being explained (Lincoln et al., 2011). Furthermore, some epistemologies foreground participants and their voices (e.g., constructivism), while others place primary emphasis on exposing and interrogating overarching systems of societal power, privilege, and oppression (e.g., criticalism; Lincoln et al., 2011). Although research studies have traditionally been rooted in one episteme (e.g., constructivism), some scholars (e.g.,

Abes, 2009; Kincheloe, 2001) have begun to recognize how epistemologies overlap, converge, and can work in collaboration to provide a more complete and complex understanding of data. Because how one thinks about knowledge is rooted in how our identities intersect with one another, we must reflect on and understand how our chosen epistemes inform our own worldview as researchers but also as people. For this theoretical analysis, we as authors discuss how researchers can work together across epistemological perspectives to enhance the research process and resulting analysis.

INTERSECTIONALITY DEFINED

Dill and Zambrana (2009) framed intersectionality "as an analytical strategy—a systematic approach to understanding human life and behavior that is rooted in the experiences and struggles of marginalized people" (p. 4). Citing the increasing emergence of studies on intersectionality in higher education, Jones and Abes (2013) maintained, "with an explicit focus on locating individuals within larger structures of privilege and oppression, intersectionality as an analytic framework for understanding identity insists on … a more holistic approach to identity" (p. 135). By centering the conversations of social identities in an intersectional view, scholars begin to interrogate the "interconnected structures of inequality" (Dill & Zambrana, 2009, p. 5) by which power and privilege are granted (or not granted) based on the intersections of one's social identities, as well as how these systems are maintained and replicated within society (Berger & Guidroz, 2009; Crenshaw, 1995). Elaborating on this point, Weber (1998) highlighted that one's own internalized understanding of one's identity (e.g., gender, race) "depends on one's *simultaneous* location in the race, class, gender, and sexuality hierarchies" (p. 26). As a result, power intrinsically plays a role in the identity politics at both an individual and collective/societal level (Crenshaw, 1995; Weber, 1998).

The Concept of Systemic Power

The notion of power is deeply implicated in intersectionality. Baca Zinn and Dill (1996) argued that intersections of identity create a confluence of privilege and oppression for individuals. Shields (2008) expanded on this idea, stating that the intersection of identities "instantiate social stratification" whereby identities "may be experienced as a feature of individual selves, but [they] also reflect … the operation of power relations among groups that comprise that identity category" (p. 302). In their work, Dill and Zambrana (2009) offered four domains by which power structures subordinate others based on dimensions of their identities and maintain systems of inequality. These included the following:

1. The structural domain, which consists of the institutional structures of the society including government, the legal system, housing patterns, economic traditions, and educational structure.
2. The disciplinary domain, which consists of the ideas and practices that characterize and sustain bureaucratic hierarchies.
3. The hegemonic domain, which consists of the images, symbols, ideas, and ideologies that shape social consciousness (Collins, 2000).
4. The interpersonal domain, which consists of patterns of interaction between individuals and groups. (p. 7)

Any discussion of intersectionality without due consideration given to the implications and effects of systemic power misses the proverbial mark. Rather than talking about intersectionality, which includes the ways in which power mediates the lived experiences of people based on dominant and/or subordinated identities, the lack of focus on the effects of systemic power often leads researchers to equate intersectionality with how people's various identities come together at the individual level (Bowleg, 2008; Nash, 2008) or the exploration of individuals' multiple identities without considering their social contexts and the influence of power on their experiences and, thus, the livability of their lives (Butler, 2004).

INTERSECTIONAL IDENTITIES ⇐⇒ INTERSECTIONAL RESEARCH

Who a researcher is—one's worldview, life experiences, and social identities—often influences the research one undertakes (Jones, Torres, & Arminio, 2006; Stewart, 2010). Moreover, a researcher rarely if ever conducts data collection and analysis in isolation. Instead, researchers work within a community of scholars, examples of which include not only the conferences at which research results are disseminated but also the personal interactions researchers have with one another to discuss and work through the particularities of one's work. Therefore, not only is there a synergistic relationship between who one is as a researcher and one's work but also how one interacts with others in a community of scholars and one's work. In other words, while we are not suggesting every research project needs to have multiple researchers, we are suggesting that researchers' identities do influence the ways in which they make meaning and view their own research from a variety of epistemological foundations (e.g., those of our colleagues).

Dill (2009) stated, "Intersectional work is dependent upon collaborations, alliances, and networks among scholars with similar intellectual interests, visions, ideas, and values" (p. 234). Additionally, Kincheloe (2011) suggested researchers bring together multiple ways of thinking and collecting data as a way to engage in inquiry with emancipatory aims. Here, it becomes clear that who one is as a researcher and how one interacts with others in the community of scholars directly influences the way one thinks, constructs, and enacts research. As examples of how these intersectional relationships enhance one's research, we as authors will now reflect on how our own thinking has been altered as a result of our ongoing dialogue and collaboration with each other.

The Evolution of Dan's Research

As a qualitative researcher, I (DT) have come to understand the importance of reflexivity and its role within my work. Being a White, gay, cisgender male from a middle-class, rural farm family in upstate New York, I know that my own lived experiences and multiple social identities play a significant role in how I make meaning of myself and others. My research interests are really passion areas of mine that stem from my personal life. The feminist slogan of "the personal is political" (Hanisch, 2006, p. 1) resonates with me in that my research is informed by my personal life and vice versa. My interest in intersectionality in higher education stems from my interest in student development and my critique that much of the traditional theories used in practice in higher education subjugate and splinter aspects of one's identities into fragmented parts rather than encouraging one to take a holistic approach. To me, intersectionality provided an outlet for understanding one's multiple identities within the context of the larger systems of power in which one lives.

My line of research has been largely focused on how sexual minority men in college make meaning of their multiple identities, particularly their sense of masculinities and sexuality (see Tillapaugh, 2012). As a researcher who tends to identify as a constructivist, I embrace the notion of social construction of identities. Therefore, in my research, I place an emphasis on understanding data (e.g., students' personal narratives) in the social contexts in which they live as well as examine the construction of knowledge between the participants and myself (Charmaz, 2006). Exploring my own meaning making process of my social identities illuminated important aspects of my positionality, which certainly helped me check some biases and assumptions; certainly reading key works on intersectionality and research (see Bowleg, 2008; Crenshaw, 1995; Dill & Zambrana, 2009; McCall, 2005; Stewart, 2010) also informed my epistemological stances and the ways I wanted to conduct my research using intersectionality as an analytical lens. At the same time, my peer review team—of which Z was a member—also played an important role in the evolution of my work.

Z's role within my research shifted my work forward tremendously, particularly in thinking critically about aspects of identity, especially the location of power and difference. As a critical researcher entrenched in critical trans politics—a critical theoretical perspective centered on increasing the life chances of trans[*1] individuals via broad-based coalitions and movements for social change (Spade, 2015)—I appreciate Z's interrogation of aspects of my work that I often take for granted or on which I did not push back. The tensions between our different theoretical paradigms may be present, but they have allowed for a blending—an epistemological bricolage (Kincheloe, 2001), of sorts—that has certainly helped my own thinking around intersectionality. As a constructivist, I appreciated the aspects of one's multiple identity development within the work but often would find myself bringing in aspects of Z's critical approaches to the systemic parts of my research. For example, in discussions of heteronormativity experienced by many of my participants in college, conversations with Z heightened my ability to dig into how heteronormativity tended to be replicated within the LGBT (lesbian, gay, bisexual, transgender) community and its advocacy for same-sex marriage rather than issues that may take higher priorities for others within our community (e.g., employment nondiscrimination laws, immigration laws for same-sex partners, access to health care for trans* people). This epistemological bricolage has provided a more nuanced and complex examination into the ways in which intersectional approaches to research can provide significant implications for practice, policy, theory, and research in higher education, which we discuss further in this chapter.

The Evolution of Z's Research

When positioning myself (ZN) within my research, I often struggle to provide "something other than a list of attributes separated by those proverbial commas (gender, sexuality, race, class), that usually mean that we have not yet figured out how to think [about] the relations we seek to mark" (Butler, 2011, p. 123). Although I am a queer, trans* researcher with an invisible disability who, due to my educational attainment, has transcended the lower middle-class background I was thrown into when my parents divorced, stating these identities does little to shed light on who I am. Similarly, stating that Dan, as a gay cisgender man, has influenced my work also seems devoid of meaning. I am not saying that social identities do not matter. Quite the opposite; I am suggesting that they matter too much to just string them together with commas and think one has explored fully one's positionality.

In reflecting on my work with Dan, what does seem important is that we simultaneously converge regarding some identities (e.g., we are both White) while diverging across other categories of difference (e.g., Dan is cisgender and I am trans*). Additionally, we negotiate dominant and subordinate identities, both individually and between us. As such, my relationship with Dan, which has spanned more than a decade, has set the stage for us to support each other as our identities shift over time as well as challenge how our thinking, life experiences, and social identities mediate our worldviews and how we make meaning of our research. Specifically, Dan's commitment to constructivist grounded theory (Charmaz, 2006) has reminded me of the importance of listening to the voices of my participants and building strong, reciprocal relationships with them. Concurrently, in keeping with the tenets of critical trans politics (Spade, 2015), I also maintain a focus on interrogating the genderism in which the trans* students with whom I research are culturally embedded to increase the livability of our lives. Furthermore, Dan has impressed upon me the importance of focusing on my own feelings, reactions, and responses throughout the research process. As a result of this new affective orientation toward my research, I am continually drawn back to my participants and the process of working alongside of them rather than solely foregrounding the systemic forms of oppression on which my critical theoretical perspective centers.

Thinking Through Intersectionality Together

It is evident in reflecting on our own experiences as researchers that our work has been enhanced by recognizing not only the connections we have to our lines of inquiry but also to each other as scholars. Nevertheless, because we have slightly different epistemological groundings (e.g., I [DT] am a critical constructivist and Z a criticalist), which tend to foreground different things (e.g., constructivism foregrounds participants' voices while criticalism foregrounds a thorough critique of social inequity), we have to negotiate what our working together means. For example, we want study participants to share their stories in whatever way they make meaning of them (a constructivist tenet), but we also realize that how they tell these stories, and the context in which these stories are placed, are often laced with elements of power, privilege, and oppression (a critical tenet). Put another way, participants' stories may be studded with elements of power, privilege, and oppression that they may not know how to articulate or make meaning of but may be highlighted by a critical analysis. As such, our working together in an intersectional way has mandated that we address questions regarding how each of us approaches research, the ways we structure research questions, and how we collect and analyze data. Furthermore, we were constantly cycling back to how our social identities, life experiences, and social contexts were mediating our responses both to each other and our work. For example, the salience of my (ZN) trans* identity allowed me to recognize a theme of gender policing grounded in transphobia that emerged from the data obtained in Dan's research (Tillapaugh & Nicolazzo, 2015). Our own vantage points as researchers have been informed by our multiple identities and the institutional and societal systems in which we are embedded, which is consistent with taking an intersectional approach to the research process. Although thinking through intersectionality requires consistent and intense reflection in all phases of the research process, we have found the resulting effects to be worthwhile.

Due to the lack of emphasis on power as a mediating force in educational research on intersectionality, we now turn to do some backward thinking on its influence on the research process prior to data collection and analysis. In doing so, it is important to recognize the way power has the potential to influence participants despite them not articulating the connection. In other words, the constellation of identities for any given researcher (see Iverson, 2014), along with one's epistemological and methodological choices for any given study, influence the following: which participants seek to join a study, which participants are selected, what experiences they share, how they share their experiences, and what meaning is made from their sharing on behalf of the researcher, participant(s), and for them as co-constructors of knowledge. For example, my (ZN) epistemological choice to use critical trans politics (Spade, 2015) likely had an influence in who I was able to recruit for my dissertation study as well as the meaning(s) me and my participants reached as a result of our collaboration. How one talks about one's work, the questions one uses to frame one's inquiry, and the places one seeks (and does not seek) participants not only impacts what data one collects (and does not collect), but they also are directly related to one's personal identities as an individual and researcher as well as one's interactions among one's scholarly community.

These are not idle decisions, and they are not without consequence. Power not only mediates the direction in which a study goes and how meaning making in the data analysis process occurs. Additionally, power also affects how the research is perceived, the extent to which it is welcomed, by whom it is welcomed, and the access one may or may not get to publish and/or present in certain venues. Scholars have pointed out that the complex intersections of personal identities and overarching social contexts (e.g., neoliberalism) may influence one's ability to be recognized as a knowledge producer in the academy (Elia & Yep, 2012; Pasque, Carducci, Kuntz, & Gildersleeve, 2012). Furthermore, although researchers on the margins certainly do gain access to publish their work, questions of in what venue, at what cost, and if such access acts as a form of "buffer zone" (Kivel, 2007; Spade, 2010) that occludes the continued pervasiveness of systemic oppression (e.g., sexism, genderism, heterosexism, ableism, classism) embedded within the institutions through which such knowledge is shared persist. As Dill (2009) reinforced, research on intersectionality should actively call for and maintain social justice and the disruption of these pervasive systems of oppression for the benefit of those marginalized within society. For example, Tierney's (1997) commentary on whether gay scholars should look to publish in mainstream journals or queer publications, and the effects of such decisions, shows how power mediates not only how one approaches research and the research process but the extent to which one's research is viewed as valid, appropriate, and useful by others in one's respective field of study.

IMPLICATIONS FOR EDUCATIONAL RESEARCH

What does all of this mean for those individuals interested in conducting research through the lens of intersectionality? We believe the process of backward thinking has several important implications for one's individual and collective work. Taking an intersectional perspective in one's work is deeply enriching and rewarding in that everyone has multiple competing identities and multiple ways of thinking. Thus, intersectional approaches seem natural as a means of engaging in and with research. At the same time, conducting research informed through the lens of intersectionality is extremely difficult to do (Jones & Abes, 2013).

As researchers and scholars, one needs to engage those aspects of oneself through reflexivity by considering one's positionality as well as one's work with collaborators, when possible, to help examine and illuminate potential biases. Additionally, one needs to also have a keen awareness of the contexts in which participants live and learn and become well-versed in considering those while engaged in data analysis. For example, one of my (DT) participants, a first-generation Cambodian American gay male from a working-class family, discussed his experiences of taking out additional student loans to provide money to his family back home for their expenses, working two part-time jobs, and thus not being connected to student organizations on campus. In the interviews, the student discussed this as being connected to his Buddhist upbringing, but I, from my positionality of being from a White middle-class background, felt as though these behaviors were indicative of the student's social class. During the study's focus group, I asked the student directly about his social class and its potential impact on his college experience; the student once again pressed back and said his faith had more to do with his personal engagement with family and college and that his social class played very little into his identity. This experience was significant because it pointed to what McCall (2005) referred to as *intracategorical complexity*, or the ways differing identities within a social group (i.e., gay men) create uniquely textured experiences that desire to be teased apart. This encounter also reminded me that ultimately, the power I had as a researcher could easily have been used to manipulate the student's truth that his faith was more salient than his social class. As a result, I had a transformative learning experience related to his own reflexivity as well as how his meaning-making of his shared experiences and my understanding of that same data were *both necessary* in providing a fuller, more complex, and more complete picture for the research study.

McCall's (2005) notion of intracategorical complexity also connects to Warner's (2008) discussion of master categories versus emergent categories in intersectional research. Warner stated, "Before researchers make the assumption that the master category validly represents all or most groups, the researcher must first establish the merit of that assumption" (p. 458). As with the aforementioned example, my (DT) positionality ultimately played into an incorrect assumption around the master category of the participant. The participant's religious beliefs combined with his racial identification as well as his status as a first-generation American played a much more significant role in his own master narrative than his socioeconomic status. Through the act of suspending my own judgment and engaging with my participant around his own meaning making of his intersectional identities, his truth was validated rather than my own incorrect assumptions. By engaging in reflexive work, I (DT) came to understand that it is essential that individuals become vigilant in understanding their own reflexivity as it relates to how they think about research, who they are, and how they approach their work.

Another implication of using intersectionality in educational research is to understand the political ramifications of that work on a micro and macro level. Truly intersectional research must address the micro and macro levels in concert with one another to frame one's multiple social identities in the larger context of systems of inequality in which one is a part (Dill & Zambrana, 2009; Jones & Abes, 2013). This relates back to Bowleg's (2008) point that "intersectionality researchers are charged with the responsibility of making the intersections between ethnicity, sex/gender, sexual orientation (to name just a few) and the social inequality related to these identities, explicit" (p. 322). Similarly, Choo and Ferree (2010) posited, "The complexity of multiple institutions that feed back into each other—both positively and negatively—can become obscured when the macrostructures of inequality are separated from the microstructures of social construction of meaning" (p. 146). When thinking backward, it becomes critical to situate one's work at both the micro and macro levels to allow for the visibility inherent at illuminating the phenomenon being studied. As Warner (2008) cautioned, "One of the central issues in the study of intersectionality is that of visibility—who is granted attention, who is not, and the consequences of these actions for the study of social issues" (p. 462). Therefore, care must be taken as one sets forth with one's research to ensure that questions of visibility are addressed in the name of research that interrogates social structures and attempts to forward human dignity and social equity.

CONCLUSION

In articulating the importance of intersectionality, Dill and Zambrana (2009) stated the following:

> We argue that intersectionality challenges traditional modes of knowledge production in the United States and illustrate how this theory provides an alternative model that combines advocacy, analysis, theorizing, and pedagogy—basic components essential to the production of knowledge as well as the pursuit of social justice and equality. (p. 1)

As researchers who are heavily invested in intersectional approaches to research, we agree with this statement. Yet, rather than just thinking about how intersectionality can be used as an analytical tool, we place emphasis on the notion of backward thinking, or identifying how intersectionality is essential to thinking through one's epistemological, axiological, and/or ontological groundings. These aspects of one's thinking are foundational for the ways in which research studies are framed and carried out. Whether one does research alongside other researchers, in collaboration with participants, or by oneself, backward thinking is one strategy to engage in deeper reflection about the research *process* rather than just using intersectionality as a lens for analyzing research *content*. In doing so, scholars are able to provide richer and more complex analyses of their research—both the process by which research was done and the data co-constructed with participants—and to promote equity and justice for those participants with whom one researches.

NOTE

1. The use of the asterisk in the word *trans** is used to symbolize the multiplicity of gender identities, expressions, and embodiments within the trans* community. For more information about the use of the asterisk in the term trans*, see Tompkins (2014) and Nicolazzo (2017).

REFERENCES

Abes, E. S. (2009). Theoretical borderlands: Using multiple theoretical perspectives to challenge inequitable power structures in student development theory. *Journal of College Student Development, 50*, 141–156.

Baca Zinn, M., & Dill, B. T. (1996). Theorizing difference from multiracial feminism. *Feminist Studies, 22*, 321–331.

Berger, M. T., & Guidroz, K. (Eds.). (2009). *The intersectional approach: Transforming the academy through race, class, and gender.* Chapel Hill: University of North Carolina Press.

Bowleg, L. (2008). When Black + lesbian + woman ≠ Black lesbian woman: The methodological challenges of qualitative and quantitative intersectionality research. *Sex Roles, 59*(5–6), 312–325.

Butler, J. (2004). *Undoing gender.* New York, NY: Routledge.

Butler, J. (2011). *Bodies that matter: On the discursive limits of "sex."* New York, NY: Routledge.

Charmaz, K. (2006). *Constructing grounded theory: A practical guide through qualitative analysis.* Los Angeles, CA: Sage.

Choo, H. Y., & Ferree, M. M. (2010). Practicing intersectionality in sociological research: A critical analysis of inclusions, interactions, and institutions in the study of inequalities. *Sociological Theory, 28*(2), 129–149.

Collins, P. H. (2000). *Black feminist thought: Knowledge, consciousness, and the politics of empowerment* (2nd ed.). New York, NY: Routledge.

Crenshaw, K. W. (1995). Mapping the margins: Intersectionality, identity politics, and violence against women of Color. In K. W. Crenshaw, N. Gotanda, G. Peller, & K. Thomas (Eds.), *Critical race theory: The key writings that formed the movement* (pp. 357–383). New York, NY: New Press.

Dill, B. T. (2009). Intersections, identities, and inequalities in higher education. In B. T. Dill & R. E. Zambrana (Eds.), *Emerging intersections: Race, class, and gender in theory, policy, and practice* (pp. 229–252). New Brunswick, NJ: Rutgers University Press.

Dill, B. T., & Zambrana, R. E. (2009). Critical thinking about inequality. In B. T. Dill & R. E. Zambrana (Eds.), *Emerging intersections: Race, class, and gender in theory, policy, and practice* (pp. 1–21). New Brunswick, NJ: Rutgers University Press.

Elia, J. P., & Yep, G. A. (2012). Sexualities and genders in an age of neoterrorism. *Journal of Homosexuality, 59,* 879–889.

Hanisch, C. (2006). Introduction: The personal is political. Retrieved from http://www.carolhanisch. org/CHwritings/PersonalisPol.pdf

Iverson, S. V. (2014). Identity constellations: An intersectional analysis of female student veterans. In D. Mitchell, Jr., C. Y. Simmons, & L. A. Greyerbiehl (Eds.), *Intersectionality and higher education: Theory, research, and praxis* (1st ed., pp. 135–145). New York, NY: Peter Lang.

Jones, S. R., & Abes, E. S. (2013). *Identity development of college students: Advancing frameworks for multiple dimensions of identity.* San Francisco, CA: Jossey-Bass.

Jones, S. R., Torres, V., & Arminio, J. (2006). *Negotiating the complexities of qualitative research in higher education.* New York, NY: Routledge.

Kincheloe, J. L. (2001). Describing bricolage: Conceptualizing a new rigor in qualitative research. *Qualitative Inquiry, 7*(6), 679–692.

Kincheloe, J. L. (2011). Critical ontology: Visions of selfhood and curriculum. In K. Hayes, S. R. Steinberg, & K. Tobin (Eds.), *Key works in critical pedagogy* (pp. 201–217). Rotterdam, the Netherlands: Sense.

Kivel, P. (2007). Social service or social change? In INCITE! Women of Color against violence (Eds.), *The revolution will not be funded: Beyond the non-profit industrial complex* (pp. 129–149). Cambridge, MA: South End.

Lincoln, Y. S., Lynham, S. A., & Guba, E. G. (2011). Paradigmatic controversies, contradictions, and emerging confluences, revisited. In N. K. Denzin & Y. S. Lincoln (Eds.), *The Sage handbook of qualitative research* (4th ed., pp. 97–128). Thousand Oaks, CA: Sage.

McCall, L. (2005). The complexity of intersectionality. *Signs: Journal of Women in Culture and Society, 30*(3), 1771–1880.

Nash, J. C. (2008). Re-thinking intersectionality. *Feminist Review, 89,* 1–15.

Nicolazzo, Z. (2017, February 1). To use or not use the asterisk [Blog post]. Retrieved from https:// znicolazzo.weebly.com/trans-resilience-blog/-to-use-or-not-to-use-the-asterisk.

Pasque, P. A., Carducci, R., Kuntz, A. M., & Gildersleeve, R. E. (2012). *Qualitative inquiry for equity in higher education: Methodological innovations, implications, and interventions* (ASHE Higher Education Report). San Francisco, CA: Jossey-Bass.

Renn, K. A. (2010). LGBT and queer research in higher education: The state and status of the field. *Educational Researcher, 39*(2), 132–141.

Shields, S. A. (2008). Gender: An intersectionality perspective. *Sex Roles, 59*(5–6), 301–311. doi:10.1007/s11199-008-9501-8

Spade, D. (2010). Be professional! *Harvard Journal of Law & Gender, 33,* 71–84.

Spade, D. (2015). *Normal life: Administrative violence, critical trans politics, and the limitations of law* (2nd ed.). Durham, NC: Duke University Press.

Stewart, D. L. (2010). Researcher as instrument: Understanding "shifting" findings in constructivist research. *Journal of Student Affairs Research and Practice, 47*(3), 291–306.

Tierney, W. G. (1997). *Academic outlaws: Queer theory and cultural studies in the academy.* Thousand Oaks, CA: Sage.

Tillapaugh, D., & Nicolazzo, Z. (2015). "It's kind of apples and oranges": Gay college males' conceptions of gender transgression as poverty. *Journal of Critical Scholarship on Higher Education and Student Affairs, 1*(1), 67–81.

Tillapaugh, D. W. (2012). *Toward an integrated self: Making meaning of the multiple identities of gay men in college* (Unpublished doctoral dissertation). University of San Diego, San Diego, CA.

Tompkins, A. (2014). Asterisk. *TSQ: Transgender Studies Quarterly, 1*(1–2), 26–27.

Warner, L. R. (2008). A best practices guide to intersectionality approaches in psychological research. *Sex Roles, 59*(5–6), 454–463. doi:10.1007/s11199-008-9504-5

Weber, L. (1998). A conceptual framework for understanding race, class, gender, and sexuality. *Psychology of Women Quarterly, 22,* 13–22.

CHAPTER NINE

Metaphorically Speaking

Being a Black Woman in the Academy Is Like …

CHRISTA J. PORTER

> There is a kind of strength that is almost frightening in Black women. It's as if a steel rod runs right through the head down to the feet.
> —MAYA ANGELOU (1973, AS CITED IN ELLIOT, 1989, P. 22)

Critical scholarship examining Black women's experiences in the academy has increased over the past several decades. Scholars have specifically examined how Black women have traversed into and through the academy through the following research foci: historical perspectives of Black women's' trajectories (Gregory, 2001); existence, resistance, and transformation (Hull, Bell-Scott, & Smith, 1982; Mabokela & Green, 2001; Perlow, Wheeler, Bethea, & Scott, 2018); fatigue and resilience through tenure and promotion (Carter Andrews, 2015; Croom & Patton, 2012); mentorship (Fries-Britt & Kelly, 2005; Grant & Ghee, 2015); self-efficacy (McNeely Cobham & Patton, 2015); and the redefinition of professional socialization and roles (Sulé, 2009, 2014). Researchers must learn from and build upon previous scholarship in order to further explore the nuanced ways Black women navigate(d) and negotiate(d) their place and space in the academy. The purpose of this chapter is to illuminate the narratives of three Black women faculty at predominately white[1] institutions through the use of metaphor.

INTERSECTIONALITY

The historical and social location of Black women has been (and must continue to be) situated at the nexus of identity and the oppressive structures within which we survive (Collins, 1990; Crenshaw, 1991; hooks, 1981). Black women's experiences in the academy mirror that of our positioning within the history of American society—the historical legacy of marginalization and exploitation Black women have carried as members of society does not change once we enter the ivory towers of academia. Black women hold an *outsider-within status* (Collins, 1986) in the academy as the intersections of our minoritized identities as Black women academics relegate us to the margins of the system. Marginalization is increased once additional identities (and subsequent 'isms) are layered such as full-time non-tenure track (NTT) or contingency in academic appointment (Boss, Davis, Porter, & Moore, 2019), age, marital status, gender identity, sexual orientation, and socioeconomic status (just to name a few). "Because the intersectional experience is greater than the sum of racism and sexism, any analysis that does not take intersectionality into account cannot sufficiently address the particular manner in which Black women are subordinated" (Crenshaw, 1989, p. 140). Crenshaw (1989, 1991) coined the term *intersectionality* in reference to Black women who experienced sexual violence and navigated the structural oppressions present within the justice system in ways that were distinctly different than their white women peers. "When there's no name for a problem, you can't see a problem. When you can't see a problem, you can't solve it" (Crenshaw, 2016). There was no name for what these Black women were experiencing at the intersections of their marginalized identities in the legal system.

Intersectionality as a tool of analysis, however, has been used more recently by scholars to expand the discussion and emphasize unveiling power structures and systems of inequality for people of Color (Collins, 2000; Collins & Bilge, 2016; Dill & Zambrana, 2009).

> Intersectional analysis explores and unpacks relations of domination and subordination, privilege and agency, in the structural arrangements through which various services, resources, and other social rewards are delivered; in the interpersonal experiences of individuals and groups; in the practices that characterize and sustain bureaucratic hierarchies; and in the ideas, images, symbols, and ideologies that shape social consciousness. (Dill & Zambrana, 2009, p. 5)

For Black women faculty in the academy, intersectionality is a critical lens through which to view our experiences, yet analyses must also be situated within the context of these systems, power structures, hegemony, and hierarchies that shape the individual and collective consciousness of the academy and those with whom we interact.

METHOD

Findings for this chapter are from a larger study on the experiences of Black women faculty at predominately white institutions, where my colleagues and I served as researcher participants (Boss et al., 2019). We—Grace, Danai, and Amanda (pseudonyms)—graduated from a higher education student affairs related doctoral program between 2013–2014, we each have held full-time contingent (NTT) and/ or tenure-track faculty appointments, and have remained in community with one another since beginning our doctoral program in 2010. While we were able to locate the literature on Black women's experiences in the academy, we specifically noticed a dearth in scholarship on contingent Black faculty women. This lack of literature provoked us to write ourselves into existence using scholarly personal narratives. Scholarly personal narrative (SPN) as a critical qualitative approach, has been used to assist the scholar-writer affirm their experiences via personal essay organized by categories and themes connected to a larger worldview (Nash, 2004). SPN has served as an optimal technique for faculty of Color in the academy to not only write themselves into existence, but to also identify themes and implications in their rich narratives that were relevant to one another, future faculty, and those with whom worked alongside faculty of Color to better understand their experiences and improve the academic climate for faculty of Color (Boss et al., 2019; Fries-Britt & Kelly, 2005; Louis et al., 2016).

In this chapter, I specifically highlight extended excerpts from our individual narratives that contribute to a collective and intersectional analysis through the use of metaphors. As discussed earlier in the chapter, we bear the burden of proof as Black women. We find ourselves having to name, explain, and describe our own experiences as real and true (Crenshaw, 2016). The purpose of conceptual metaphors is to represent one thing with something else; they provide structure into how we understand our experiences (Lakoff & Johnson, 1980). Using metaphor is a meaning-making process; individuals engage metaphors in our daily lives to guide how we relate to others, how we navigate the world, and what we perceive. The coupling of scholarly personal narratives with metaphor not only permitted the space to authentically reflect, but it also challenged us to think more deeply about the tangible ways intersectionality became/becomes real for us as Black women in the academy.

I offered the following prompt:

> Using metaphor(s), how would you describe what it is like to be a Black woman in the academy? What specific experiences influence your description while teaching, researching, or serving as a faculty member? Discuss how intersectionality has influenced the way(s) you show up as a Black woman in the academy? How do you define and identify with intersectionality in your identities?

After compiling the narratives, I reviewed the following four theoretical interventions of intersectionality (Dill & Zambrana, 2009): centering the experiences of people of Color, complicating identity, unveiling power in interconnected structures of inequality, and promoting social justice and change. Our narratives were stored in an online shared folder; we each engaged in member checking for accuracy and each researcher participant reviewed my analysis and interpretation of data. While I was reading our metaphorical analogies, the majority of our narratives centered on the relationship between identity and power (or inequities in power), so I employed focus coding (Charmaz, 2006) by organizing relevant chunks of data under the two theoretical interventions: (1) complicating identity and (2) unveiling power in interconnected structures of inequality. Complicating identity refers to not only individual and group identities, but also the complex and nuanced relationships between them (Dill & Zambrana, 2009). Unveiling power in interconnected structures of inequality can be described as a force to oppress others and an intangible entity that operates in various domains of society (e.g., hegemonic and interpersonal; Collins, 2000).

FINDINGS

This section is separated into three parts. The first part consists of excerpts from Grace and Danai broadly reflecting on their definitions of intersectionality. The second portion presents the theoretical intervention, complicating identity, in which Amanda, Danai, and Grace articulated the ways intersectionality influenced how they show(ed) up as Black women faculty in the academy. The third and final part of this findings section introduces metaphor through the theoretical intervention, unveiling power in interconnected structures of inequality.

Danai and Grace defined intersectionality respectively,

> I define intersectionality as the thing that makes me more than just another Black woman in the academy. I am a Black woman, but I am also the daughter of a former foster kid whose scrappy, independence taught me to never trust in the system to take care of/care for me but to carve out my own places of belonging. I am a Southerner whose feet tread daily over land where violence was perpetrated over my ancestors and where it was not uncommon to see confederate flags flown high and proud. I am a thousand other things that make my Black womanness simultaneously my own experience and yet still a collective connection. Intersectionality provides me a way of talking both about what it is to be a Black woman and who I am as a Black woman.

Grace reflected,

> When I reflect on intersectionality, my first thought goes to the ways in which I show up as a Black woman with a PhD, and how I experience racism, sexism, and ageism

daily as a faculty member. My identities color the way I am received and at the same time are the lenses through which I exist. As sister Collins discussed, my identities are inextricably linked, thus the marginalization I experience daily, both locally and broadly, are a result of intersectionality as a theoretical framework that encapsulates all of the isms.

Complicating Identity–Influence of Intersectionality as a Black Women in the Academy

Amanda acknowledged,

For me, navigating the academy is an amalgam of the different positions that I hold. I embrace both intersectionality and intersections of my identity in the academy. Although to be fair, most of the identities that are most salient are those that lack power in the academy: Black, woman, and contingent (NTT). I am also very aware of my being young (I appear younger than I am, constantly being told "oh my gosh, you look like a student" or "my children are older than you" and it being laughed off). Since I've been a faculty member, all of these intersections of my identity have been present in ways that I don't believe they were as much as an administrator. There were defined jobs, roles, and responsibilities in administrative life. In faculty life, there's stuff that needs to get done, yet who actually does them is a bit more of a gray area, because they fall under "faculty work." However, these intersections begin to become magnified in the gray area. In my own experience, the women ended up taking on more of the labor of "caring" for the program in terms of recruitment, meeting with students, serving as advisor, developing community, etc. As a contingent faculty member, this was assumed to be my sole responsibility, yet isn't faculty life inclusive of program and departmental service as well?

Danai shared,

The best way I can discuss how intersectionality has influenced the way I show up in the academy is through hyperawareness. My Blackness, womanness, youth, socioeconomic status are ever present in my mind as I interact with colleagues and students. I find myself constantly considering whether to code switch around both colleagues and students, because I realize there are many who still deem Black vernacular English as lazy and ignorant. Yet, I value authenticity and expressing myself in ways that feel comfortable to me, and often more effectively convey the power of my meaning is also important. But, I am not only Black, I am a woman, and I appear youthful. This particular trifecta causes me to constantly think about what I have to do to get a seat at the table and whether getting to the table is even worth it. This trifecta makes me think about how privileged I am to be in academia, especially now that I am in a tenure-track role, because I know the numbers would suggest I am an anomaly. AND, I want to redefine the pathway; so that generations of Black and women of Color academics do not feel like anomalies, but can come into academia and find home. Home, a place where they are accepted for who they are fully and what they have to offer. So, I would say intersectionality places me in a place of questioning if authenticity is attainable for me in the academy.

Grace asserted,

> Specifically, in the academy, because tenure line roles are so coveted, it's almost as if I gained a medal of some sort. Like regardless of my identities, I am "smart" enough and have enough potential to secure one of these spots based on "their" system of judgment and performance. So, I can get in the door and now I am now invited to the table. But because of my identities as Black, woman, and 35, I am still questioned, critiqued, and often marginalized for my ways of knowing, thinking, and producing knowledge based on both my experiences and the experiences of my research participants.

Amanda, Danai, and Grace reflected on their marginalized identities, yet the complex relationships, intersections among identities, and situations of power, nuance their experiences even more. Our identities are complicated because they are inextricably linked, interconnected, and cannot exist on their own, nor can our identities exist outside of power structures. The use of metaphor within our scholarly personal narratives challenged us to objectify our realities more clearly.

Unveiling Power in Interconnected Structures of Inequality—Through the Use of Metaphor

Danai emphasized,

> Being a Black woman in the academy is putting the wooden spoon over the pot to keep it from boiling over. It's the everyday microaggressions, death by a thousand cuts, of being disregarded, dismissed or invisible that lead me to my metaphor. When I think of my experience I think of a boiling pot just on the brink of overflowing, but realizing I cannot let that happen, I reach for whatever guidance I can to prevent it. I remember hearing long ago, that putting a wooden spoon over a boiling pot would stop it from boiling over. I have actually tried this a few times, and a couple of those times the pot boiled over anyway. Yet, I still reach for that solution overall. You would think that just turning down the heat would be my first go to, but it rarely seems like a viable option. As it relates to the prompt, I think about all the times I have been at the height of my frustration in academia, particularly tied to my Blackness and my womanness, and I realize, rarely do I think about turning down the heat (do less service, not caring about teaching quality or evaluations, not striving for top-tiered publications), because in my mind I have to do all those things. I have to serve students, especially Black and Brown students. I have to be great; I cannot let my colleagues or students confirm what I always fear they think: I do not belong. So in lieu of turning down the heat, I reach for the spoon (connecting with a community of peers, prayer, therapy, poetry, dance). Sometimes, I still boil over, but it helps.

Amanda articulated,

> Being a Black woman in the academy is like using a curling iron in the morning and forgetting whether you turned it off when you've left your home for work (the same thing happens when you question whether you left any electric appliance on). It's the nagging thought that you might have left the curling iron on and thinking about all of the bad

METAPHORICALLY SPEAKING | 105

things that could happen. Did you leave it near a towel, could it catch fire, would it blow a fuse, etc. It's all the back-and-forth, the "did I?" or "did I not?" that you have to engage in to determine whether you will go back home to ensure that you did indeed turn off the curling iron and be late for work or a meeting or whether you hope for the best and that your home is still standing when you get home. Essentially, it comes down to how much risk I am willing to take and the mental acrobatics that I must engage in to reconcile my decision. I've come to think of being a Black woman in the academy in the same way: how much of what I believe, who I am, and how I show up am I willing to risk to be seen, heard, and valued in the academy and thinking about all the scenarios that might play out depending on how I "behave." Will I be seen as the proverbial "help," will I be responsible for providing the emotional labor on behalf of the program, will I be viewed as "challenging" when I bring up issues of process, equity, and/or inclusion, will I be viewed as scholarly and just as credible as my white colleagues, will students challenge my authority in the classroom?, and a very real question that stays just below the surface, "will any of these very real possibilities affect whether my annual contract will be renewed?" Being Black, being a woman, and being a non-tenure track faculty member means that I grapple with these "what ifs" all the time as I'm often the only one or one of two Black women in the academic space within my department. When you are thinking about whether you turned something off in your home, most of the time you end up mentioning it to a friend or colleague and they will say, "I'm sure that you did! It's fine." That doesn't make it any easier to get the thought out of your mind. There's still the nagging thought, is it worth the risk? For me, right now, it is worth the risk. I've learned how to show up authentically and recognize the implications and consequences of standing in my truth and integrity. I've learned that while I'm in the academy, I have a responsibility to help change and transform the culture and practices so that they become more equitable and inclusive for Black women and contingent faculty. It's been because I have a strong community that serves as my sounding boards and allows me to process and vent. Being a Black woman in the academy, finding community is critical.

Grace illustrated,

Being a Black woman in the academy is like being a doormat …
    The environment and those within it, step on, step over, and force their so(u)les into us, while we hold up, protect, experience wear and tear as a result of the elements.
    It is a rarity that someone or something picks us up or dusts us off—from the same elements that/who wear and tear (on) us, we are strengthened, learn to self-clean, and must preserve ourselves for the changing climate(s). I felt this metaphor daily. It could have been the environment within which I was positioned, or it could have been the toxicity of those persons who sat at the same table. Either way, the feelings of isolation and marginalization were ever-so-present. I was silenced, yet my voice mattered when it was beneficial to others. I was overlooked for opportunities, yet it was my responsibility to increase experiences for students. I was tired, yet I found strength to maximize my efforts for the students and my professional trajectory. I was isolated, yet I found those who remain necessary and great company for the journey. The company I kept then and keep at this point in my career push, pull, encourage, and strengthen.
    Being a Black woman in the academy is like receiving the professoriate badge on a brownie shawl (in the girl scouts) … except the badge is worthless by itself. It only has meaning and value once its sewn onto the shawl and it's not sown onto the shawl until you

receive tenure and promotion. So you work and write, teach, and publish, and repeat ... do all what's necessary and then some, to wear the shawl, but the badge remains in your hand. You are earning and building, creating and influencing, but without the greater reward until someone else deems you worthy by actually sewing the badge onto the shawl you wear.

DISCUSSION AND IMPLICATIONS

Collins (2009) challenged researchers engaging in intersectional analyses to repo-sition identity narratives outward to elucidate social inequalities and structures within which the individuals or group is situated. The purpose of this chapter was to illuminate the scholarly personal narratives of Grace, Amanda, and Danai as we specifically discussed our experiences as Black women faculty in the academy. The two theoretical interventions permitted me to illuminate a both/and paradigm of Collins' (2009) critique of individuals identifying their research as intersectionality and/or engaging an intersectional analysis—both the individual narratives and the positioning within an inequitable social structure. First, the narrative excerpts I organized under the complicating identity intervention high-lighted not only the unique individual and collective identities Black women hold, but also the relationships among them—the ways they are inextricably linked (Collins, 1990) and the ways those identities manifest in the academy (Boss et al., 2019). Grace, Danai, and Amanda mentioned their age as being (or appearing) younger than colleagues and the ways youthfulness is demoralized only adding to the marginalization of Black women. Amanda shared that her contingency (NTT) status (and one's responsibility for administrative labor) often relegates her to the margins and is the subject of ongoing microaggressions from her colleagues.

Second, the narrative reflections I organized under the theoretical interven-tion, unveiling power in interconnected structures of inequality, metaphorically illustrated the social inequalities that exist within the structure of the academy in which Black women hold an outsider-within status (Collins, 1986). Danai com-pared her experience in the academy to a boiling pot. As a Black woman who is untenured and lacks positional power she is unable to decrease the academic heat (e.g., pressure or expectations), instead, she must place a wooden spoon over the top to sustain her daily existence. Amanda analogized the mental acrobatics and constant reconciliation that Black women endure as similar to forgetting whether you turned off the curling iron after leaving for work. This consistent questioning however is not simply because Black women feel their identities are underrepre-sented or valued less than their colleagues; the marginalization of Black women in the academy is systemic and deeply rooted in our historical and social location in American society (Carter Andrews, 2015; Collins, 1986, 1990; Croom & Patton, 2012; Gregory, 2001; hooks, 1981; Hull et al., 1982; Mabokela & Green, 2001). Grace's reflections revealed both the sacrificial investment Black women make and the inequitable evaluation structure we must persist in order to obtain (and maintain) legitimacy in the academy. Her comparison of our bodies to doormats and us earning (fighting for) a professoriate badge on a brownie shawl captured the juxtapositioning of our outsider-within status (Collins, 1986) and the realities of our resiliency to remain in the academy (Boss et al., 2019).

The longitudinal study of our experiences as Black women in the academy has expanded the work of previous scholarship by examining our experiences in unconventional ways. Coupling scholarly personal narrative with metaphor provided us the language to make meaning of our experiences in an abstract, yet intentional way. Whether a wooden spoon over a boiling pot, turning off a curling iron, being a doormat, or receiving a badge on a brownie shawl, our individual and collective communities were not only crucial in shaping how we interacted with the system, our colleagues, and students, but were also necessary parts of our survival.

Implications

Two implications from this scholarship on Black women in the academy is through mentoring and individuals who are willing to serve as advocates on behalf of Black women to change the system piece-by-piece. Mentorship of Black women doctoral students into the professoriate by Black women faculty has been evidenced as crucial to their success (Fries-Britt & Kelly, 2005; Grant & Ghee, 2015). Peer mentorship of Black women faculty who form writing groups, sister circles, accountability groups, and additional ways to commune with one another assist in supporting one's trajectory in the academy (Boss et al., 2019; Porter, Davis, & Boss, 2018). The onus should not be placed solely on Black women, who are already isolated at their respective institutions, to figure out the academic terrain on their own. Academic affairs departments need to formally establish mentoring structures whereby contingent and tenure-track faculty are provided guidance and ongoing support throughout the duration of their academic appointment at the institution. Having a critical contingency of Black women at an institution would help the pairing process, specifically when discussing identity intersections and how one experiences interactions with colleagues and students within their respective departments.

The inequitable social structure of the academy is not going to change itself—the individuals who hold positional and influential power must influence (and be) the change. Despite our strength and resiliency throughout history, Black women faculty do not hold the necessary political power to change the academy. Even when we reach full professorship, Black women's historical legacy of marginalization preclude a positional authority different than their white peers (Croom & Patton, 2012). Black women faculty across rank, must "develop an arsenal of emotional and psychological weaponry against the cumulative effects of the gendered racism and racist sexism that many of us experience" (Carter Andrews, 2015, p. 79). This gendered racial battle fatigue is exhausting, and Black women need others who hold authentic, equitable, and critical intentions, to use their positional and political power and advocate on our behalf within their respective spheres of influence(s). Being a Black woman in the academy is acknowledging the system for which we are signing up; we may not physically know what "it" looks like to be at the table, but because of the narratives of those who have paved (and are paving) the way for us, we have some insight. This does not mean, however, we are in complete agreement with the structure, governance, and inner workings of the system; but we do need to understand its/our history. Black women persevered the academy as doctoral students and intentionally continue our trajectories into the professoriate, just as Black women have pushed through hundreds of years of marginalization. In a 1973 interview, Maya Angelou referred to the frightening strength of Black women as similar to a steel rod running through her body (as cited in Elliot, 1989). The strength Black women have maintained throughout history is powerful to say the least, despite the frightening, inequitable, and exploitive social structures within which we have been forced (and chosen) to occupy.

NOTE

1. The author has chosen not to capitalize "white" to resist white supremacy.

REFERENCES

Boss, G. J., Davis, T. J., Porter, C. J., & Moore, C. M. (2019). Second to none: Contingent women of Color faculty in the classroom. In R. Jeffries (Ed.), *Diversity, equity, and inclusivity in contemporary higher education* (pp. 211–225). Hershey, PA: IGI Global.
Carter Andrews, D. J. (2015). Navigating raced-gender microaggressions: The experiences of tenure-track Black female scholars. In F. A. Bonner II, A. F. Marbley, F. Tuitt, P. A. Robinson, R. M. Banda, and R. L. Hughes (Eds.), *Black faculty in the academy: Narratives for negotiating identity and achieving career success* (pp. 79–88). New York, NY: Routledge.
Charmaz, K. (2006). *Constructing grounded theory: A practical guide through qualitative analysis*. London, UK: Sage.
Collins, P. H. (1986). Learning from the outsider within: The sociological significance of Black feminist thought. *Social Problems, 33*(6), S14–S22.
Collins, P. H. (1990). *Black feminist thought: Knowledge, consciousness, and the politics of empowerment*. New York, NY: Routledge.
Collins, P. H. (2000). *Black feminist thought: Knowledge, consciousness, and the politics of empowerment* (2nd ed.). New York, NY: Routledge.
Collins, P. H. (2009). Foreword: Emerging intersections–Building knowledge and transforming institutions. In B. T. Dill and R. E Zambrana (Eds.), *Emerging intersections: Race, class, gender, in theory, policy, and practice* (pp. vii–xiv). New Brunswick, NJ: Rutgers University Press.

Collins, P. H., & Bilge, S. (2016). *Intersectionality*. Cambridge, UK: Polity Press.

Crenshaw, K. (1989). Demarginalizing the intersection of race and sex: A Black feminist critique of antidiscrimination doctrine, feminist theory, and antiracist politics. *University of Chicago Legal Forum, 1989*(8), 139–167.

Crenshaw, K. (1991). Mapping the margins: Intersectionality, identity politics, and violence against women of Color. *Stanford Law Review, 43*(6), 1241–1299.

Crenshaw, K. (2016). The urgency of intersectionality [video file]. Retrieved from https://www.ted.com/talks/kimberle_crenshaw_the_urgency_of_intersectionality

Croom, N. N., & Patton, L. D. (2012). The miner's canary: A critical race perspective on the representation of Black women full professors. *Negro Educational Review, 62–63*(1–4), 13–39.

Dill, B. T., & Zambrana, R. E. (2009). *Emerging intersections: Race, class, gender, in theory, policy, and practice*. New Brunswick, NJ: Rutgers University Press.

Elliot, J. M. (1989). *Conversations with Maya Angelou*. Jackson: University Press of Mississippi.

Fries-Britt, S., & Kelly, B. T. (2005). Retaining each other: Narratives of two African American women in the academy. *Urban Review, 37*(3), 221–242.

Grant, C. M., & Ghee, S. (2015). Mentoring 101: Advancing African-American women faculty and doctoral student success in predominantly White institutions. *International Journal of Qualitative Studies in Education, 28*(7), 759–785.

Gregory, S. T. (2001). Black faculty women in the academy: History, status and future. *The Journal of Negro Education, 70*(3), 124–138.

hooks, b. (1981). *Ain't I a woman?: Black women and Feminism*. Boston, MA: South End Press.

Hull, G. T., Bell-Scott, P., & Smith, B. (1982). *All the women are White, all the Blacks are men, but some of us are brave: Black women's studies*. New York, NY: The Feminist Press.

Lakoff, G., & Johnson, M. (1980). *Metaphors we live by*. Chicago, IL: University of Chicago Press.

Louis, D. A., Rawls, G. J., Jackson-Smith, D., Chambers, G. A., Phillips, L. L., & Louis, S. L. (2016). Listening to our voices: Experiences of Black faculty at predominantly White research university with microaggressions. *Journal of Black Studies, 47*(5), 454–474.

Mabokela, R. O., & Green, A. L. (2001). *Sisters of the academy: Emergent Black women scholars in higher education*. Sterling, VA: Stylus.

McNeely Cobham, B. A., & Patton, L. D. (2015). Self-will, power, and determination: A Qualitative study of Black women faculty and the role of self-efficacy. *NASPA Journal about Women in Higher Education, 8*(1), 29–46.

Nash, R. J. (2004). *Liberating scholarly writing: The power of personal narrative*. New York, NY: Teachers College Press.

Perlow, O. N., Wheeler, D. I., Bethea, S. L., & Scott, B. M. (2018). *Black women's liberatory pedagogies: Resistance, transformation, and healing within and beyond the academy*. Cham, Switzerland: Springer Nature.

Porter, C. J., Davis, T. J., Boss, G. J. (2018, December 13). My sister's keeper: Advancing scholarship and sustaining one another through an academic writing (life) group [Web log post]. Retrieved from https://medium.com/national-center-for-institutional-diversity/my-sisters-keeper-1c814c96ce5d

Sulé, V. T. (2009). Black female faculty: Role definition, critical enactments, and contributions to predominantly White research institutions. *NASPA Journal about Women in Higher Education, 2*(1), 93–121.

Sulé, V. T. (2014). Enact, discard, and transform: A critical race feminist perspective on professional socialization among tenured Black female faculty. *International Journal of Qualitative Studies in Education, 27*(4), 432–453.

CHAPTER TEN

Challenges Conducting Intersectional Research WITH LGBQ Students

Reflecting on Studies Exploring Spirituality and Disability

RYAN A. MILLER AND ASHLEY P. JONES

Research on college students' multiple social identities has expanded in recent years, most notably since the introduction of the model of multiple dimensions of identity (Jones & McEwen, 2000) and subsequent revisions and additions (Abes, Jones, & McEwen, 2007; Jones & Abes, 2013). While moving from consideration of a single social identity in isolation to considering multiple identities in tandem arguably represented an important advance in higher education scholarship, multiple identity frameworks still treated identities as discrete entities that can be compared, ranked, or considered more or less salient or important given shifting contexts. By contrast, the increased usage of intersectionality as a framework for connecting students' social identities with their experiences navigating multiple forms of oppressions calls for the treatment of identities as inseparable and mutually reinforcing. Further, use of intersectionality theory necessarily highlights multiple, overlapping systems of oppression that inform the distinct experiences of individuals and groups at the intersections of two or more marginalized social identities, with this theoretical perspective rooted in analysis of the combination of racism and sexism affecting Black women (Crenshaw, 1991). Scholars taking up such a perspective in recent years have produced studies addressing the identities and experiences of Black students (e.g., Stewart, 2008, 2009), trans* and queer students of Color (e.g., Means & Jaeger, 2015; Nicolazzo, 2016), lesbian, gay, and bisexual students (e.g., Payne Gold & Stewart, 2011), and students with disabilities (e.g., Tevis & Griffen, 2014).

These scholars have produced exemplars for the field, yet conducting research using an intersectionality framework remains complex and challenging (Bowleg, 2008; Stewart, 2010). Continued reflection upon research design and method- ological approaches toward understanding intersectionality is needed. Addressing this need, the central question guiding this chapter is: What challenges and lessons learned from two studies focused on understanding intersectional identities of les- bian, gay, bisexual, and queer (LGBQ) students can be applied to future intersec- tional research and practice in higher education? In this chapter, we consider how we, as researchers, approached methodological issues in conducting intersectional studies with LGBQ students including research design, sampling and data collec- tion, and data analysis and interpretation.

More specifically, this chapter is guided by two scholars' reflections on their research (Bowleg, 2008; Stewart, 2010). Bowleg (2008) reflects on two pre- vious studies of stress and resilience experienced by Black lesbian women to derive implications for measurement, analysis, and interpretation of data. The article's title, "When Black + Lesbian + Woman ≠ Black Lesbian Woman," suggests tensions in adopting either additive or intersectional approaches to the study of identity. Bowleg offers concrete suggestions for qualitative and quantitative researchers to use in adopting an intersectional approach to rec- ognize that "social identities and inequality are interdependent for groups such as a Black lesbians, not mutually exclusive" (p. 312). For instance, she suggests that questions must be worded in an intersectional manner that positions iden- tities as inseparable and that data must be analyzed within social and histor- ical context, including analysis of "how individual [participant] accounts are shaped by their location within social hierarchies based on race, sex, and sexual orientation" (p. 318).

We are also guided by Stewart's (2010) reflections on two qualitative stud- ies of Black collegians' multiple identities, both guided by constructivism but conducted four years apart. Stewart considered his role as research instrument and how his growth and evolving perspectives a researcher, as well as differ- ences in context and climate, may have informed the "similar studies [that] yielded different findings" (p. 291). These differences in the two study's find- ings included "the language participants used to describe the multiple facets of their identities; how they negotiated identity; what participants identified as the animating essence of their personalities; and the participants' goals for identity development" (Stewart, 2010, p. 297). Stewart, drawing upon Bowleg's (2008) insights, examined whether and how he asked additive questions, used additive assumptions, and made additive interpretations in his studies. Using Stewart's (2010) work as an exemplar, we take up his call for "researchers to revisit previous findings and interpretations continually as their research skills mature and develop" (p. 303).

METHODS AND BACKGROUND ON TWO ORIGINAL STUDIES

We draw upon our personal reflections of conducting two research studies on college student identities utilizing intersectionality as a framework. We recorded and analyzed our reflections for this chapter using scholarly personal narratives (SPNs) as conceived by Nash (2004) to consider our respective experiences conducting the studies. SPN writers "ask a series of personal, narrative-grounded, contextual questions that are too often ignored by researchers who use the more established frameworks" (Nash, 2004, p. 5). Accordingly, we found writing scholarly personal narratives fit with our goal of critically reflecting upon and assessing our own attempts at conducting qualitative research using intersectionality as a theoretical framework. We also attempted to heed Nash's elements of "truth criteria" (p. 41) in SPN writing, including striving for "open-endedness, plausibility, vulnerability, narrative creativity, interpretive ingenuity, coherence, generalizability, trustworthiness, caution, and personal honesty" (p. 41). While we reflect on our own processes as researchers, we hope that by conveying our narratives in an honest and vulnerable manner—highlighting our missteps as well as our successes—readers can find applications to their own work with students using intersectionality theory as practitioners and scholars.

We begin with background on the two original studies we conducted—one on disability, sexual orientation, and gender identity among LGBQ and trans* students with disabilities and the other on intersections of sexual orientation and spirituality among LGBQ students—for context, including brief synopses of relevant findings. We reflect upon our paths conducting intersectional research and draw upon documents and artifacts from our research studies including IRB applications, recruitment materials, interview protocols, coded data, and presentations and manuscripts emerging from the studies.

Background on Study #1: Disability and Queer/Trans* Identities

My (RM) dissertation study focused on how queer and trans* undergraduate and graduate students with disabilities understood their social identities (particularly disability, gender identity, and sexual orientation) and how they perceived the influence of context in shaping their experiences at a large, predominantly White research university in the South. I conducted one-on-one, in-depth interviews with 25 students. I primarily used the principles of constructivist grounded theory to guide the study (Charmaz, 2014), in large part because few scholars had considered the lives of LGBTQ students with disabilities. Grounded theory entails analyzing qualitative data inductively "to construct theory from the data themselves" (Charmaz, 2014, p. 1) rather than simply using existing theory, while a constructivist approach "acknowledge[s] subjectivity and the researcher's involvement in the construction and interpretation of data" (Charmaz, 2014, p. 14). I have also drawn on additional frameworks and theories to interpret data and approach related collaborations and extensions of the initial study, including situational analysis (Clarke, 2005; Miller, 2017) and theories of identity management and disclosure (Miller, Wynn, & Webb, 2018). For the purposes of this chapter, I focus on the primary finding from this study in which I proposed five intersectional identity perspectives on disability and LGBTQ identities that students articulated: intersectional (10 participants), interactive (18 participants), overlapping (18 participants), parallel (21 participants), and/or oppositional (17 participants; Miller, 2018). Every student drew upon multiple perspectives to describe their identities. As I conducted the study and began to analyze data, I wondered why students might create and use multiple discourses to describe their identities and experiences. I was also surprised that an explicit focus on intersectionality informed only the first of five perspectives. I eventually concluded that using multiple perspectives enabled students "to resist oppression, navigating changing contexts, and build resilience and community" (Miller, 2018, p. 327). I noted in the study:

> These five perspectives functioned as discourses that students used to make sense of their experiences living at the intersections of identities. ... Sometimes these discourses suggested that identities did not neatly intersect or inform each other. However, these experiences must be placed into a context of intersecting forms of oppression, not just of intersecting identities on an individual level. (Miller, 2018, pp. 341–342)

Background on Study #2: Spirituality and Sexuality

The conceptual framework for this study was comprised of two theories: intersectionality (see Crenshaw, 1991; Museus & Griffin, 2011) and queer theory (see Browne & Nash, 2010; Nicolazzo, 2016; Olive, 2015). This analysis was grounded in the understanding of intersectionality, or the "process through which multiple social identities converge and ultimately shape individual and group experiences" (Museus & Griffin, 2011, p. 7) and the roles of power and oppression of marginalized identities. In addition, queer theory, which "by its very nature ... resists defining" (Olive, 2015, p. 22) was utilized to question the use of dominant language and power relationships on intersectional identity development in the context of the collegiate environment. Fifteen of the 16 participants completed two semi-structured interviews and one participant completed one in-depth interview designed to understand ways in which students explored potential tensions between these two intersecting identities.

The ways in which LGBQ undergraduate students experienced tension between spirituality and sexual orientation identity exploration were represented in three distinct categories: (a) resolution of dissonance, (b) exploration of dissonance, and (c) living within dissonance. It is important to note that the representation of the themes does not indicate a stage model or a particular progression of identity development. Rather, the themes illustrate a snapshot of ways in which participants articulated their experiences of intersectional identity exploration at a particular point in time during data collection.

Six of the 16 participants represented the resolution of dissonance theme based on their articulation of ways in which they viewed their sexual orientation and spirituality as not conflicting or at odds with one another. This distinction does not mean that students never experienced tension between their sexual orientation and spirituality, but rather that they had taken intentional steps in bringing the identities together in a variety of ways. In addition, four participants represented the exploration of dissonance theme, which highlighted their recognition that there was some level of tension present between these two identities, but also specific action focused on exploration of both identities. Along with the presence of questioning whether or not it is possible to maintain current spiritual/faith identity and sexual orientation identity, there was a common experience of seeking additional information through personal research and questioning. Finally, six participants represented the living within the dissonance theme, which is representative of perceived separateness of spirituality and sexual orientation. A common thread among all participants was that at some point during their sexual orientation identity development, they recognized that their intersectional identities were in potential conflict with one another.

FINDINGS: CHALLENGES AND LESSONS LEARNED

With the background from the two studies in mind, we offer our considerations of the challenges we faced in designing our studies, recruiting participants, conducting interviews, and analyzing data. Accompanying each challenge, we share our respective personal reflections (excerpts of our scholarly personal narratives).

Challenge 1: Devising Research Approaches and Design

Both researchers reflect on how epistemologies, theoretical frameworks, and researcher positionalities influenced the design of our studies. Both studies aimed to illuminate the experiences of participants in regards to multiple aspects of identity exploration. Although each of the studies focused on LGBQ students, one study explored disabilities while the other study investigated perceptions of spirituality/faith. From the beginning of the research design process, a particular challenge was appropriately bounding the scope with intersectionality at the forefront of consideration. Honing in on multiple aspects of identity while also recognizing that identity is far more complex than the scope of any one particular study proved difficult.

Researcher 1 (RM) reflection

Guided by a constructivist grounded theory approach, I sought to design a study that would create a space for participants to share their experiences living at the intersections of disability and queer identities in their own words. When students would express interest in the study, I would share information about my background, my own identities, and my motivations and goals for conducting the study. I provided this information both to be honest and transparent, as well as to try and build rapport before participants had shared any information about themselves. I hoped that any commonalities we might share would encourage participants to feel comfortable participating and sharing within the subsequent interviews.

I shared with participants that my identities as a White, queer, cisgender man, and first-generation college graduate, deeply influenced my perspectives and informed my activism and eventual career in higher education, but that I needed to reflect more on my status as a temporarily able-bodied person. I told students that this study found its roots in my time directing an LGBT resource center on a college campus. During that time, I learned much from the students who frequented the center, led student organizations, and advocated for themselves and their communities. Students were ready to have in-depth conversations about race, class, religion, and disability, and how each of these aspects of identity related to sexuality and gender identity. When I realized my own gap in knowledge around disability and its intersections with sexuality and gender identity in particular, a colleague and I began having discussions about launching a study to better understand students' experiences, particularly since the literature base in this area was so thin. I thought that being an "outsider" to experiencing disability personally would distance me from participants, but I found that in many cases students generously shared their experiences with me despite (or perhaps because of) this difference.

Researcher 2 (AJ) reflection

Due to my role as a student affairs administrator, my inclination was to offer advice throughout the interview either based on my own experiences or awareness of campus resources. As the interviewer, I was intentional about removing my input from the interview as much as possible. However, several participants shared that they were unaware of resources on campus that focused on spirituality and sexual orientation or of spiritual communities in the area in which the study took place that are welcoming and affirming of LGBTQ identities. In these instances, I reached out to the students following the interview to offer information about available campus and community resources.

Initially drawing from concepts of interpretive phenomenology (Creswell, 2013), I bracketed out my personal experiences with the focus of the study as much as possible. For example, although I identify as both gay and as Christian, I chose to not share this information with participants in the invitation to participate and explanation of the project during the pilot study phase of the project. However, after completion of the pilot study and discussion with my research supervisor, I chose to provide broad information about my identities and positionality with participants during the introduction of the study. I sought to balance providing support and building positive rapport with participants while also remaining aware of my potential influence as the researcher on the interview process.

Challenge 2: Sampling Participants and Collecting Data

Because both studies called for recruiting students with specific intersecting identities, we sought to reach potential participants through multiple venues that might resonate with their identities. In both studies, we contacted the campus LGBTQ center and requested that e-mail invitations be sent to students, and we also contacted leaders of LGBTQ student organizations. Data collection for both studies primarily entailed semi-structured interviews, guided by open-ended questions attempting to explore students' experiences of their intersecting identities. Beyond these commonalities, we share some of our specific approaches below. We now realize that we were limited in our ability to capture intersectionality by the "anchor points" of the identities we sought to address (sexual orientation and spirituality in the first study, LGBTQ identities and disability in the second study; Christensen & Qvotrup Jensen, 2012, p. 112). As Stewart (2010) reflected, "race guided my participant selection, not race *and* gender or race, gender, *and* sexuality. In other words, intersectionality ... did not inform my research" (p. 303). In terms of data collection, Bowleg (2008) advised that the "wording of questions shapes how participants respond to them" (p. 314) and that questions should be worded in an open-ended way so that "no part of the question should even hint at addition" (p. 316).

Researcher 1 reflection

Open-ended protocol questions included: "What are some of your social and cultural identities? How do you describe or identify yourself to others?" These questions followed Bowleg's (2008) advice and did not limit participants to sharing particular aspects of their identities or ask participants to rank their identities. However, given the study's advertised purpose to explore the experiences of LGBTQ students with disabilities, it is not surprising that most participants listed their queer identities and disabilities in response. Many participants also shared other identities including race, ethnicity, socioeconomic status, first-generation student status, and religion. Students often shared how identities beyond queer and disability identities informed their experiences, but I am left wondering to what degree this conversation was limited given the stated purpose of the study.

The protocol also included questions such as: "Of the identities we have discussed, which are significant to you? How would you describe the relationship among your multiple identities?" While I attempted to make these questions as broad as possible, upon reflection, I realize that these questions asked participants to rank their identities as though they were separate (i.e., which are important or unimportant?) and to craft a narrative of multiple identities as though they were discrete and could be compared. Even though participants provided rich, complex stories, particularly in response to the question about relationship among their identities, the very premise of the question assumes identities can be separated and compared. I also asked, "How strongly do you identify with LGBTQ communities?" and "How strongly do you identify with disability communities?," questions that, when asked separately, implied that participants would view these communities as distinct and might place an implicit value judgment on involvement in one or both communities.

Researcher 2 reflection

One of the challenges I anticipated at the beginning of the pilot study was gaining access and recruiting participants. I reached out to administrators at the campus LGBTQ center to ask for suggestions about posting the invitation to available list-servs, emailed student leaders from LGBTQ-related student organizations, and connected with several student leaders that I had worked with in other contexts on campus to recruit participants for the pilot study. Based on the limited diversity in the sample of the pilot study, for the dissertation, I broadened the scope of how the invitation was distributed. I began with reaching out to participants from the pilot study who remained enrolled as an undergraduate student two years later (two participants) and also reached out to student government organizations, Greek-letter organizations, and campus programming groups.

Despite learning important lessons about participant recruitment and the interview protocol from completion of a pilot study, several limitations in regards of the sample remained in the dissertation. The goal of this exploratory study was to understand intersectional identity exploration from diverse worldview perspectives, sexual orientations, as well as other salient aspects of identity. However, all participants in the study represented a variation of Christian worldviews with the exception of one Jewish participant and one Muslim participant. Also, all participants in the study identified as Hispanic, Latino/a/x, or White. Although multiple perspectives were collected, the sample did not reflect the overall population at the institution.

Challenge 3: Analyzing Data and Deriving Implications

Even though we both sought to design intersectional studies, we faced specific challenges when we began to analyze the data collected and derive relevant implications for higher education. During the analysis and subsequent reflective phases of these studies we realized broader limitations of our research design and data collection methods. However, we were encouraged by Bowleg (2008) to interpret implicit data related to intersectionality, recognizing that interlocking systems of oppression might prevent participants from explicitly articulating intersectional identities. To adequately analyze data from an intersectional standpoint, Bowleg (2008) charged researchers to "broaden their analytical scope beyond the collected data to become intimately acquainted, if they are not already, with the sociohistorical realities of historically oppressed groups" (p. 318), thus analyzing intersectionality not at only the individual level but at the larger level of systems of oppression.

Researcher 1 reflection

An intersectionality framework does not make use of additive or rank-ordered approaches to identity (Bowleg, 2008). Yet, as I noted in the discussion section of my article on LGBTQ/disability intersectional identity perspectives, "four of the five intersectional identity perspectives (i.e., interactive, overlapping, parallel, oppositional) that emerged from participants rely, at least minimally, on the idea that identities can be compared or even considered 'separate threads,' in the words of one participant" (Miller, 2018, p. 343). While writing up the results, and subsequently revising and resubmitting my manuscript, I struggled with the question: Could intersectionality appropriately be applied as a framework to understand the experiences of people who largely frame their experiences in ways that might not be consistent with intersectionality theory? Though I have not found a sufficient answer to this question, through reflection and dialogue with other scholar-practitioners and students, I have come to some tentative realizations.

Students' identity journeys are deeply shaped by the presence of multiple, overlapping systems of power and privilege. To truly operate within an intersectional framework, these systems must be acknowledged and viewed not as separate but as inseparable from individual narratives of identity. Students in my study contended with pervasive ableism, genderism, and heterosexism from peers, faculty and staff, families of origin, institutional processes, oppressive policies and laws, and the larger society. I began to wonder whether devising multiple approaches to discussing one's own identities and experiences functioned as strategies to build resilience and community. Rather than paternalistically dismiss student narratives that may appear to draw more on a multiple identity framework (or even a single identity framework) rather than intersectionality, perhaps these narratives illustrate the influence of oppression and students' creative responses to navigating spaces that often excluded or marginalized them.

Researcher 2 reflection

Applying an intersectionality framework was helpful to conceptualize the complex and dynamic identity exploration processes described by participants. However, it was difficult in some ways to remain focused on the two specific research questions of the study. As participants shared their stories about their spiritual/faith and sexual orientation identity exploration, certainly other aspects of identity surfaced. From an intersectional perspective, it was necessary to interrogate systems of power that perhaps privileged certain aspects of one's identity while other aspects of identity may have been oppressed. For example, one participant who identified as Latino, gay, and evangelical Christian noted that they felt as though they could not discuss their sexual orientation with their peers of Color and also felt as though they could not fully discuss their ethnicity in spaces dedicated to support of LGBTQ individuals. Ultimately, at the conclusion of data analysis for the dissertation, I generated a list of additional questions based on the data because utilization of an intersectional framework yielded far more questions than answers concerning complex identity development processes.

DISCUSSION: ADDRESSING THE CHALLENGES

Through reflections on conducting intersectional research studies, we considered aspects of the research process including design, researcher positionality and rapport building, sampling and participant recruitment, and data analysis. Considering our narratives together, we note several common challenges. Recruiting participants with specific identity intersections means that we, as researchers, will inevitably share and not share some identities with participants; that is, we may be both insiders and outsiders. Though we initially had divergent approaches in terms of bracketing personal experiences or sharing our personal perspectives, in accordance with our respective research approaches, we conclude that operating with a solid, ethical rationale for such decisions that aligns with one's epistemological and methodological commitments is key. In terms of sampling and recruitment, we find ourselves balancing the ideal research scenario with the realistic research scenario: We recognize that by advertising specific identity intersections as points of interest, we will inevitably miss or exclude potential participants. However, we were encouraged in both of our studies that participants went beyond discussion of the primary identities that grounded our studies and took advantage of open-ended questions to share their experiences. Such challenges point to the need for cross-identity collaborations and commitments to building trust and rapport with communities. Lastly, we struggled to interpret the experiences of students who did not necessarily frame their experiences in a way that aligned with intersectionality theory. In these instances, we sought to understand the obstacles students might have to overcome to place their own experiences in an intersectionality framework, and also took tentative steps to overlay participant experiences with theory and social and historical context.

We now return to the literature on conducting intersectional research and connect these challenges with our tentative steps to address them.

"The wording of questions shapes how participants respond to them. ... Ask an additive question, get an additive answer" (Bowleg, 2008, p. 314).

Rather than asking first about specific identities (e.g., "How do you identify your sexual orientation?"), researchers can ask participants broadly about how they identify and follow up if particular identities of interest as "anchor points" (Christensen & Qvotrup Jensen, 2012, p. 112) in the study were not mentioned.

"[The] concept of salience is an additive construction. It rests on the assumption that the facets of identity can be separated, are independent of one another, and are uni-dimensional" (Stewart, 2010, p. 302).

Researchers may be tempted to ask students which identity(ies) are more or less important, significant, or noteworthy given time, place, or context. Taking intersectionality into account, researchers might avoid asking questions that imply ranking or separating identities. Questions can assume that identities are inseparable, and participants can be free to describe their identities in whichever ways they choose.

"Questions about intersectionality should focus on meaningful constructs such as stress, prejudice, discrimination rather than relying on demographic questions alone" (Bowleg, 2008, p. 316).

We attempted to move beyond simply how participants identify to understanding their experiences in context. To do this, researchers can ask students to identify strategies they employ to manage the construct being examined (i.e., academic experiences, stress, community building, discrimination).

Multiple identities ≠ intersectionality (Jones & Abes, 2013; Stewart, 2010): "When interviewees did not articulate the experience of intersectionality explicitly, data analysis became more perplexing" (Bowleg, 2008, p. 317).

Participants may discuss their experiences and identities in ways that reflect a multiple identity (or additive) framework rather than an intersectional framework. However, scholars can help place participants' narratives and experiences in broader social and historical context, taking into account systems of power and privilege operating within their lives, on campus and in society.

"Despite coming from an approach of intracategorical complexity ... my interview protocol still used additive prompts. I was committed to an identity narrative that located race in the center. I believed that race was the lens through which other facets of self were understood" (Stewart, 2010, p. 297).

Because our studies focused on particular intersections of identities to the exclusion of others (even when we asked open-ended questions about students' identities and experiences), participants and readers might assume the primacy of sexual orientation, spirituality, and/or disability in the studies. We have not resolved this tension; participants responded to particular recruitment language that emphasized identity intersections we hoped to focus on. It is likely that potential participants did not respond if they did not view these particular identities as central to their lives.

"[S]tudents did share that how they performed their identities depended on the setting. The students chose performances that set others at ease, both Blacks and Whites, not out of personal ambivalence or confusion about their own identities" (Stewart, 2010, p. 299).

We struggle with how to ask questions about, analyze, and interpret the differential performance and understanding of particular identities while employing an intersectional frame. When participants described their experiences in additive/ multiple identity terms, we attempted to consider multiple strategies for analysis and interpretation that could acknowledge intersectionality and reflect participants' lived realities of oppressive systems that demand they parse their identities in particular spaces.

CONCLUSION: MORE QUESTIONS THAN ANSWERS

As we noted at the start of this chapter, conducting research with an intersectionality framework is challenging and potentially fraught with difficulty at all phases of the research process: design, data collection, analysis, and application. Though we have explored some of our own challenges and successes as early-career researchers, we recognize that intersectionality research in higher education often prompts more questions than settled answers. We remind ourselves, and invite readers, to embrace this complexity as we continue to attempt to understand, critique, and transform our social worlds through research employing an intersectionality framework.

REFERENCES

Abes, E. S. (2012). Constructivist and intersectional interpretations of a lesbian college student's multiple social identities. *Journal of Higher Education, 83*(2), 186–216.
Abes, E. S., Jones, S., & McEwen, M. (2007). Reconceptualizing the model of multiple dimensions of identity: The role of meaning-making capacity in the construction of multiple identities. *Journal of College Student Development, 48*(1), 1–22.

Bowleg, L. (2008). When Black + lesbian + woman ≠ Black lesbian woman: The methodological challenges of qualitative and quantitative intersectionality research. *Sex Roles: A Journal of Research, 59*(5–6), 312–325.

Browne, K., & Nash, C. J. (2010). Queer methods and methodologies: An introduction. In K. Browne & C. J. Nash (Eds.), *Queer methods and methodologies: Intersecting queer theories and social science research* (pp. 1–25). New York, NY: Ashgate.

Charmaz, K. (2014). *Constructing grounded theory* (2nd ed.). Thousand Oaks, CA: Sage.

Christensen, A.-D., & Qvotrup Jensen, S. (2012). Doing intersectional analysis: Methodological implications for qualitative research. *NORA – Nordic Journal of Feminist and Gender Research, 20*(2), 109–125.

Clarke, A. (2005). *Situational analysis: Grounded theory after the postmodern turn.* Thousand Oaks, CA: Sage.

Crenshaw, K. (1991). Mapping the margins: Intersectionality, identity politics, and violence against women of Color. *Stanford Law Review, 43*(6), 1241–1279.

Creswell, J. W. (2013). *Qualitative inquiry and research design: Choosing among five approaches* (3rd ed.). Los Angeles, CA: Sage.

Jones, S. R., & Abes, E. S. (2013). *Identity development of college students: Advancing frameworks for multiple dimensions of identity.* San Francisco, CA: Jossey Bass.

Jones, S. R., & McEwen, M. K. (2000). A conceptual model of multiple dimensions of identity. *Journal of College Student Development, 41*(4), 405–414.

Jones, S. R., Torres, V., & Arminio, J. (2014). *Negotiating the complexities of qualitative research in higher education* (2nd ed.). New York, NY: Routledge.

Means, D. R., & Jaeger, A. J. (2015). Spiritual borderlands: A Black gay male college student's spiritual journey. *Journal of Student Affairs Research and Practice, 52*(1), 11–23.

Miller, R. A. (2017). "My voice is definitely strongest in online communities": Students using social media for queer and disability identity-making. *Journal of College Student Development, 58*(4), 509–525.

Miller, R. A. (2018). Toward intersectional identity perspectives on disability and LGBTQ identities in higher education. *Journal of College Student Development, 59*(3), 327–346.

Miller, R. A., Wynn, R. D., & Webb, K. W. (2018). "This really interesting juggling act": How university students manage disability/queer identity disclosure and visibility. *Journal of Diversity in Higher Education.* Advance online publication. doi: 10.1037/dhe0000083

Museus, S. D., & Griffin, K. A. (2011). Mapping the margins in higher education: On the promise of intersectionality frameworks in research and discourse. In K. A. Griffin & S. D. Museus (Eds.), *Using mixed-methods approaches to study intersectionality in higher education* (New Directions for Institutional Research, No. 151, pp. 5–13). San Francisco, CA: Jossey-Bass.

Nash, R. J. (2004). *Liberating scholarly writing: The power of personal narrative.* New York, NY: Teachers College Press.

Nicolazzo, Z. (2016). "It's a hard line to walk": Black non-binary trans* collegians' perspectives on passing, realness, and trans*-normativity. *International Journal of Qualitative Studies in Education, 29*(9), 1173–1188.

Olive, J. L. (2015). Queering the intersectional lens: A conceptual model for the use of queer theory in intersectional research. In D. J. Davis, R. J. Brunn-Bevel, & J. L. Olive (Eds.), *Intersectionality in educational research* (pp. 19–31). Sterling, VA: Stylus.

Payne Gold, S., & Stewart, D.-L. (2011). Lesbian, gay, and bisexual students coming out at the intersection of spirituality and sexual identity. *Journal of LGBT Issues in Counseling, 5*(3–4), 237–258.

Stewart, D.-L. (2008). Being all of me: Black students negotiating multiple identities. *Journal of Higher Education, 79*(2), 183–207.

Stewart, D.-L. (2009). Perceptions of multiple identities among Black college students. *Journal of College Student Development, 50*(3), 253–270.

Stewart, D.-L. (2010). Researcher as instrument: Understanding "shifting" findings in constructivist research. *Journal of Student Affairs Research and Practice, 47*(3), 291–306.

Tevis, T., & Griffen, J. (2014). Absent voices: Intersectionality and college students with physical disabilities. *Journal of Progressive Policy and Practice, 2*(3), 239–254.

CHAPTER ELEVEN

Identity Collisions

An Intersectional Analysis of Students' Experiences in the McNair Scholars Program

SUSAN V. IVERSON, CHINASA ELUE,
KELLY E. CICHY, AND EMILY P. McCLAINE

Low-income and first-generation students are far less likely to enter, and complete, graduate school than their peers (Kniffin, 2007). The Ronald E. McNair Postbaccalaureate Achievement Program (McNair Scholars Program or MSP) seeks to interrupt that trend. The overall goal of the McNair Scholars Program is to "increase the attainment of Ph.D. degrees by students from underrepresented segments of society" (U.S. Department of Education, 2017, para. 1). This federally funded initiative within the U.S. Department of Education's Federal TRIO Programs prepares undergraduates from disadvantaged backgrounds (e.g., low-income, first-generation, and/or racially minoritized) for doctoral work by providing mentored research experiences and graduate school preparation.

A dimension of MSP is to facilitate students' development of a scholar identity which has been found to be particularly salient to their perceived preparedness to attend graduate school (Gazley et al., 2014). McNair Scholars are paired with faculty mentors who focus on developing students' skills as researchers, and, in turn, develop their identity as scholars. Strikingly, however, the dimensions of identity that afford entrée to MSP—being low-income, first-generation, and/or racially minoritized—are rarely engaged. In this chapter, we draw upon an intersectional lens to illuminate the McNair Scholars' embodiment and enactment of their complex and intersectional identities and how these scholars are "multiply disadvantaged by numerous systems of inequality" (Ferber, 2012, p. 64).

Mindful of the paradoxical role of identity in the McNair Scholars Program, the authors of this chapter developed purposeful intergroup dialogue curriculum

(Gurin-Sands, Gurin, Nagda, & Osuna, 2012) in which students were able to reflect on and dialogue about how their identities intersected with their development and aspirations as scholars. Our thinking about this dialogue is undergirded by the work of critical scholars and educators who argue that "through dialogue, people unveil their world" (Kiragu & McLaughlin, 2011, p. 421). Such dialogue can push individuals toward what Freire (1970) termed "conscientization"— meaning, to perceive social, political, and economic contradictions and awaken critical consciousness (p. 36).

As part of the McNair Scholars busy eight-week summer research program, the students convened each Monday morning for facilitated dialogue. The curriculum was designed to introduce students to concepts such as privilege, stereotype threat, social capital, imposter syndrome, and grit. Through the use of various tools (e.g., video clips, readings, writing "I am" poems), students reflected on their backgrounds, academic experiences, barriers, and aspirations. The facilitated dialogues encouraged them to unpack how these concepts related to their experiences as developing scholars and their preparation for graduate study. These conversations provided the scholars with critical opportunities to grapple with how the intersections of their identities shape how they view themselves not only as emerging scholars, but as future graduate students. In order to delve deeper into our understanding of the impact of these conversations and their experiences, our guiding question for this piece was: How do MSP scholars grapple with the intersections of their identity when conceptualizing their views of themselves as scholars and potential graduate students? In this chapter, we provide a brief overview of intersectionality theory and describe the research design for this case study. We then discuss our findings, drawing upon an intersectional lens illuminating how the development of their scholar identity and preparation for graduate school may be affected by their various dimensions of identity such as race, gender and social class and how racism, sexism, classism, and societal inequities impact their development. In conclusion, we offer implications for student scholar development.

THEORETICAL FRAME

Researchers are increasingly critical of inquiry that foregrounds particular identity dimensions as singular analytic categories, and instead, draw upon intersectionality theory to expose the complexity of and inter-related forces acting on dimensions of identity (e.g., Berger & Guidroz, 2009; Iverson, 2017; Ken, 2007; McCall, 2005). Crenshaw's (1991) analogy of traffic through an intersection remains a dominant way of conceptualizing how individuals' experiences are frequently the product of interlocking systems of oppression (e.g., racism, classism, sexism) that constrain and marginalize.

The body of intersectional work continues to grow. While some conceptualizations and metaphors diverge from Crenshaw's traffic analogy (e.g., Iverson's 2014 metaphor of constellations for understanding the experiences of women veterans; or Ken's 2008 culinary metaphor to illustrate how identities are produced and processed), several shared elements of this theory exist. Social categories, such as race, gender, sexuality, and ability, are socially constructed and are too often seen as separate spheres of experiences. The challenge then, for scholar-practitioners, is how to "retain and deconstruct" (Harris, 2016, p. 113) the interlocking systems of oppression that construct and sustain them.

An intersectional analysis is not an additive analysis; researchers do not just "add up" effects of race + class + gender (Bowleg, 2013; Brewer, 1999; Zerai, 2000). Rather, attention to "how power and power relations are maintained and reproduced" is paramount (Hankivsky et al., 2010, p. 3). Ken (2008), using sugar as a metaphor, illuminates how race, class, and gender "bump up against each other throughout the production process" (p. 153). Ken adds that having received these "products … into our institutional and human 'bodies,' either voluntarily or as the result of force or hegemony, these combinations come to structure us" (p. 153). The challenge, for researchers and practitioners, is to make these raced, gendered, and classed structures visible and then determine what to "do" with them. We sought to understand, through our use of an intersectional lens in our analysis, what these undergraduates do with the "taste" of what has been produced and prepared in their MSP experience (Ken, 2008, p. 164).

METHOD

Data for this chapter are drawn from a larger, multi-phase, qualitative case study (Flyvbjerg, 2006; Merriam & Tisdale, 2015) that examined the experiences of 14 undergraduate students in the McNair Scholars Program Summer Research Institute at one large, public research university in the Midwest. The case study was bound by location and time with the unit of analysis being each participant (Flyvbjerg, 2006). For the purposes of this chapter, we draw upon data from one-hour interviews with the 14 McNair Scholars to investigate how the scholars' personal identities shaped and informed their experiences.

In order to qualify and be selected for the MSP, students must submit a program application that includes sections on demographic details, academic and extracurricular experiences, and educational goals. Eligibility requirements for students to participate in the program include having a minimum 2.80 grade point average and meeting federal demographic guidelines such as: students must be a U.S. citizen or permanent resident as well as a first-generation college student who meets income guidelines or is from a racial or ethnic underrepresented group enrolled in a doctoral program. The MSP application must be accompanied by a statement of interest, two academic recommendations, an official transcript, proof of financial eligibility, and an in-person interview. Of the 15 students selected for MSP, 14 consented to participate in this study. These 14 scholars participated on a voluntary basis without compensation and received the invitation to participate from the principal investigator of the project (who was not part of MSP) to avoid potential coercion from MSP staff and administration.

The 14 participants included eight women and six men who were sophomore through senior class standings (see Table 11.1). Their racial composition was 12 students from a minoritized race or ethnicity (primarily African American or Black with a couple of students identifying as Hispanic/Latino) and two White participants. Most (10 of 14) met the TRIO federal guidelines for being considered from a low-income background, and nine of the 14 identified as a first-generation college student (using the U.S. Department of Education definition meaning students whose parents have never earned a bachelor's degree).

Table 11.1. Identity Characteristics of Respondents.

Name	First-generation	Low Income	Citizenship	Race/Ethnicity	Gender
Aileen	No	No	US Citizen	African American	Woman
Carla	No	Yes	Permanent Resident	Black	Woman
Donna	No	No	US Citizen	African American	Woman
Elana	Yes	Yes	US Citizen	Hispanic/Latino	Woman
Ellis	Yes	No	US Citizen	African American	Man
Faith	Yes	Yes	US Citizen	White	Woman
Gus	Yes	Yes	US Citizen	African American	Man
Jacob	No	No	US Citizen	African American	Man
Johnny	Yes	Yes	US Citizen	African American	Man
Joy	Yes	Yes	US Citizen	African American	Man
Misty	Yes	Yes	US Citizen	African American	Woman
Naomi	No	Yes	US Citizen	African American and Hispanic/Latino	Man
Ralph	Yes	Yes	US Citizen	White	Man
Yvonne	Yes	Yes	US Citizen	African American	Woman

Source: Authors.

Our analytic process was comprised of direct interpretation of the data, as "the qualitative researcher concentrates on the instance, trying to pull it apart and put it back together again more meaningfully" (Stake, 1995, p. 75). Analysis involved inductive coding that was initially done independently by four coders. "The search for meaning," Stake (1995) explains, "often is a search for patterns, for consistency within certain conditions" (p. 78). We then brought together our independent codes into broad themes that captured the lived experiences of the scholars. (Miles, Huberman, & Saldana, 2014). In the next section, we describe the findings from our analysis, including illustrative quotes from the transcripts together with an interpretation of our findings.

FINDINGS AND DISCUSSION

In 2016, one month before the McNair Scholars Program Summer Research Institute began, Duckworth released her book, *Grit: The Power of Passion and Perseverance*. According to Duckworth, "grittier adults were more likely to get further in their formal schooling" (p. 11), and this lead us to wonder: What role could grit play in graduate school preparation? During the second week of the summer research institute, scholars learned about and discussed the concept of grit, completed the grit scale, and through facilitated dialogue shared examples and stories of their passion and perseverance through challenge. Yet, we were quick to realize, and an intersectional lens further illuminated, that an exclusive focus on grit as a predictor of success leaves out how the participants' social identities and cultural backgrounds are rooted within multiple systems of oppression. Grit fosters notions of meritocracy, suggesting that just by simply pulling oneself up by the bootstraps will ensure success. In contrast, systemic and intersecting inequities produce marginalization and discrimination. For instance, Misty described systemic educational inequities in her high school. She shares:

> my high school did not get me ready for college at all. I felt like I breezed by high school. ... I would never go back. It wasn't a good curriculum, we didn't have very good teachers, our counselors weren't that good, you were lucky, like, I was lucky to find two teachers that like, cared about you.

This is a common story shared by students who come from low-income and under-resourced schools (Ordu, 2014).

We do not want to suggest that grit does not matter. Strayhorn (2014), in his study of Black male students' success at PWIs, found that "grit level was positively related to Black males grades in college" (p. 7). However, we argue that grit alone does not account for and will not overcome the structural barriers that the McNair students encountered. For example, Joy described the paradoxical role of her mother who would both encourage her to pursue college, while concurrently asking, "Why don't you have a baby?" leaving Joy to wonder, "Whose interest does she have?" It was common for women in her community to have children by this young age and oftentimes forgo a college education. These occurrences plagued her mind with self-doubt and she would often wonder, "Am I doing the right thing?" Faith also shared how being part of MSP afforded her a space to speak about her father's incarceration and financial struggles that resulted in her moving "20 times"—details that she would otherwise guard against sharing. These experiences illuminate how these participants are subjected to the complex interplay of sexism, classism, and racism. Their academic aspirations conflict with messages they have received throughout the educational pipeline and pose challenges to their ability to develop scholar identities (Charleston, Adserias, Lang, & Jackson, 2014).

An intersectional analysis further illuminates how "social locations are inseparable and shaped by interacting and mutually constituting social processes and structures, which, in turn, are shaped by power and influenced by both time and place" (Hankivsky, Grace, Hunting, & Ferlatte, 2012, p. 17).

By example, Aileen described how systems such as income classifications linked with financial aid categorize individuals, and how these classifications and categorizations socially construct constraints and barriers:

> I feel like I'll never fit the full, you know, ideal TRIO student because it is first-generation, low-income background and somehow, I, with all my $50,000 in debt, I'm not low income background 'cause my mom's a nurse and you know, you make to a certain pay level even though I don't know where the money goes 'cause we've got to live paycheck by paycheck.

LaKeisha provides a critical vignette to further illustrate this point. She stated:

> Like, when we're, well, looking for internships is really hard, because of the color of my skin. Like, most of them are predominantly [White]. And, it's really hard, like with my name and everything, like, people automatically know, like, she's African American.

LaKeisha was worried that her "Black sounding" name, and the pernicious effects of stereotypes, would yield fewer opportunities for her. Such concerns are not rooted in falsehoods. Studies have shown that there is a racial gap in the labor market in regard to perceptions around applicants' names that are uniform across occupation, industry, and employer (Bertrand & Mullainathan, 2004). Further, being a racially minoritized woman can be viewed as stereotype-incongruent with her scholar identity. Viewing through an intersectional lens illuminates "the process by which social structures and power relations are written into identities and bodily repertoires and thus *shape* experience" (Phipps, 2010, p. 360, italics in original).

The multiple, overlapping sources of subjugation that afforded the scholars' entry into the MSP program and subjected participants to multiple marginalities in academia also fueled their aspirations for what they might contribute to their field. For instance, Gus, a Black man, stated, "I wanna produce more positive images of people of Color." Ellis, a Black man majoring in fashion, shared, "I want to use my research to further sustainable fashion in the African American community." From his experience observing landfills in Black communities (among other injustices), he wondered, "Why not use your resources to kind of power through?" Some foresaw their potential for leadership and advocacy, such as Elana who observed:

> So, basing my research around, like, minority students, but specifically Latino students in higher education, kind of brings awareness to the problem a little bit more, and since nobody really is paying too much attention, I feel like I can be that voice.

Yet, as they strive to reject the stereotypes that might constrain their capacity, they are concurrently aware and reminded of their multiple marginalities. For instance, Jacob was cognizant of "being a Black man—those outer and inner characteristics that you know make us all different—that's who I represent, and not only that, but that's kind of who I am politically." Aileen, a student who identifies as an African American woman, illustrates this point further:

> I'm essentially like one of the only people who you know, is a Black woman in [my major]. So, it also felt like it was being geared towards them [white women] and not necessarily me. And just like, they found solidarity within themselves, they had those study groups that nobody invited me to and like, in the end I don't care, but it felt like I wasn't close to my cohort, felt like I didn't feel as much uh, connection with the professors at that time either ... the Black race or you know, people of Color, that, that's just a barrier right there.

Racism and other systems of oppression undermine the scholars' abilities to establish themselves and gain legitimacy as scholars.

The adversities that participants had experienced in their lives served as a gateway for connecting with each other in very deep and meaningful ways. Gus provides this example:

> We may have come from different backgrounds, but there's, there's some similarities in struggles and stuff like that we connect on. ... I see that you know, *I'm not the only one* that's experienced ... hardship and stuff ... That was definitely dope for us to sit back and then elaborate on what we thought. (emphasis added)

For Gus, he found solace in knowing that he had fellow scholars to connect with. His comment—"I'm not the only one"—is striking in its contrast to existing literature on minoritized students' feelings of isolation in resisting and responding productively to stereotype threat (Harper et al., 2011; Steele & Aronson, 1995). For instances, Carla, an African immigrant from Tanzania, thought that her socioeconomic experiences were isolated only to her particular context until she discovered that other scholars had similar stories to hers, despite her nationality. She further reflected, "You hear stories that, heavy, rich, stories of people that are telling you their background, and, you know I thought I was alone." Being a member of MSP and realizing the shared adversities MSP students encounter, shifted some (potentially) internalized burdens to an awareness of institutional factors and systemic oppressions (Massey & Owens, 2014).

IMPLICATIONS AND CONCLUSION

These scholars' stories, analyzed through an intersectional lens, illuminate how race, gender, and social class work together to construct identities that are both vulnerable and empowered, stigmatized, and political. In the final section of this chapter, we suggest implications, or rather praxis—the enactment of a field of thought and provide directions for further research.

The Personal Is Political

Our findings clearly illustrate that for students in the MSP, the personal is political. The students in MSP "get it"—their identities are inextricably linked to social processes and structures that construct and sustain marginalization and advantage. Programs, like MSP, that recruit based upon identity characteristics cannot then be delivered as if the program and its participants are identity-neutral. Curriculum, generally designed to prepare students for graduate study, specifically through interactions with faculty mentors, must recognize how privilege operates to sustain identity-neutral façades to conducting research and being a scholar. Systematic erasure of identity not only can contribute to academic isolation, but also fails to account for the structural subordination that constructs such isolation. Intentional efforts to attend to issues related to identity, privilege, and racial and socioeconomic factors (such as what we implemented through the "Monday meeting" curriculum) can provide students with space to process their experiences and to expose the academic, social, and institutional barriers that produce the shared adversities they faced. Tillapaugh, Mitchell, and Soria (2017), stemming from their intersectional analysis of student leadership, recommend that educators facilitate purposeful reflection using questions about how students' social identities affect student leadership; we argue such questions could be similarly deployed to make visible the systems of oppression that intersect with scholar identity.

   In addition to the curriculum, interactions with faculty mentors and research teams must also acknowledge, or rather explicitly address, systemic erasures of intersectional identities. It is not uncommon for McNair Scholars to be the only researchers of their race/ethnicity in their research team or in their discipline.

and for faculty mentors to have an incomplete understanding of students' backgrounds and experiences with regard to gender, race/ethnicity, or socioeconomic status (Prunuske, Wilson, Walls, & Clarke, 2013). Therefore, we recommend that programs, like MSP, provide training and support to empower faculty who mentor students' research experiences to facilitate conversations with students that acknowledge how intersectional identities and societal structures inform social interactions in research settings and long-term goals for graduate study.

Developing Social Networks

Our findings also underscore the need for more programs like MSP to work to disrupt the traditional hierarchies that exist in academia. Most of academia assumes that students' learning and development occurs through the dissemination of knowledge from a more seasoned expert to a less knowledgeable person. Even when educators reject the *banking method* of education (Freire, 1970) and adopt constructivist approaches (von Glasersfeld, 2012), hierarchies typically remain (e.g., students learning from faculty mentors). Yet, our study revealed that peer-to-peer interactions were powerful. We argue for the need to disrupt dominant notions of hierarchical mentoring and elevate the lateral/co-mentoring found in social networks. Specifically, we need to move beyond privileging the "expert knowledge" of faculty mentors to acknowledge the unique, significant role of peer-to-peer mentoring. Prior research emphasizes the significance of strong peer support for underrepresented students' persistence, particularly within STEM fields (e.g., see Chang, Sharkness, Hurtado, & Newman, 2014; Ong, Wright, Espinosa, & Orfield, 2011). For instance, Fries-Britt (1998) found evidence that social networks can ameliorate the isolation that is experienced as a racially minoritized scholar. We, too, found that academic and emotional support emerged from scholars' awareness of their shared adversities. We recommend creating spaces where networks can be established so that students can reflect on negative and isolating experiences, develop responses to adversity, and overcome systemic barriers that emerge from marginalized intersecting identities.

CONCLUSIONS

In closing, our hope is that readers will see the value of intersectionality as not only an analytic lens in research, but also as a pedagogical tool for developing curriculum. In this case study, curriculum and research foregrounds the complex interplay of intersectional identities and how these social constructs are produced and sustained through practices—even those designed to ameliorate inequities (like MSP). Students in the MSP excel academically and are leaders within the campus community; yet, these exceptional students still face structural barriers that no amount of "grit" can completely overcome. In order for programs like MSP to successfully meet the goal of diversifying the professoriate, it is important that faculty mentors recognize their own biases and, in many cases, their own privileges and oppressions, and how those operate when working with students to foster their scholar identity. In addition to training faculty, additional research is needed that explores how faculty mentors facilitate students' scholarly identity development, including how mentors' own identity characteristics shape their interactions with MSP students. Perhaps, more importantly, programs like MSP simultaneously need to disrupt dominant notions of hierarchy and cultivate social networks that recognize students' multiple and intersectional identity-based needs (Rockquemore, 2013, 2016). In sum, our findings underscore how programs like MSP that recruit based on identity characteristics must adopt an intersectional lens in order to fully engage these intersecting systems of identity in praxis.

REFERENCES

Berger, M. T., & Guidroz, K. (Eds.). (2009). *The intersectional approach: Transforming the academy through race, class, and gender.* Chapel Hill, NC: The University of North Carolina Press.

Bertrand, M., & Mullainathan, S. (2004). Are Emily and Greg more employable than Lakisha and Jamal? A field experiment on labor market discrimination. *American Economic Review, 94*(4), 991–1013.

Bowleg, L. (2013). "Once you've blended the cake, you can't take the parts back to the main ingredients": Black gay and bisexual men's descriptions and experiences of intersectionality. *Sex Roles, 68*(11–12), 754–767.

Brewer, R. (1999). Theorizing race, class, and gender: The African American experience. *Race, Gender, and Class: An Interdisciplinary and Multicultural Journal, 6*(2), 29–47.

Chang, M. J., Sharkness, J., Hurtado, S., & Newman, C. B. (2014). What matters in college for retaining aspiring scientists and engineers from underrepresented racial groups. *Journal of Research in Science Teaching, 51*(5), 555–580.

Charleston, L., Adserias, R., Lang, N., & Jackson, J. (2014). Intersectionality and STEM: The role of race and gender in the academic pursuits of African American women in STEM. *Journal of Progressive Policy & Practice, 2*(3), 273–293.

Crenshaw, K. (1991). Mapping the margins: Intersectionality, identity politics, and violence against women of Color. *Stanford Law Review, 43*(6), 1241–1299.

Duckworth, A. (2016). *Grit: The power of passion and perseverance.* New York, NY: Scribner/Simon & Schuster.

Ferber, A. L. (2012). The culture of privilege: Color-blindness, postfeminism, and christonormativity. *Journal of Social Issues, 68*(1), 63–77.

Freire, P. (1970). *Pedagogy of the oppressed.* Trans. Myra Bergman Ramos. New York, NY: Continuum.

Fries-Britt, S. (1998). Moving beyond Black achiever isolation: Experiences of gifted Black collegians. *The Journal of Higher Education, 69*(5), 556–576.

Flyvbjerg, B., (2006). Five misunderstandings about case-study research. *Qualitative Inquiry, 12*(2), 219–245.

Gazley, J. L., Remich, R., Naffziger-Hirsch, M. E., Keller, J., Campbell, P. B., & McGee, R. (2014). Beyond preparation: Identity, cultural capital, and readiness for graduate school in the biomedical sciences. *Journal of Research in Science Teaching, 51*(8), 1021–1048.

Gurin-Sands, C., Gurin, P., Nagda, B. R. A., & Osuna, S. (2012). Fostering a commitment to social action: How talking, thinking, and feeling make a difference in intergroup dialogue. *Equity & Excellence in Education, 45*(1), 60–79.

Hankivsky, O., Grace, D., Hunting, G., & Ferlatte, O. (2012). Introduction: Why intersectionality matters for health equity and policy analysis. In O. Hankivsky (Ed.), *An intersectionality-based policy analysis framework* (pp. 7–30). Vancouver, BC: Institute for Intersectionality Research and Policy, Simon Fraser University.

Hankivsky, O., Reid, C., Cormier, R., Varcoe, C., Clark, N., Benoit, C., & Brotman, S. (2010). Exploring the promises of intersectionality for advancing women's health research. *International Journal for Equity in Health, 9*(5), 1–15.

Harper, S. R., Davis, R. J., Jones, D. E., McGowan, B. L., Ingram, T. N., & Platt, C. S. (2011). Race and racism in the experiences of Black male resident assistants at predominantly White universities. *Journal of College Student Development, 52*(2), 180–200.

Harris, K. L. (2016). Reflexive voicing: A communicative approach to intersectional writing. *Qualitative Research, 16*(1), 111–127.

Iverson, S. V. (2017). Mapping identities: An intersectional analysis of sexual violence policies. In J. Harris & C. Linder (Eds.), *Intersections of identity and sexual violence on campus: Centering minoritized students' experiences* (pp. 214–232). Sterling, VA: Stylus.

Iverson, S. V. (2014). Identity constellations: An intersectional analysis of female student veterans. In D. Mitchell, Jr., C. Y. Simmons, & L. A. Greyerbiehl (Eds.), *Intersectionality and higher education: Theory, research, and praxis* (1st ed., pp. 135–145). New York, NY: Peter Lang.

Ken, I. (2008). Beyond the intersection: A new culinary metaphor for race-class-gender studies. *Sociological Theory, 26*(2), 152–172.

Ken, I. (2007). Race-class-gender theory: An image(ry) problem. *Gender Issues, 24*(2), 1–20.

Kiragu, S., & McLaughlin, C. (2011). Unveiling their worlds: The use of dialogue as a health-promotion tool for HIV/AIDS education in a poor community in Kenya. *Sex Education, 11*(4), 419–430.

Kniffin, K. (April 24, 2007). Accessibility to the Ph.D. and professoriate for first-generation college graduates: Review and implications for students, faculty, and campus policies. *American Academic, 3*, 49–79. Retrieved from http://ssrn.com/abstract=2150662

Massey, D. S., & Owens, J. (2014). Mediators of stereotype threat among Black college students. *Ethnic and Racial Studies, 37*(3), 557–575.

McCall, L. (2005). The complexity of intersectionality. *Signs: Journal of Women in Culture and Society, 30*(3), 1771–1800.

Merriam, S. B., & Tisdell, E. J. (2015). *Qualitative research: A guide to design and implementation* (4th ed.). San Francisco, CA: Jossey-Bass.

Miles, M., Huberman, A. M., & Saldana, J. (2014). *Qualitative data analysis: A methods sourcebook* (3rd ed.). Thousand Oaks, CA: Sage.

Ong, M., Wright, C., Espinosa, L., & Orfield, G. (2011). Inside the double bind: A synthesis of empirical research on undergraduate and graduate women of Color in science, technology, engineering, and mathematics. *Harvard Educational Review, 81*(2), 172–208.

Ordu, C. (2014). *The perceptions of increased student loan debt on the college choice and enrollment of rural low-income students* (Doctoral dissertation). Retrieved from https://tigerprints.clemson.edu/cgi/viewcontent.cgi?article=2396&context=all_dissertations

Phipps, A. (2010). Violent and victimized bodies: Sexual violence policy in England and Wales. *Critical Social Policy, 30*(3), 359–383.

Prunuske, A. J., Wilson, J., Walls, M., & Clarke, B. (Fall 2013). Experiences of mentors training underrepresented undergraduates in the research laboratory. *CBE-Life Sciences Education, 12*, 403–409.

Rockquemore, K. A. (2013, July 22). A new model of mentoring. *Inside Higher Ed.* Retrieved from https://www.insidehighered.com/advice/2013/07/22/essay-calling-senior-faculty-embrace-new-style-mentoring

Rockquemore, K. A. (2016, February 3). Why mentor matches fail. *Inside Higher Ed.* Retrieved from https://www.insidehighered.com/advice/2016/02/03/most-mentoring-today-based-outdated-model-essay

Stake, R. E. (1995). *The art of case study research.* Thousand Oaks, CA: Sage.

Steele, C. M., & Aronson, J. (1995). Stereotype threat and the intellectual test performance of African Americans. *Journal of Personality and Social Psychology, 69*(5), 797–811.

Strayhorn, T. L. (2014). What role does grit play in the academic success of black male collegians at predominantly White institutions? *Journal of African American Studies, 18*(1), 1–10.

Tillapaugh, D., Mitchell, D., Jr., & Soria, K. M. (2017). Considering gender and student leadership through the lens of intersectionality. In D. Tillapaugh & P. Haber-Curran (Eds.), *Critical perspectives on gender and student leadership* (New Directions for Student Leadership, No. 154, pp. 23–32). San Francisco, CA: Jossey-Bass.

U.S. Department of Education. (2017). *Ronald E. McNair Postbaccalaureate Achievement Program: Purpose.* Retrieved from http://www2.ed.gov/programs/triomcnair/index.html

von Glasersfeld, E. (2012). A constructivist approach to teaching. In L.P. Steffe & J. Gale (Eds.), *Constructivism in education* (pp. 21–34). New York, NY: Routledge.

Zerai, A. (2000). Agents of knowledge and action: Selected Africana scholars and their contributions to the understanding of race, class and gender intersectionality. *Cultural Dynamics, 12*(2), 182–222.

CHAPTER TWELVE

Intersectionality AND Student Leadership Development

Advancing the Quantitative Research Agenda

JASMINE D. COLLINS

Higher education and leadership development have long been connected in two important ways. For one, the earliest colleges often served as training grounds for young men who would go on to fill important roles in clergy, law, and the public sector. In recent decades, higher education mission statements have reflected a duty of postsecondary institutions to facilitate social transformation through the development of civic-minded leaders who are dedicated to solving social issues. Although social actors are an integral component of the social justice *process*, ensuring both equitable access to and distribution of resources as well as the physical and psychological safety of all members of society are important social justice *goals* (Bell, 2013). If leadership research and practice are to be used as tools of social transformation, scholars and practitioners must contend to both understanding the development of students as social actors, as well as uncovering systems of oppression that serve as roadblocks to social justice goals.

It is no secret that, on the whole, postsecondary institutions in the United States, are becoming less White and less male. For the first time in U.S. history, the percentage of U.S. women aged 25 and older with a bachelor's degree or higher (33%) is not statistically different from that of men (32%; Ryan & Bauman, 2016). Of the over 20.2 million students enrolled in 2- and 4-year postsecondary institutions in the United States today, women make up roughly 57% (Kena et al., 2014). Within the past decade, native-born 25-to-34-year -old White, Black, Hispanic and Asian women have become significantly more likely than their male counterparts in each respective racial group to obtain at least a bachelor's degree (Ryan & Bauman, 2016).

Recent research efforts have made important contributions to our understandings of how social identities such as gender and race may influence student leadership attitudes and behaviors. Yet, these research studies largely fail to root identity-based findings within the context of social power and inequality. This is particularly true of quantitative research designs, which comprise most of the current body of leadership education literature (Collins, 2017).

Drawing on principles of critical quantitative inquiry (Rios-Aguilar, 2014 Stage, 2007a; Wells & Stage, 2015), this chapter engages with, and problematizes, a small body of widely-cited quantitative student leadership development articles published in the past twenty years. Moving from conceptualization to interpretation, this chapter poses the following questions in an effort to (re)orient the contemporary study of student leadership development toward more transformative ends:

1. How might research questions be reframed to focus less on differences in leadership outcomes by social group membership, and more on power structures that influence development?
2. How do processes of data collection support or inhibit intersectional approaches to data analysis?
3. In what ways might current data analysis procedures elide effects of multiple axes of privilege and oppression on leadership-related outcomes for students in postsecondary settings?

The overarching objective of this chapter is to bring intersectionality, as an analytical tool, into the nexus of higher education and leadership studies in an effort to unveil complex power dynamics that, when left unmasked, make the equitable development of student leaders an elusive aim.

THE STUDY OF LEADERSHIP NEEDS
AN INTERSECTIONAL LENS

As a theoretical and analytic tool, intersectionality empowers scholars and practitioners to recognize that "people's lives and the organization of power in a given society are better understood as being shaped not by a single axis of social division be it race or gender or class, but by many axes that work together to influence each other" (Collins & Bilge, 2016, p. 2). This recognition is crucial to the advancement of anyone who possesses race, gender, class, sexual orientation, ability, age, and religious identities that place them in a subordinate social group. That is, social identities are more than common labels—they signify group memberships that are linked to larger systems of power (Collins & Bilge, 2016; Jones & Abes, 2013). Tatum (1999) elaborates:

> Each of these categories has a form of oppression associated with it: racism, classism, religious oppression/anti-Semitism, heterosexism, classism, ageism, and ableism … In each case, there is a group considered dominant (systematically advantaged by the society because of group membership) and a group considered subordinate or targeted (systematically disadvantaged). (p. 11)

Women are systemically disadvantaged in the pursuit of leadership advancement by the very nature of prevailing ideologies of what leadership means in Western contexts (Eagly & Carli, 2007; Kezar, Carducci, & Contreras-McGavin, 2006). This is because conceptualizations of what leadership "looks like" and who is "qualified" to be a leader are largely informed by dominant patriarchal ideologies. Such conceptualizations become evident in traditional articulations that characterize *processes* of leadership as hierarchical, unidirectional, and used to maintain order and that connote *images* of leaders as those who possess masculine traits such as assertiveness, charisma, intelligence, and gregariousness (Eagly & Carli, 2007; Kezar et al., 2006; Ospina & Foldy, 2009). These ideologies—the assemblage of "images, concepts, and premises which provide the frameworks through which we represent, interpret, understand and 'make sense' of some aspect of social existence" (Hall, 2000, p. 271)—function as a means to protect and maintain this status quo (Mills, 1997; Walsh, 1993). That definitions and images of leadership continue to reflect those who are already in power, illustrates the ability of ideology to reproduce the current social order.

This also means that intersectionality is needed because initiatives to advance women leaders continue to treat women as a homogenous group—failing to account for the double oppression faced by non-White women. A notable example of this is the seminal book by Eagly and Carli (2007), *Through the Labyrinth: The Truth about how Women become Leaders*. Herein, Eagly and Carli examine key assumptions about leadership differences between men and women such as: men are naturally better leaders, women are less dedicated to their careers because of responsibilities at home, and women lack the tenacity needed to succeed in competitive environments. Within this text, chapters on discrimination and prejudice bring together research on gender stereotypes and hiring preferences. Meanwhile, race-related oppression is never mentioned. In the book's final paragraphs, Eagly and Carli (2007) give recognition to the feminist activism that taught women to be resourceful, creative, brave, and smart—presumably the same feminist activism that has expressly excluded the liberation of Black women (Collins, 1990).

Intersectionality is needed in leadership work because intersections of race and gender exacerbate the material consequences of patriarchy that simultaneously praise Whiteness (Collins, 1990; Crenshaw, 1989). Consequently, focusing only on gender oppression or only on racism (or classism, or ableism, etc.) serves to ignore the plight of those who experience multiple oppressions simultaneously. With respect to student populations, intersectionality may serve as a useful tool for educators and practitioners to guide students through processes which challenge them to think more deeply about how they, and others, experience privilege and oppression, and how these lived experiences relate to their development as leaders (Tillapaugh, Mitchell, & Soria, 2017).

RACE, GENDER, AND STUDENT LEADERSHIP DEVELOPMENT

With respect to gender, research has identified several driving forces behind college women's aspirations for leadership including the opportunity to develop communication skills (Rosch, Boyd, & Duran, 2014), a desire to foster meaningful connections with others (Boatwright & Egidio, 2003; Renn & Ozaki, 2010), and the determination to advocate for social justice issues (Broido, 2000; Renn & Ozaki, 2010). Fear of negative evaluation has emerged as a significant negative predictor of college women's aspirations for leadership (Boatwright & Egidio, 2003), with higher leadership aspirations being correlated with lower fear. This finding may support additional research that shows White women focusing more on trait-related leadership development goals, such as increasing their confidence to speak up in groups, than White men, who were more interested in developing skills to advance their goals (Rosch et al., 2014). These gender-related findings are consistent with prior research from Kezar and Moriarty (2000) who found that African American and White male college students possess more confidence in their leadership abilities than African American and White women; and, research conducted by Liu and Sedlacek (1999) who reported that incoming Asian Pacific American (APA) women students more strongly agreed that they did not possess the skills necessary to be a leader on campus than their male APA peers.

Race-related differences in leadership attitudes, motivations, and behaviors have also emerged in the literature. Prior research has shown that students of Color tend to possess a stronger awareness of their racial identity (Komives, Owen, Longerbeam, Mainella, & Osteen, 2005) and are more likely to increase in their cultural knowledge during college relative to White students (antonio, 2001). For some students of Color, the decision to become involved in student organizations on campus stems from the encouragement of peers or mentors (Garcia, Huerta, Ramirez, & Patrón, 2017; Renn & Ozaki, 2010). Students of Color also join campus organizations to meet peers with similar interests (Renn & Ozaki, 2010); deepen understanding of their personal and/or social identities (Renn & Ozaki, 2010; Sutton & Terrell, 1997); learn about and/or how to interact with other cultures (Arminio et al., 2000; Harper & Quaye, 2007); and advocate for issues important to them (Harper & Quaye, 2007; Renn & Ozaki, 2010). Although students of Color may possess a stronger sense of their social identities and the privileges and forms of oppression they are likely to face because of them, several studies exist pertaining to the social justice ally development of White students as well as other members of dominant groups who work to end the oppression of marginalized groups (Broido, 2000; Munin & Speight, 2010; Broido & Reason, 2005). For these White students, awareness of social issues and processes of meaning-making around their own identity served as important precursors to social justice action (Broido, 2000). Several factors in the college context contribute to cultural awareness and knowledge for White students including participation in diversity workshops (antonio, 2001; Kezar & Moriarty, 2000), interacting students of another race (antonio, 2001; Broido, 2000), and developing interracial friendships (antonio, 2001). Moreover, precollege influences such as the intentional education about diversity and privilege by parents were crucial to the development of White students' orientations toward social justice (Broido, 2000; Munin & Speight, 2010; Reason et al., 2005).

CRITICAL QUANTITATIVE INQUIRY

The brief review of identity-related research above highlights important differences in the ways that students may think about and practice leadership given their social vantage points. The collection of studies above also raise important questions about what prevailing epistemological and methodological approaches allow scholars to uncover about the role of identity in processes of student leadership development. Moreover, it is worth considering how the use of critical paradigms might shift the conversation away from examinations based on social differences, and toward the investigation of systems of power that perpetuate privilege, marginalization, and oppression.

Critical scholarship is often thought of as a qualitative endeavor; however, several researchers have made significant contributions to current understandings of the ways critical thought can be applied through the use of quantitative methods (e.g., Bensimon & Bishop, 2012; Carter & Hurtado, 2007; Covarrubias & Vélez, 2013; Hernández, 2015; Stage, 2007a, 2007b; Wells & Stage, 2015). According to Stage and Wells (2014), quantitative criticalists must work toward three important ends:

1. First, they must "use data to represent educational processes and outcomes on a large scale to reveal inequities and to identify social or institutional perpetuation of systematic inequalities in such processes and outcomes" (p. 2).

2. Secondly, critical quantitative inquiry seeks to "question the models, measures, and analytic practices of quantitative research in order to offer competing models, measures, and analytic practices that better describe the experiences of those who have not been adequately represented" (p. 3).
3. Lastly, critical quantitative scholars are called to, "conduct culturally relevant research by studying institutions and people in context" (p. 3).

To engage in critical quantitative inquiry is recognize the interplay between research questions, methodological approaches, and policy, advocacy and/or practice (Rios-Aguilar, 2014). The remainder of the chapter uses critical quantitative inquiry as a guiding framework for the application of intersectionality to student leadership development research.

RESEARCH QUESTIONS, DATA COLLECTION
AND DATA ANALYSIS

In a recent critical literature review of 21 empirical studies of student leadership development by gender and race, Collins (2017) found that 60% (n = 10) used quantitative analytic methods, 28% (n = 8) used qualitative approaches, and 12% (n = 3) used mixed methods designs. Of the quantitative and mixed methods studies, over half (n = 8) used large national data sets such as the Cooperative Institution Research Program (CIRP) or the Multi-Institutional Study of Leadership (MSL). There are many benefits to research designs that employ such large data sets; however, these data also tend to dictate the kinds of questions researchers ask, and in turn, the conclusions drawn from the findings of those inquiries. Consider the following examples:

- "Are there relationships between key demographic variables (e.g., race, gender, sexual orientation) and student scores across eight leadership measures?" (Dugan, Komives, & Segar, 2008, p. 480).
- "To what extent do differences exist in incoming levels of and long-term gains in leadership capacity by gender, race, class status, and prior leadership experience?" (Rosch, Stephens, & Collins, 2016, p. 46)

These kinds of inquiries, while common, are limiting in their implications for social transformation for two important reasons. First and foremost, these questions appear to presume that students can parse out individual pieces of their identities, and that each piece will subsequently have a unique impact or interaction with the outcome variable in question. Bowleg (2008) acknowledges the difficulty in wording quantitative research questions in such ways that account for intersectionality without resorting to an additive approach. She writes,

The additive approach posits that social inequality increases with each stigmatized identity. Thus, a Black lesbian woman would be multiply oppressed because of the combination of her ethnicity, sexual orientation, and sex/gender (i.e., triple jeopardy). Critics reject the additive approach because it conceptualizes people's experiences as separate, independent, and summative ... Alas, what holds in theory does not always easily translate into practice. Indeed, I would contend that it is virtually impossible, particularly in quantitative research, to ask questions about intersectionality that are not inherently additive. (p. 314)

Of course, students do not live their lives as only a function of their gender or race or sexual orientation, or any other single identity. They walk through the world experiencing a host of gendered, classed, raced, and sexualized experiences that simultaneously shape the ways they interact with their learning environment, and the ways that others in the learning environment interact with them. Thus, research that focuses on single-axis differences does little to advance understandings of students' developmental needs.

Secondly, research questions that are worded in the manner above to do not account for the structural implications that may accompany the possession of any one or more identity categories in question. What's more, research questions that only focus on differences by categories of identity may even appear to suggest that students belonging to certain categories are to blame for differences that show up (deficit-thinking) rather than addressing implications for dynamics of inequality and oppression that may significantly contribute to said differences. According to Bowleg (2008), "Questions about intersectionality should focus on meaningful constructs such as stress, prejudice, discrimination rather than relying on demographic questions alone" (p. 316). It has been shown through a number of higher education studies, for instance, that students of Color often perceive campus climates as more hostile than White students (Harper & Hurtado, 2007), yet quantitative leadership studies do not routinely include measures of stress, experiences with racial microaggressions, or even measures of identity salience. Intersectionality as a theoretical and analytical tool can add a layer of nuance to quantitative research designs by acknowledging the impact of intersecting forms of oppression that extend beyond demographic questionnaires.

DATA ANALYSIS AND INTERPRETATION

Research studies designed to measure differences habitually rely on a handful of methods that uphold to a seemingly objective standard of rigor (Carter & Hurtado, 2007; Hernández, 2015; Wells & Stage, 2015). Such statistical methods, however, are ultimately rooted in White supremacy (Covarrubias & Vélez, 2013) and—when left uninterrogated—can perpetuate "an understanding of the world that further solidifies racial hierarchies" (Covarrubias & Vélez, 2013, p. 273). One way this happens is through the analytic technique of dummy coding. Through dummy coding procedures, the average score of one categorical group (usually the dominant social group—men, Whites, etc.) becomes the reference group. Findings for other groups are then interpreted in relation to the reference group, making the experiences of the non-dominant group understood only within the context of the dominant group's outcomes (Mayhew & Simonoff, 2015). This practice leads to a perpetuation of deficit-narratives of student of Color underachievement (Bensimon & Bishop, 2012; Harper, 2009; Solórzano & Yosso, 2002). An example of findings written in this way comes from a 2015 study of students' motivation to lead that reported that affective identity motivation to lead for Asian American students "lagged behind" their peers (Rosch, Collier, & Thompson, 2015, p. 289).

Lastly, research questions such as those mentioned above focus on differences in outcomes on the basis of race or gender or class or age and so on, not adequately accounting for the impact of intersecting systems of oppression that are tied to these identities. This approach can hinder scholars' ability to draw meaningful conclusions about leadership development processes, especially for women students of Color. Covarrubias and Vélez (2013) explain, "non-intersectional analyses conceal the intra-group differences and elide the fact that different status identity holders within any given social group are differently situated with respect to how much, and the form of discrimination they are likely to face" (p. 276). Focusing on only one axis of identity also creates false homogenization—creating a narrative that all women, for example, experience processes of leadership development in the same way regardless of race.

For instance, Boatwright and Egidio (2003) offer findings about the influence of 213 female college students' aspirations for leadership in their future careers. The sample included 213 female college students at a predominantly White liberal arts college, 200 (94%) of whom identified as White, 8 (4%) who identified as African American, and 4 (2%) who identified as Asian American. Boatwright and Egidio explain that "due to our sample's racial/ethnic homogeneity, ethnicity was not included in the primary design" (p. 661). Nonetheless, the incorporated constructs of *femininity*, *connectedness needs*, *fear of negative evaluation*, and *self-esteem* would likely have very different implications for these women depending on their racial group membership.

RECOMMENDATIONS AND NEXT STEPS

The present chapter used principles of intersectionality and critical quantitative inquiry to wrestle with the idea of bringing the quantitative study of student leadership development into a new paradigmatic frontier. With regard to the first key question, *how might research questions be reframed to focus less on differences in leadership outcomes by social group membership, and more on power structures that influence development?* One recommendation would be to move past the default interest in differences to consider the difference that difference makes. In the spirit of Tillapaugh and Nicolazzo (2014), it is important to recognize that "intersectional thinking that begins and ends with research participants' identities misses an important step" (p. 111). Instead of asking "are there differences by race, gender, and sexual orientation on reported leadership self-efficacy of participants of this program?", try looking for relationships between more meaningful constructs such as self-reported experiences with racism, homophobia, and sexism as they relate to leadership outcomes of interest.

In speaking to the second and third questions, *how do processes of data collection support or inhibit intersectional approaches to data analysis?* and *in what ways might current data analysis procedures elide effects of multiple axes of privilege and oppression on leadership-related outcomes for students in postsecondary settings?* scholars are encouraged to seek data sources beyond the large, public, four-year PWIs. Moreover, scholars are encouraged to design with the end in mind. In order to combat the familiar "there were not enough Black, Latinx, and Asian American students for effective disaggregation so we lumped them all together in the non-White group" trope, be intentional about seeking out the campus spaces where the Black, Latinx, and Asian American students are on campus. If they are not well-represented in the campus or program context in which the research study is being done—adjust the research plan until there are enough students in the sample to support a more complex research design. Additionally, Carter and Hurtado (2007) suggest studying one specific population at a time so that more of the group's internal variability can be accounted for. Lastly, Mayhew and Simonoff (2015) suggest effect coding rather than dummy coding, in an effort to avoid using the experiences of the dominant group as the meaning-making context for a non-dominant group's experiences.

Additional questions not addressed in this chapter, but are worth considering further are: What roles do theory and epistemology play in current conceptualizations of quantitative leadership development research designs? Are critical and constructivist analytic paradigms at odds with the nature of quantitative research designs? If so, how might this tension be reconciled to conduct socially responsive leadership research? How do current interpretations of quantitative research findings perpetuate dominant leadership ideologies? How might these interpretations be reoriented in service to social transformation?

Research is not value-free. Findings are a function of the interaction between researcher and the researched—often operating in ways that affirm dominant cultural narratives (Bensimon & Bishop, 2012; Covarrubias & Vélez, 2013; Harper, 2012; Hernández, 2015; Solórzano & Yosso, 2002; Stage, 2007a; Zuberi & Bonilla-Silva, 2008). Social transformation cannot occur without critically examining scholarship the scholarship that informs our approaches to educating the next generation of leaders, and intersectionality is one tool that may be used to that end. Together, leadership educators, student affairs practitioners, and critical higher education scholars can work toward the equitable development of diverse leaders.

REFERENCES

antonio, a. l. (2001). The role of interracial interaction in the development of leadership skills and cultural knowledge and understanding. *Research in Higher Education, 42*(5), 593–617.

Arminio, J. L., Carter, S., Jones, S. E., Kruger, K., Lucas, N., Washington, J., … Scott, A. (2000). Leadership experiences of students of Color. *NASPA Journal, 37*(3), 496–510.

Bell, L. A. (2013). Theoretical foundations. In M. Adams, W. J. Blumenfeld, R. Castañeda, H. W. Hackman, M. L. Peters, & X. Zúñiga (Eds.), *Readings for diversity and social justice* (3rd ed., pp. 21–34). New York, NY: Routledge.

Bensimon, E. M., & Bishop, R. (2012). Introduction: Why "critical"? The need for new ways of knowing. *The Review of Higher Education, 36*(1), 1–7.

Boatwright, K. J., & Egidio, R. K. (2003). Psychological predictors of college women's leadership aspirations. *Journal of College Student Development, 44*(5), 653–669.

Bonilla-Silva, E. (2009). *Racism without racists: Color-blind racism and the persistence of racial inequality in the United States* (3rd ed.). Lanham, MD: Rowman & Littlefield.

Bowleg, L. (2008). When Black + Lesbian + Woman ≠ Black Lesbian Woman: The methodological challenges of qualitative and quantitative intersectionality research. *Sex Roles: A Journal of Research, 59*(5–6), 312–325.

Broido, E. (2000). The development of social justice allies during college: A phenomenological investigation. *Journal of College Student Development, 41*(1), 3–18.

Broido, E. M. & Reason, R. D. (2005). The development of social justice attitudes and actions: An overview of current understandings. In R. D. Reason, E. M. Broido, T. L. Davis, & N. J. Evans (Eds.), *Developing social justice allies* (New Directions for Student Services, No. 110, pp. 17–28). San Francisco, CA: Jossey-Bass

Carter, D. F., & Hurtado, S. (2007). Bridging key research dilemmas: Quantitative research using a critical eye. In F. K. Stage (Ed.), *Using quantitative data to answer critical questions* (New Directions for Institutional Research, No. 133, pp. 25–35). San Francisco, CA: Jossey-Bass.

Collins, J. D. (2017). *Exploring intersectional influences of race and gender on student leadership capacity development: A critical quantitative approach* (Doctoral dissertation). Retrieved from https://www.ideals.illinois.edu/handle/2142/99089

Collins, P. H. (1990). *Black feminist thought: Knowledge, consciousness, and the politics of empowerment.* Boston, MA: Unwin Hyman.

Collins, P. H., & Bilge, S. (2016). *Intersectionality.* Malden, MA: Polity.

Covarrubias, A., & Vélez, V. (2013). Critical race quantitative intersectionality: An anti-racist research paradigm that refuses to "let the numbers speak for themselves." In M. Lynn & A. D. Dixson (Eds.), *Handbook of critical race theory in education* (pp. 270–283). New York, NY: Routledge.

Crenshaw, K. (1989). Demarginalizing the intersection of race and sex: A Black Feminist critique of antidiscrimination doctrine, feminist theory and antiracist politics. *The University of Chicago Legal Forum, 1989*(8), 139–167.

Dugan, J. P., Komives, S. R., & Segar, T. C. (2008). College student capacity for socially responsible leadership: Understanding norms and influences of race, gender, and sexual orientation. *NASPA Journal, 45*(4), 475–500.

Eagly, A. H., & Carli, L. L. (2007). *Through the labyrinth: The truth about how women become leaders.* Boston, MA: Harvard Business Press.

Garcia, G. A., Huerta, A. H., Ramirez, J. J., & Patrón, O. E. (2017). Contexts that matter to the leadership development of Latino male college students: A mixed methods perspective. *Journal of College Student Development, 58*(1), 1–18. doi:10.1353/csd.2017.0000

Harper, S. R. (2009). Niggers no more: A critical race counternarrative on Black male student achievement at predominantly White colleges and universities. *International Journal of Qualitative Studies in Education, 22*(6), 697–712.

Harper, S. R. (2012). Race without racism: How higher education researchers minimize racist institutional norms. *The Review of Higher Education, 36*(1), 9–29.

Harper, S. R., & Hurtado, S. (2007). Nine themes in campus racial climates and implications for institutional transformation. In S. R. Harper & L. D. Patton (Eds.), *Responding to the realities of race on campus* (New Directions for Student Services, No. 120, pp. 7–24). San Francisco, CA: Jossey-Bass.

Harper, S. R., & Quaye, S. J. (2007). Student organizations as venues for Black identity expression and development among African American male student leaders. *Journal of College Student Development, 48*(2), 127–144.

Hernández, E. (2015). What is "good" research? Revealing the paradigmatic tensions in quantitative criticalist work. In R. S. Wells & F. K. Stage (Eds.), *New scholarship in critical quantitative research—Part 2: New populations, approaches, and challenges* (New Directions for Institutional Research, No. 163, pp. 93–101). San Francisco, CA: Jossey-Bass.

Jones, S. R., & Abes, E. S. (2013). *Identity development of college students: Advancing frameworks for multiple dimensions of identity.* San Francisco, CA: John Wiley & Sons.

Kena, G., Aud, S., Johnson, F., Wang, X., Zhang, J., Rathbun, A., … Kristapovich, P. (2014). *The condition of education 2014* (NCES 2014–083). Washington, DC: U.S. Department of Education, National Center for Education Statistics.

Kezar, A. J., Carducci, R., & Contreras-McGavin, M. (2006). *Rethinking the "L" word in higher education: The revolution of research on leadership* (ASHE Higher Education Report). San Francisco, CA: Jossey-Bass.

Kezar, A., & Moriarty, D. (2000). Expanding our understanding of student leadership development: A study exploring gender and ethnic identity. *Journal of College Student Development, 41*(1), 55–68.

Komives, S. R., Owen, J. E., Longerbeam, S. D., Mainella, F. C., & Osteen, L. (2005). Developing a leadership identity: A grounded theory. *Journal of College Student Development, 46*(6), 593–611.

Liu, W. M., & Sedlacek, W. E. (1999). Differences in leadership and co-curricular perception among entering male and female Asian-Pacific-American college students. *Journal of the First Year Experience, 11*(2), 93–114.

Mayhew, M. J., & Simonoff, J. S. (2015). Non-White, no more: Effect coding as an alternative to dummy coding with implications for higher education researchers. *Journal of College Student Development, 56*(2), 170–175.

Munin, A., & Speight, S. (2010). Factors influencing the ally development of college students. *Equity & Excellence in Education, 43*(2), 249–264.

Ospina, S., & Foldy, E. (2009). A critical review of race and ethnicity in the leadership literature: Surfacing context, power and the collective dimensions of leadership. *Leadership Quarterly, 20*(6), 876–896.

Renn, K. A., & Ozaki, C. C. (2010). Psychosocial and leadership identities among leaders of identity-based campus organizations. *Journal of Diversity in Higher Education*, *3*(1), 14–26.

Rios-Aguilar, C. (2014). The changing context of critical quantitative inquiry. In F. K. Stage, & R. S. Wells (Eds.), *New scholarship in critical quantitative research—Part 1: Studying institutions and people in context* (New Directions for Institutional Research, No. 158, pp. 95–107). San Francisco, CA: Jossey-Bass.

Rosch, D. M., Boyd, B. L., & Duran, K. M. (2014). Students' self-identified long-term leadership development goals: An analysis by gender and race. *Journal of Leadership Education*, *13*(3), 17–33.

Rosch, D. M., Collier, D., & Thompson, S. E. (2015). An exploration of students' motivation to lead: An analysis by race, gender, and student leadership behaviors. *Journal of College Student Development*, *56*(3), 286–291.

Rosch, D. M., Stephens, C. M., & Collins, J. D. (2016). Lessons that last: LeaderShape-related gains in student leadership capacity over time. *Journal of Leadership Education*, 15(1), 44–59.

Ryan, B. C. L., & Bauman, K. (2016). *Educational attainment in the United States: 2015*. Washington, DC: U.S. Census Bureau.

Solórzano, D. G., & Yosso, T. J. (2002). Critical race methodology: Counter-storytelling as an analytical framework for education research. *Qualitative Inquiry*, *8*(1), 23–44.

Stage, F. K. (2007a). Answering critical questions using quantitative data. In F. K. Stage (Ed.), *Using quantitative data to answer critical questions* (New Directions for Institutional Research, No. 133, pp. 5–16). San Francisco, CA: Jossey-Bass.

Stage, F. K. (2007b). Moving from probabilities to possibilities: Tasks for quantitative criticalists. In F. K. Stage (Ed.), *Using quantitative data to answer critical questions* (New Directions for Institutional Research, No. 133, pp. 95–100). San Francisco, CA: Jossey-Bass.

Stage, F. K., & Wells, R. S. (2014). Critical quantitative inquiry in context. In F. K. Stage, & R. S. Wells (Eds.), *New scholarship in critical quantitative research—Part 1: Studying institutions and people in context* (New Directions for Institutional Research, No. 158, pp. 1–7). San Francisco, CA: Jossey-Bass.

Sutton, E. M., & Terrell, M. C. (1997). Identifying and developing leadership opportunities for African American men. In M. J. Cuyjet (Ed.), *African American men on college campuses: Their needs and their perceptions* (New Directions for Student Services, No. 80, pp. 55–64. San Francisco, CA: Jossey-Bass.

Tatum, B. D. (1999). *Why are all the Black kids sitting together in the cafeteria? And other conversations about race.* New York, NY: Basic Books.

Tillapaugh, D., Mitchell, D., Jr., & Soria, K. (2017). Considering gender and leadership through an intersectionality lens. In D. Tillapaugh & P. Haber-Curran (Eds.), *Critical perspectives on gender and student leadership* (New Directions for Student Leadership, No. 154, pp. 23–32). San Francisco, CA: Jossey-Bass.

Tillapaugh, D., & Nicolazzo, Z. (2014). Backward thinking: Exploring the relationship among intersectionality, epistemology, and research design. In Donald Mitchell, Jr., C. Y. Simmons, & L. A. Greyerbiehl (Eds.), *Intersectionality & higher education: Theory, research, & praxis* (1st ed., pp. 111–122). New York, NY: Peter Lang.

Wells, R. S., & Stage, F. K. (2015). Past, present, and future of critical quantitative research in higher education. In R. S. Wells & F. K. Stage (Eds.), *New scholarship in critical quantitative research— Part 2: New populations, approaches, and challenges* (New Directions for Institutional Research, No. 163, pp. 103–112). San Francisco, CA: Jossey-Bass.

Zuberi, T., & Bonilla-Silva, E. (Eds.). (2008). *White logic, white methods: Racism and methodology.* Lanham, MD: Rowman & Littlefield.

CHAPTER THIRTEEN

Gaps IN THE Rainbow

Finding Queer Women of Color in Higher Education

COBRETTI D. WILLIAMS

According to the Association of Governing Boards of Colleges and Universities (Trammell, 2014), there are over one million lesbian, gay, bisexual, transgender, and queer (LGBTQ) students in higher education. Based on reports from the rise in LGBTQ centers on U.S. college campuses and target recruitment of LGBTQ students (Cegler, 2012), it seems likely the representation of LGBTQ students will continue to increase as society becomes more progressive and welcoming of queer identity (Pratt, 2014), specifically naming queer identity for students with non-heteronormative sexuality and gender identities traditionally underrepresented in higher education (Jagose, 1996; Purvis, 2012). To that end, Renn (2017) contends that higher education can be a positive environment for queer identity development; however, there are caveats to this statement. Specifically, Renn wrote:

> For some LGBTQ students, sexual orientation or gender identity are not the most salient identities during their time in college … Acknowledging such diversity within the LGBTQ community is as important as recognizing sexual orientation and gender diversity within the campus community as a whole. (para. 5)

Indeed, acknowledgement of marginalized identities in the queer community—namely race and gender—represent a smaller portion of larger literature base on queer college students. Furthermore, in cases where literature supports the narratives of queer people of Color–that is queer people with racial and ethnic identities historically underrepresented in higher education—data in these studies often narrowly represent cisgender, men of Color (e.g., see Means & Jaeger, 2013; Misawa, 2010b). As such, there is a current dearth of research that fully encompasses the identities of queer women of Color (QWOC)—particularly at the cross section of interlocking systems of oppression based on race, gender, and sexuality (Collins, 1989). In the midst of a hostile climate for LGBTQ students with high rates of harassment, violence, and cyber-bullying (Renn, 2017), this is an area that requires our direct and critical attention.

The purpose of this chapter is to explore the experiences of QWOC in regard to their identity development and navigation through U.S. higher education institutions. Furthermore, I hope to articulate the ways intersectionality theory further complicates these experiences, pointing to racism, sexism, heterosexism, and other interlocking systems of oppression they incur. To achieve this purpose, I present critical, qualitative research from narratives of QWOC attending a U.S. higher education institution. Through discussion and analysis of research findings, my hope is students, faculty, and administrators reading this chapter will have a better sense of some QWOC experiences and examples of how they learn, develop, grow, and survive as college students.

LITERATURE REVIEW

The identity development and experiences of QWOC require analysis of literature from ideological and organizational perspectives to fully assess their identities as QWOC and how they navigate higher education institutions. *Intersectionality*, as coined by Kimberlé Crenshaw (1989), has been a prominent analytical tool significant to the development of critical social theories including critical race feminism and quare theory (e.g., see Johnson, 2001; Wing, 1997). In higher education, intersectionality has only recently been used as a framework. There are some notable exceptions, including *Queer People of Color in Higher Education* by Moon and Javier (2017) and the previous volume of *Intersectionality and Higher Education* by Mitchell, Simmons, and Greyerbiehl (2014). In addition, the creation of the model of multiple dimensions of identity (MMDI) by Abes, Jones, and McEwen (2007), while not grounded in intersectionality, does offer an interpretation of identity construction that accounts for external factors of identity that cannot be understood from a singular standpoint. This framing of multiple identities provide a helpful start to understand intersectionality—which moves beyond identity and explores interlocking social oppressions—as a theory to accurately explore the lives of QWOC. Still, the majority of student development theories have focused singularly on identities of race, gender, and sexuality as opposed to their simultaneous intersection and marginalization (Torres, Jones, & Renn, 2009). In a similar vein, in cases where there is a potential for intersectionality to be implemented as a framework, most studies undergird the perspectives of men of Color (e.g., Means & Jaeger, 2013). Given this, the representation of QWOC in the literature is sparse (e.g., see King, 2011; Patton & Simmons, 2008; Revilla, 2010) and warrants further exploration.

In their study of Black lesbian students in the college environment, Patton and Simmons (2008) asserted that a major challenge of students that identify as racial, gender, and sexual minorities is finding space to both develop these identities, acceptance and affirmation of these identities, and balancing the multiple oppressed identities of being a queer person of Color. For instance, students encounter situations where their racial identity is not accepted in predominantly White queer communities on campus, where their queer identity is ignored in communities of Color, or where students experience gendered bias within both spaces (Revilla, 2010). As such, the analysis for students with multiple, intersecting identities, as it concerns QWOC, is often invisible in higher education literature and scholarship.

Though identity development is a crucial area of consideration for critical researchers, there is a tendency in higher education literature to view identity development in a vacuum from the surrounding college environment. Conversely, understanding campus climate in tandem with identity development expands our understanding of college environments impacted by peers, faculty, and administrators with investment in the campus community (Brown, Clarke, Gortmaker, & Robinson-Keilig, 2004; Nora, Urick, & Cerecer, 2011).

Multiple studies show students racial, gender, or queer minoritized identities often perceive their respective campus climates as less welcoming when compared to students with privileged identities (e.g., see Misawa, 2010a; Rankin, 2005; Rankin & Reason, 2005). Unfortunately, an unfavorable campus climate negatively influences the sense of affirmation and belonging for marginalized students, especially those with multiple, intersecting marginalized social identities (Johnson & Quaye, 2017; Strayhorn & Mullins, 2012). Still, despite a hostile climate for queer students, students are finding different ways to persist and maintain hope, particularly through affirmative and non-discriminatory campus policies and campus leadership positions that effectuate social change (Pitcher, Camacho, Renn, & Woodford, 2016; Renn, 2007; Revilla, 2010).

As mentioned before, the representation of QWOC students in the literature is few and far in between, particularly studies that acknowledge and affirm the multiple intersections of identity while honing a framework cognizant of simultaneous and compounding systems of oppression. This chapter offers perspectives and experiences from QWOC and contributes to intersectionality theory and practice.

METHOD

To explore the experiences of QWOC participants, I utilized a critical, qualitative methodology of participants. As Merriam and Tisdell (2015) assert about critical research designs, "The point is that in the design of the study and in the analysis of the study, the researcher would be specifically examining the nature of power relations" (p. 60). Furthermore, Pasque and Pérez (2015) contend that critical, qualitative methodologies should embody a multiplicity of interpretations and contexts while avoiding fulfilling a linear or fixed conceptualization. Employing this methodology allowed me to focus on the experiences of these women's lives at the center of analysis without the influence of gendered, heterosexist institutions of higher education impacting their narratives (Ropers-Huilman & Winters, 2011).

The research question underscoring this study was: how do QWOC navigate the campus environment of U.S. higher education institutions? Concurrently, how do these experiences inform their identity development as QWOC, if at all? As such, the study began by eliciting participation from college students identified as QWOC. More specifically, in order to participate, participants had to identify as a woman with a racial or ethnic identity historically underrepresented in higher education. In this case, a purposeful, snowball sampling technique was utilized (Rapley, 2014) by connecting with administrators, staff, and students that could recommend and promote the study to interested participants. Seven students ultimately participated in the study. From those seven, the narratives of five graduate and undergraduate women of Color with non-heteronormative sexual identities are included in the findings for this chapter.

The method for data collection included in-depth, semi-structured, in-person interviews with each participant. In accordance with qualitative inquiry, interviews can be a significant part of data collection that provides a rich description of first-hand accounts incurred by participants (Creswell, 2009). Furthermore, a semi-structured format "allows the researcher to respond to the situation at hand, to emerging worldview of the respondent, and to new ideas on the topic" (Merriam & Tisdell, 2015, p. 111). Using this method created an opportunity for the women in the study to exercise agency in terms of revealed information and flexibility of language and emotions expressed during the interviews. Table 13.1 provides demographic information for each participant.

Interviews lasted approximately one-hour and each participant self-selected a pseudonym to help safeguard their identity. Each interview was audio-recorded with consent from the participant, and those audio files were then transcribed for the coding process. In an effort to fully immerse myself in the data, I decided to use an inductive coding style, beginning with an initial round of open codes and first impressions of the manuscript. Then, I categorized codes with similar

Table 13.1. Participant Demographics.

Pseudonym	Race/Ethnicity	Pronouns	Sexuality	Other Salient Identities
Mariana	Puerto Rican	She/Her/Hers	Bisexual	Feminist
Amelia	Mexican/Thai	She/Her/Hers	Bisexual	First-generation student
KT	Indian	She/Her/Hers	Bisexual	First-generation student, immigrant
Rose	Afro-Latina	She/Her/Hers	Bisexual/Queer	
Yanise	Puerto Rican/ Colombian	She/Her/Hers	Queer	Bruja, Chingona

Source: Author.

emotions and essences. Finally, overarching themes emerged that attempt to create a story for how QWOC navigate, exist, and develop in higher education (Merriam & Tisdell, 2015). In the development of codes for analysis, intersectionality was a pivotal component. The experiences named by participants often involved navigating power and privilege in the context of their higher education institution and U.S. society. Therefore, the construction of their racial, gender, and sexual identities were layered with one another to honor the complexity, fluidity, and different worldviews each participant evokes within the sociopolitical setting of U.S. higher education (Hunting, 2014). Since this study was conducted in earnest as a social justice research endeavor, part of my responsibility as a researcher includes sharing my positionality in relation to the study (Milner, 2007). As a queer, cisgender, Black man, I acknowledge how my privileged gender identity potentially biases the results of the study. Additionally, my identification with the queer community as a person of Color also has implications for how I view the findings, potentially leading to generalization that is not typically seen in qualitative research. Therefore, to limit this bias, I undertook a number of methods to ensure validity. To emphasize a collaborative research process (see Cornish, Gillespie, & Zittoun, 2014), at the conclusion of the transcription process, each participant was invited to a second, informal meeting with me to discuss their interview transcript as well as convey additional details they wanted included in the dissemination of findings. Furthermore, after the completion of the coding process, I collaborated with an external evaluator who identifies as a QWOC to verify and revise any conclusions I drew from the transcripts that may lead to impartial or biased conclusions (Milner, 2007).

FINDINGS

Once analysis and validation of data were complete, three prominent themes emerged: (1) cultural dissonance, (2) the politics of identity, and (3) finding authenticity in identity. The findings reveal the journey of identity development begins well before college and are heavily informed by communities of practice. In turn, the development and actualization of identity becomes inherently political up until students are able to make meaning and connection between their queerness, gender identity, and race.

Cultural Dissonance

An important element to the experiences of QWOC in the study was their upbringing prior to college. Family culture, friends, and peers all proved to be pivotal communities of socialization for the participants. Some participants named family as an influence in their decision to attend their current institution. When asked about her family's reception to queer identity, Yanise plainly stated:

> There's so much homophobia in my family, we just don't talk about it at all. It is very taboo in my Latino culture too. With Catholicism or Christianity views overshadowing what is seen—what is deemed evil or good practices of spirituality.

As the quote highlights, negative perceptions of queer sexuality were embedded in her family, given the importance of religion and spirituality in her Latino culture. These perceptions exacerbated the disclosure process for participants, with some choosing not to involve or tell members of their communities because of their ignorance. Speaking about her bisexuality, Mariana confirmed:

> I usually experience ignorance about bisexuality on a frequent basis, partly because of them and also because of who I choose to reveal my identity to. With family, they just want to know that I'm safe and doing well so no need to really talk about it. If you don't know me, then you don't know I'm bi myself because I've actually been dating a guy for a while, so if you don't know me, people just assume I'm straight and I'm like okay, if you want to assume that, that's cool, I don't care.

Participants exercised certain selectivity when being vulnerable about their sexuality, either because it will be received negatively by community members, people in their lives lack enough knowledge about queerness to not make assumptions or stereotypes about the participants, or they are limited by expectations of what their sexuality should be based on expectations of race and gender. As such, a dissonance is created, separating participants from making meaningful connections between their layered identities based on socialization within their social community of peers, family, and educational institutions. This dissonance inevitably became the starting point of development for participants entering the college environment.

The Politics of Identity

As participants engaged in the college environment, and gained a better awareness of their identity, they also learned about the sociopolitical nature of identity; markedly, how higher education institutions reflect the systemic oppression of QWOC in U.S. society. Inherently, by the time participants arrived at college, they learned to politically maneuver different spaces not receptive to their holistic identity. KT was vocal about her lack of connection with the Asian community at the university. As a result, KT strategically avoided community specific to her racial and ethnic identity, opting to focus more on her convictions as a bisexual woman. During the interview, she said:

> I tend to gravitate towards non-Asian, or non-Indian specifically, people, because I feel like ... I don't know, I just feel like there's too much baggage that goes with some parts of my community, so much that I can't be open and vulnerable with the Asian or Indian community, at times. Some certain issues in my community that get kind of heavy, strong thoughts about marriage and children sometimes, so ... I've always been very alternative from that path, so sometimes it makes it hard for me to be around Asian or Indian people who have very strong convictions about things like that.

What KT exemplifies are select interactions with people, communities, and environments depending on their views of certain social issues, seeking to share only a small aspect of their whole identity as a queer woman of Color. Therefore, they begin to compartmentalize parts of their identity—whether it is race, gender, or sexuality—in order to fit in or assimilate into a certain space. Likewise, Amelia, who identifies as biracial, Mexican, and Thai, was candid about her experience in the theater community that seems to be open to queer sexuality and less about issues of race and migration. She revealed:

> The theater community tends to be majority White and focused on Western forms of theater and art. Because of that, it can be hard to discuss Eastern forms of theater or incorporate narratives of migration, because not a lot of people want to talk about it because it is controversial in a way from LGBTQ issues. Not that LGBTQ things are less controversial now, they're just slightly more accepted I feel like and more prevalent in the theater community, that there are not a lot of immigrants in it so it's hard to kind of express and be vocal about that.

A major issue and reason for compartmentalization is often a lack of space to fully explore intersectionality of race, gender, and sexuality or a visibility of people and images that evoke a diverse representation of these intersections.

Finding Authenticity in Identity

The final finding of this study briefly touches on the power and challenges of visible intersectionality and how it operates in spaces deemed safe for exploration and development of identity. While the life experiences of participants provided barriers to their identity development, each were able to name and identify people—family, friends, and mentors—that helped them to grow and learn how to authentically embrace their QWOC identity through spaces that affirm the multiplicity and challenges of intersectionality. For instance, Amelia recalled being heavily influenced by her friend's gender transition during their senior year of high school and became more aware of gender fluidity and queer sexuality, as a result. As she described:

> I met one of my best friends through theater and he eventually disclose that he was trans. At that point I was like, "What? There is more than one gender identity?" So, once I became aware of the possibilities, I started to learn more on my own and really embrace being fluid with my own gender and my own expression and start calling out transphobia and homophobia when I see it.

Similar, after her experiences of being marginalized based on her sexuality from the Black cultural center on campus, Rose was able to find a community of QWOC in another organization within the multicultural affairs office. She recounted:

> It's actually quite refreshing being in a space and going on retreats where literally everyone is a woman of Color and queer. Like that never happens. Even having the staff being queer people of Color helps to put me at ease. I feel like I can be honest about the racism and sexism and homophobia I encounter without having to hide pieces of myself to make others feel comfortable. Not sure if this will be the case in the future, but you bet I'm gonna take advantage of it while I have the opportunity!

As some of the participants recounted their experiences since entering college and process their development before graduation, they felt more empowered to be authentic in every part and space of their life without compromising parts of their identity. As Yanise positively affirmed:

> Everything that I do is always integrated. It feels great to be sustained in that way and not feel so pressured to always have to fit some type of mold or do things to fit a standard that will appease some type of institution or hierarchy, or whatnot. Wherever I go, I wanted to feel rooted and grounded that I could bring all those parts with me to the work. That's what being worthy feels like to me and it's a beautiful place to be in.

DISCUSSION

Based on the findings of the study, there are a number of dynamics to consider that are relevant to the study and higher education literature. Foremost, it cannot be emphasized enough how cultural factors preceding college can influence the development of QWOC during college. As participants talked implicitly and explicitly about homophobia and sexism they encountered from family, friends, and peers, it confirms a connection between cultural environments that espouse ignorance about social issues and the development of queer and gender identities (Jeyasingham, 2008). Furthermore, it is often race that was centered in the consciousness of identity for participants, as critical race theory asserts (Delgado & Stefancic, 2017). While an important and critical perspective to center race, emphasizing one aspect of a person's marginalized identity above other marginalized identities does not necessarily imply an understanding of how these identities intersect, influence one another, and reinforce interlocking systems of oppression (Collins, 1989).

Findings also suggest that while colleges can be a conducive environment for identity development of QWOC (Renn, 2017), identities are still political and has implications for where QWOC feel safe and affirmed. Amelia and KT spoke assertively about the tension between their identities as QWOC during college, often with race at the center of consciousness. Their need to separate these identities to survive may imply that the college environment is not always a positive place for growth. While participants experienced positive aspects of their college experiences, such as finding exploratory spaces for identity development or community with similar, salient identities, quotes from participants and students suggests there are challenges QWOC must overcome to grow and be successful.

Finally, it is evident that space in all its forms—physical, mental, and emotional—can lay the groundwork for identity development and exploration for QWOC. In some cases, participants like Rose lauded having the ability to discover and become more aware of their identity, power, and knowledge within the institution. At the same time, other participants like Yanise experienced negativity in these spaces, whether it was due to ignorance, lack of education on gender or queer sexuality, or safety that is not granted to bodies that are raced, gendered, and perpetually heterosexualized. These kinds of physical spaces not only contribute to a hostile campus climate (Brown et al., 2004; Hurtado, Griffin, Arellano, & Cuellar, 2008; Rankin, 2005), but create additional stressors for QWOC who do not feel seen, heard, or validated in the college environment.

This study partially affirms what is known about queer students in higher education, especially as it relates to campus climate and identity development and salience in college. Building upon previous literature on the experiences of queer people of Color, I found affirmation and mattering are salient components of making QWOC feel supported on college campuses. Moreover, this study expands to uncover how QWOC survive in hostile and negative environments, particularly those that are gendered, raced, and heterosexualized where compartmentalization of identities appeared necessary for their persistence.

Future Implications

One of the most significant implications arising from this study is the need for more empirical studies on QWOC. If intersectionality continues to be prominent in critical higher education literature, attention must be paid to include women of Color, and QWOC in particular, especially as their attendance and representation in U.S. colleges and universities rises (National Center for Education Statistics, 2015). Likewise, there is even less representation of trans women in queer research, and as this population of students incurs a harsh campus and societal climate (Beemyn, Curtis, Davis, & Tubbs, 2005; Marine & Nicolazzo, 2014), centering their stories could foster positive change for institutional culture, policies, and programs.

Building from the discussion and the significance of space in the study, it would behoove higher education institutions to consider implementing programs and community spaces for QWOC to relate and share important stories of development including family relationships, the coming out process, navigation of sexism, and general understanding of queer sexuality and intersectionality. For example, dialogue circles or discussion groups that use an intersectional framework could present a format to curate welcoming spaces for QWOC.

CONCLUSION

As colleges and universities become more diverse, administrators, faculty, and staff must take more action to create and sustain inclusive environments, markedly for marginalized student populations that are not represented within the larger landscape of predominantly White higher education institutions. As a hopeful first step, this study sought to understand a perspective not commonly heard in higher education research, and one that expands what is known about intersectionality in higher education. With more research on QWOC experiences, consistent implementation of critical frameworks that honor QWOC, and more thoughtful, concerted practices by higher education institutions that center QWOC, I am confident one day higher education will be a place for QWOC to thrive, closing current gaps in the rainbow.[1]

NOTE

1. Rainbows, first popularized by San Francisco artist Gilbert Baker in 1978, are considered a cultural symbol of the LGBTQ community (Haag, 2017). The title of this chapter signifies that despite the presence of non-heteronormative and queer sexual identities in higher education research, there are still gaps within the rainbow yet to be explored.

REFERENCES

Abes, E. S., Jones, S. R., & McEwen, M. K. (2007). Reconceptualizing the model of multiple dimensions of identity: The role of meaning-making capacity in the construction of multiple identities. *Journal of College Student Development, 48*(1), 1–22.

Beemyn, B., Curtis, B., Davis, M., & Tubbs, N. J. (2005). Transgender issues on college campuses. In R. Sanlo (Ed.), *Gender identity and sexual orientation: Research, policy, and personal* (New Directions for Student Services, No. 111, pp. 49–60). San Francisco, CA: Jossey-Bass.

Brown, R., Clarke, B., Gortmaker, V., & Robinson-Keilig, R. (2004). Assessing the campus climate for gay, lesbian, bisexual and transgender (GLBT) students using a multiple perspectives approach. *Journal of College Student Development, 45*(1), 8–26.

Cegler, T. D. (2012, Spring). Targeted recruitment of GLBT students by colleges and universities. *Journal of College Admission, 215*, 18–23.

Collins, P. H. (1989). The social construction of Black feminist thought. *Signs: Journal of Women in Culture and Society, 14*(4), 745–773.

Cornish, F., Gillespie, A., & Zittoun, T. (2014). Collaborative analysis of qualitative data. In U. Flick (Ed.), *The SAGE handbook of qualitative data analysis* (pp. 79–93). Thousand Oaks, CA: Sage.

Crenshaw, K. (1989). Demarginalizing the intersection of race and sex: A Black feminist critique of antidiscrimination doctrine, feminist theory and antiracist politics. *University of Chicago Legal Forum, 1989*(8), 139–167.

Creswell, J. W. (2009). *Research design: Qualitative, quantitative, and mixed methods approaches* (3rd ed.). Thousand Oaks, CA: Sage.

Delgado, R., & Stefancic, J. (2017). *Critical race theory: An introduction* (3rd ed.). New York, NY: New York University Press.

Haag, M. (2017, March 31). Gilbert Baker, gay activist who created the rainbow flag, dies at 65. *New York Times.* Retrieved from https://www.nytimes.com/2017/03/31/us/obituary-gilbert-baker-rainbow-flag.html

Hurtado, S., Griffin, K. A., Arellano, L., & Cuellar, M. (2008). Assessing the value of climate assessments: Progress and future directions. *Journal of Diversity in Higher Education, 1*(4), 204–221.

Hunting, G. (2014). Intersectionality-informed qualitative research: A primer. *Criminology, 4*(1), 32–56.

Jagose, A. (1996). *Queer theory: An introduction.* New York, NY: New York University Press.

Jeyasingham, D. (2008). Knowledge/ignorance and the construction of sexuality in social work education. *Social Work Education, 27*(2), 138–151.

Johnson, E. P. (2001). "Quare" studies, or (almost) everything I know about queer studies I learned from my grandmother. *Text and Performance Quarterly, 21*(1), 1–25.

Johnson, A. A., & Quaye, S. J. (2017). Queering Black racial identity development. *Journal of College Student Development, 58*(8), 1135–1148.

King, A. R. (2011). Environmental influences on the development of female college students who identify as multiracial/biracial-bisexual/pansexual. *Journal of College Student Development, 52*(4), 440–455.

Marine, S. B., & Nicolazzo, Z. (2014). Names that matter: Exploring the tensions of campus LGBTQ centers and trans* inclusion. *Journal of Diversity in Higher Education, 7*(4), 265–281.

Means, D. R., & Jaeger, A. J. (2013). Black in the rainbow: "Quaring" the Black gay male student experience at historically Black universities. *Journal of African American Males in Education, 4*(2), 124–140.

Merriam, S. B., & Tisdell, E. J. (2015). *Qualitative research: A guide to design and implementation* (4th ed.). San Francisco, CA: Jossey-Bass.

Milner, H. R. (2007). Race, culture, and researcher positionality: Working through dangers seen, unseen, and unforeseen. *Educational Researcher, 36*(7), 388–400.

Misawa, M. (2010a). Queer race pedagogy for educators in higher education: Dealing with power dynamics and positionality of LGBTQ students of Color. *International Journal of Critical Pedagogy, 3*(1), 26–35.

Misawa, M. (2010b). Racist and homophobic bullying in adulthood: Narratives from gay men of Color in higher education. *New Horizons in Adult Education and Human Resource Development, 24*(1), 7–23.

Mitchell, D., Jr., Simmons, C. Y., & Greyerbiehl, L. A. (Eds.). (2014). *Intersectionality & higher education: Theory, research, & praxis* (1st ed.). New York, NY: Peter Lang.

National Center for Education Statistics. (2015). *Digest of education statistics 2015*. Retrieved from https://nces.ed.gov/pubs2016/2016014.pdf

Nora, A., Urick, A., & Cerecer, P. D. Q. (2011). Validating students: A conceptualization and overview of its impact on student experiences and outcomes. *Enrollment Management Journal, 5*(2), 34–52.

Pasque, P. A., & Pérez, M. S. (2015). Centering critical inquiry: Methodologies that facilitate critical qualitative research. In G. S. Cannella, M. S. Pérez, & P. A. Pasque (Eds.), *Critical qualitative inquiry: Foundations and futures* (pp. 139–170). Walnut Creek, CA: Left Coast Press.

Patton, L. D., & Simmons, S. L. (2008). Exploring complexities of multiple identities of lesbians in a Black college environment. *Negro Educational Review, 59*(3–4), 197–215.

Pitcher, E. N., Camacho, T. P., Renn, K. A., & Woodford, M. R. (2016). Affirming policies, programs, and supportive services: Using an organizational perspective to understand LGBTQ+ college student success. *Journal of Diversity in Higher Education, 11*(2), 1–17.

Pratt, T. (2014, September 2). Colleges see gay students as growth market. *TIME*. Retrieved from http://time.com/3211813/lgbt-gay-colleges-resources/

Purvis, J. (2012). Queer. In C. M. Orr, A. Braithwaite, & D. Lichtenstein (Eds.), *Rethinking women's and gender studies* (pp. 189–206). New York, NY: Routledge.

Rankin, S. R. (2005). Campus climates for sexual minorities. In R. Sanlo (Ed.), *Gender identity and sexual orientation: Research, policy, and personal* (New Directions for Student Services, No. 111, pp. 17–23). San Francisco, CA: Jossey-Bass.

Rankin, S. R., & Reason, R. D. (2005). Differing perceptions: How students of Color and White students perceive campus climate for underrepresented groups. *Journal of College Student Development, 46*(1), 43–61.

Rapley, T. (2014). Sampling strategies in qualitative research. In U. Flick (Ed.), *The SAGE handbook of qualitative data analysis* (pp. 49–63). Thousand Oaks, CA: Sage.

Renn, K. A. (2007). LGBT student leaders and queer activists: Identities of lesbian, gay, bisexual, transgender, and queer identified college student leaders and activists. *Journal of College Student Development, 48*(3), 311–330.

Renn, K. A. (2017, April 10). LGBTQ students on campus: Issues and opportunities for higher education leaders. *Higher Education Today*. Retrieved from https://www.higheredtoday.org/2017/04/10/lgbtq-students-higher-education/

Revilla, A. T. (2010). Raza womyn—making it safe to be queer: Student organizations as retention tools in higher education. *Black Women, Gender & Families, 4*(1), 37–61.

Ropers-Huilman, R., & Winters, K. T. (2011). Feminist research in higher education. *Journal of Higher Education, 82*(6), 667–690.

Strayhorn, T., & Mullins, T. G. (2012). Investigating Black gay male undergraduates' experiences in campus residence halls. *Journal of College and University Housing, 38–39*(1–2), 140–161.

Torres, V., Jones, S. R., & Renn, K. A. (2009). Identity development theories in student affairs: Origins, current status, and new approaches. *Journal of College Student Development, 50*(6), 577–596.

Trammell, J. B. (2014). LGBT challenges in higher education today: 5 core principles for success. *Association of Governing Boards of Colleges and Universities.* Retrieved from https://www.agb.org/trusteeship/2014/5/lgbt-challenges-higher-education-today-5-core-principles-success

Wing, A. K. (1997). *Critical race feminism: A reader.* New York, NY: New York University Press.

CHAPTER FOURTEEN

Demographic Information Collection IN Higher Education AND Student Affairs Survey Instruments

Developing a National Landscape for Intersectionality

JASON C. GARVEY

Within the fields of higher education and student affairs, there are a select number of national surveys that provide data for a considerable amount of empirical analyses. Because of their wide recognition and publication volume, findings from these analyses have the potential to shape the discourse of research on students in higher education and student affairs. Pascarella and Terenzini (2005) wrote, "[A] number of national data sets, which produce a substantial portion of the evidence on the impact of college on students, have become targets of opportunity for large numbers of social scientists" (p. 15). These national quantitative datasets significantly permeate tier-one journals within the fields of higher education and student affairs and the disciplines of sociology, economics, and political sciences. It is possible that these national surveys not only influence the entire body of literature in these broad fields and disciplines but also policies and administrative practices.

Though these national quantitative datasets heavily permeate research publications, scholarly communities do not have a holistic or transparent understanding of how participant information is collected. With a growing emphasis on intersectional survey research (Cole, 2009; Davis, 2008; McCall, 2005), there is a need to examine the ways in which these influential surveys collect demographic information across various social identities.

Sanlo (2002) wrote, "I am concerned about the language we as professionals still use on our campuses ... these words violate boundaries of race, gender, and sexual identity, and serve to perpetuate a climate of exclusion and marginalization" (p. 171). Notably, the tension between recognizing intersectional and fluid identities while quantitatively categorizing responses is a continual struggle for survey methodologists. These assertions beget the question, how can researchers embrace a more inclusive and intersectional understanding of social identities and incorporate these strategies when collecting demographic information?

LITERATURE REVIEW

Students' social identities play a central influence in their higher education experiences (Astin, 1970a, 1970b, 1991; Pascarella, 1985; Tinto, 1975, 1987, 1993; Weidman, 1989). In their examination of how colleges impact students, Pascarella and Terenzini (2005) discussed that "diversity in the faculty and student body is a potentially powerful force in shaping important cognitive and noncognitive outcomes" (p. 631). Social identities are fundamentally important within higher education and student affairs scholarship, yet there are few established guidelines for contextualizing demographic variables into empirical analyses, particularly within quantitative research.

Intersectionality is a research paradigm that offers new ways to understand the complexity of social identities. Cole (2009) wrote, "Rather than prescribing—or proscribing—any particular research or data analysis technique, the concept of intersectionality entails a conceptual shift in the way researchers understand social categories" (p. 178). The following sections briefly outline the main tenets of intersectionality and discuss its relevance to quantitative analyses in higher education and student affairs.

Intersectionality

Developed through Black feminist thought and originally coined by Crenshaw (1989), intersectionality refers to the interaction between gender, race, and other categories of difference and the outcomes of these interactions as they relate to power. Intersectionality began in feminist and critical scholarship to acknowledge differences among women and deconstruct a history of exclusion within the field of women's studies (Davis, 2008). Davis (2008) commented, "As a concept, intersectionality is, without a doubt, ambiguous and open-ended" (p. 77). Nonetheless, scholars understand intersectional approaches to research as the relationship between people and their social locations, paying particular attention to power within social spaces (Mahalingam, 2007). Intersectionality encourages scholars to understand how systems of oppression intersect to create structures, political systems, and cultural contexts that shape the experiences of individuals with oppressed identities. More specifically, intersectional scholars are interested in the relationships among social groups defined by the inclusion of all groups in each social category (McCall, 2005).

McCall (2005) provided commentary on intersectionality from a methodological standpoint. She discussed that there are no established guidelines for empirically addressing research questions informed by an intersectional framework and recognized that the current restriction on intersectional research comes down primarily to methods. As a new frame of understanding, intersectionality has introduced new methodological difficulties. Nevertheless, Cole (2009) discussed that "[t]o translate the theoretical insights of intersectionality into psychological research does not require the adoption of a new set of methods; rather, it requires a reconceptualization of the meaning and consequences of social categories" (p. 176). Although a large portion of intersectional work employs qualitative methods, intersectional theorists must utilize quantitative techniques to advance intersectionality as a research paradigm. Dubrow (2008) wrote that "[w]e need to stop wondering whether quantitative analysis of survey data is appropriate for accounting for intersectionality. The challenge now is to strengthen the bond between intersectionality theory and quantitative techniques" (p. 99).

Regarding higher education and student affairs research, Stage (2007) described two broad tasks for quantitative scholars. First, researchers should use data to represent and uncover large-scale processes and outcomes that perpetuate systemic social or institutional inequities. Second, scholars must question quantitative models, measures, and analytic practices in order to propose competing models, measures, and analytic practices that more appropriately describe minority individuals and communities. An intersectional theorist can achieve these tasks set forth by Stage, providing a more nuanced understanding of demographic variables and recognizing power and cultural differences as influential and evolving.

The purpose of this chapter is to examine the national landscape of higher education and student affairs survey instruments in regard to demographic information collection utilizing intersectionality as a theoretical lens. The chapter addresses the following questions:

1. How prevalent are studies using quantitative methods in tier-one higher education and student affairs journals?
2. Which demographic variables do higher education and student affairs researchers include in quantitative analyses?
3. Which survey instruments are most widely used by higher education and student affairs researchers? What demographic variables are included in these widely used survey instruments?
4. (How) do current demographic data collection techniques inhibit or promote intersectional research?

METHOD

To answer the aforementioned research questions, I began by reviewing five tier-one higher education and student affairs journal volumes from 2010 to 2012. These journals included *The Journal of Higher Education, Review of Higher Education, Research in Higher Education, Journal of College Student Development,* and *Higher Education* (Bray & Major, 2011).

I first categorized the primary methods used for each article within the journals, noting whether they were quantitative, qualitative, mixed-methods, or nonempirical. Within articles that used quantitative methods, I tracked the demographic variables that researchers included in the analyses. These demographic variables included the following: gender (male/female), race/ethnicity, age, class/socioeconomic status (SES), immigration status/nationality, religion/spirituality, sexual identity, transgender identity, and ability (Adams et al., 2013). From this information, I determined the proportion of quantitative studies from 2010 to 2012 that included each demographic variable.

Also for all quantitative articles, I noted which survey instruments the researchers used in their studies. From this information, I identified the most widely used survey instruments in these top-tiered journals for the past three years. For this study, I was most interested in survey instruments that were used in analyses for three or more studies published in the aforementioned journals from 2010 to 2012. Upon identifying the most widely used survey instruments, I gained copies of the instruments by either contacting the survey distributors or downloading the survey online. After collecting the instruments, I conducted a detailed assessment of demographic information included in the surveys. For each demographic variable, I examined the prevalence across all survey instruments.

RESULTS

Figure 14.1 presents the primary analyses used across tier-one higher education and student affairs journals from 2010 to 2012. *The Journal of Higher Education* had 87 articles published from 2010 to 2012, with 47 (52.02%) using quantitative methods. *Review of Higher Education* had 65 total articles published, and of those, 29 (44.62%) used quantitative methods. In *Research in Higher Education,* there were 113 total articles and 108 (95.58%) used quantitative methods. For the *Journal of College Student Development,* 83 of the 154 total (53.90%) used quantitative methods. Finally, in *Higher Education,* there were 272 articles published from 2010 to 2012 and of those, 106 (38.97%) used quantitative methods. There were 691 articles published among all five journals from 2010 to 2012 and of those, 373 (53.98%) used quantitative methods.

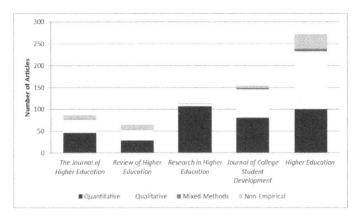

Figure 14.1. Primary Analyses Used across Tier-One Higher Education and Student Affairs Journals from 2010 to 2012.

Figure 14.2 presents the percentage of quantitative articles in tier-one higher education and student affairs journals that included demographic variables. Regarding demographic variable use in quantitative studies, a significant percentage of articles included gender (male/female; N = 201; 53.89%) or race/ethnicity (N = 157; 42.09%) in their analyses. About one in five articles included age (N = 74; 19.84%) or class/SES (N = 73; 19.57%). Fewer articles included immigration status/nationality (N = 23; 6.17%), religion/spirituality (N = 16; 4.29%), or sexual identity (N = 7; 1.88%). Finally, only two quantitative studies (0.54%) included transgender identity, and no quantitative articles included ability. Interestingly, across all five tier-one journals, only the *Journal of College Student Development* published quantitative articles that included sexual identity or transgender identity.

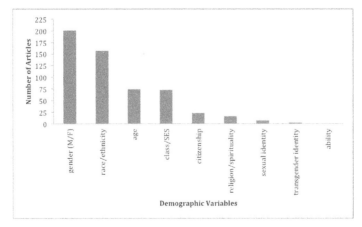

Figure 14.2. Percentage of Quantitative Articles in Tier-One Higher Education and Student Affairs Journals that Included Demographic Variables.

Results in Table 14.1 provide a list of higher education and student affairs survey instruments used three or more times across the tier-one journals from 2010 through 2012. In total, there were 19 instruments used three or more times in these journals. Of the total 373 articles that used primarily quantitative analyses, these instruments were used 135 times in 124 articles (a select number of articles used more than one instrument in their analyses). In other words, one-third of all the quantitative articles published in tier-one higher education and student affairs journals from 2010 to 2012 used data from these 19 survey instruments. From 2010 through 2012, scholars who published quantitative studies in *Research in Higher Education* used 18 of the 19 surveys for a total of 62 times. For all studies that used quantitative methods in *Research in Higher Education,* these 19 survey instruments were utilized 45.93% of the time.

Among the 19 widely used survey instruments, six were U.S. federal government surveys and 13 were administered by education nonprofit organizations. The most widely used U.S. federal government surveys were the National Education Longitudinal Study (N = 21) and the Integrated Postsecondary Education Data System (N = 19). The most used surveys from education nonprofit organizations were the Wabash National Study of Liberal Arts Education (N = 17) and the National Survey of Student Engagement (N = 12).

Table 14.1. Higher Education and Student Affairs Survey Instruments Used Three or More Times across Tier-One Journals from 2010 through 2012.

	Research in HE	TJHE	JCSD	Review of HE	HE	Total
National Education Longitudinal Study*+	11	5	–	5	–	21
Integrated Postsecondary Education Data System*+	7	6	1	1	4	19
Wabash National Study of Liberal Arts Education	5	2	7	2	1	17
National Survey of Student Engagement	7	–	3	2	–	12
Freshman Survey	4	2	2	–	–	8
College Students' Beliefs and Values Survey*	3	1	3	–	–	7
National Student Clearinghouse*	5	1	–	1	–	7
Beginning Postsecondary Students Longitudinal Study*+	2	2	–	1	1	6
National Study of Postsecondary Faculty*+	2	1	–	1	2	6

	Research in HE	TJHE	JCSD	Review of HE	HE	Total
Faculty Survey	1	1	-	1	1	4
Survey of Earned Doctorates	1	2	-	-	1	4
Current Population Study*+	2	-	-	1	-	3
Postsecondary Education Transcript Study*+	1	1	-	1	-	3
Faculty Survey of Student Engagement	3	-	-	-	-	3
Gates Millennium Scholars Tracking and Longitudinal Study	2	1	-	-	-	3
Multi-Institutional Study of Leadership	-	-	2	1	-	3
National Study of Living-Learning Programs	1	1	1	-	-	3
The College Student Experiences Questionnaire	2	-	1	-	-	3
National Association of State Student Grant and Aid Program*	3	-	-	-	-	3
Total	62	26	20	17	10	135

Note. Research in HE = *Research in Higher Education*; TJHE = *The Journal of Higher Education*; JCSD = *Journal of College Student Development*; Review of HE = *Review of Higher Education*; HE = *Higher Education*.
*not evaluated.
+federal government survey.

For the purposes of this chapter, I only assessed survey demographic information collection from education nonprofit organizations. Among the 13 survey instruments administered by education nonprofit organizations, three were from the Cooperative Institutional Research Program (Freshman Survey [*N* = 8], College Students' Beliefs and Values Survey [*N* = 7], and Faculty Survey [*N* = 4]); two were from the National Survey of Student Engagement (National Survey of Student Engagement [*N* = 12] and Faculty Survey of Student Engagement [*N* = 3]); and two were from the National Opinion Research Center (Survey of Earned Doctorates [*N* = 4] and Gates Millenium Scholars Tracking and Longitudinal Study [*N* = 3]). The remaining surveys were from other education nonprofit organizations, including the Center of Inquiry (Wabash National Study of Liberal Arts Education, *N* = 17), the National Student Clearinghouse (*N* = 7), the College Student Experiences Questionnaire Assessment Program (*N* = 3), the Multi-Institutional Study of Leadership (*N* = 3), the National Study of Living-Learning Programs (*N* = 3), and the National Association of State Student Grant and Aid Program (*N* = 3).

Three education nonprofit organization survey instruments were not included in the analyses for specific reasons. First, the College Students' Beliefs and Values Survey is administered by the Cooperative Institutional Research Program as a follow-up to their Freshman Survey. Participants' survey responses are linked across both instruments by a personal identifier. Therefore, although the only demographic question included in the College Students' Beliefs and Values Survey is religion/spirituality, researchers are able to include other demographic variables into analyses that were asked in the Freshman Survey. Second, the National Association of State Student Grant and Aid Program survey was not included because it assessed information from the programmatic level and did not include individual-level variables. Lastly, the National Student Clearinghouse Research Center does not publish and did not make available the National Student Clearinghouse survey for this study.

Table 14.2 details the demographic questions included across the 10 survey instruments utilized in the analysis. All 10 surveys included gender (male/female) and race/ethnicity in their questionnaires. Nine out of 10 included age, four included sexual identity and ability, three included religion/spirituality, and two included transgender identity. Worth noting is that the Multi-Institutional Study of Leadership was the only instrument to include all demographic questions examined in this study.

Table 14.2. Demographic Questions Included within 10 Widely Used Higher Education and Student Affairs Survey Instruments.

	Gender (M/F)	Race/Ethnicity	Age	Citizenship	Religion/Spirituality	Sexual Identity	Transgender Identity	Ability
Wabash National Study of Liberal Arts Education	yes	yes	yes	yes	no	no	no	no
Freshman Survey	yes	yes	yes	yes	yes	no	no	no
Faculty Survey	yes	yes	yes	no	no	no	no	no
Multi-Institutional Study of Leadership	yes	yes	yes	yes	yes	yes	yes	yes

	Gender (M/F)	Race/ Ethnicity	Age	Citizenship	Religion/ Spirituality	Sexual Identity	Transgender Identity	Ability
Survey of Earned Doctorates	yes	yes	yes	yes	no	no	no	yes
Gates Millennium Scholars Tracking and Longitudinal Study	yes	yes	yes	no	no	no	no	no
National Study of Living-Learning Programs	yes	yes	no	yes	yes	yes	yes	yes
National Survey of Student Engagement	yes	yes	yes	yes	no	yes	no	yes
Faculty Survey of Student Engagement	yes	yes	yes	yes	no	yes	no	no
The College Student Experiences Questionnaire	yes	yes	yes	no	no	no	no	no
Percentage	100.00%	100.00%	90.00%	70.00%	30.00%	40.00%	20.00%	40.00%

Given the variability and difficulty in determining how survey instruments operationalized class/SES, I consciously decided to remove this demographic question from this portion of my analyses. Though all 10 surveys included proxy measures for class/SES (e.g., parents' education and income, Pell Grant status), I was unable to determine how specific instruments quantified the variable. Whereas I was able to determine in analyses for individual articles based on authors' variable descriptions, I could not with certainty verify the ways in which survey instruments constructed class/SES.

Finally, Table 14.3 provides a side-by-side comparison of demographic variables included in the most widely used higher education and student affairs instruments from education nonprofit organizations with demographic variables included in articles across the tier-one journals from 2010 through 2012.

Table 14.3. Comparison of Demographic Variables Included within 10 Widely Used Higher Education and Student Affairs Survey Instruments with Quantitative Articles in Tier-One Journals that Included Demographic Variables.

	Included within Survey Instruments	Included within Quantitative Articles
Gender (M/F)	100.00%	53.89%
Race/Ethnicity	100.00%	42.09%
Age	90.00%	19.84%
Class/Socioeconomic Status	–	19.57%
Citizenship	70.00%	6.17%
Religion/Spirituality	30.00%	4.29%
Sexual Identity	40.00%	1.88%
Transgender Identity	20.00%	0.54%
Ability	40.00%	0.00%

DISCUSSION

Results from the analyses help to examine the national landscape of higher education and student affairs survey instruments in regard to demographic information collection. The following paragraphs highlight how current demographic data collection techniques inhibit or promote intersectional research.

Regarding demographic variable use across the tier-one journals, only two quantitative articles included transgender identity in their analyses. In both studies, the researchers employed the Multi-Institutional Study of Leadership as their survey instrument. Not surprisingly, sexual identity was included in both of these analyses as well. As previously stated, seven quantitative articles included sexual identity and two quantitative studies included transgender identity. The only tier-one higher education and student affairs journal to publish quantitative articles with sexual and transgender identity was the *Journal of College Student Development*. The general omission of sexual and transgender identities is highly problematic given the scope of our field. Among all the tier-one journals, the *Journal of College Student Development* is the only functional-specific publication. It concentrates largely on student development and learning, whereas the other tier-one journals are general higher education publications (Bray & Major, 2011). Renn (2010) wrote the following:

> Higher education scholars frequently divide their work into categories of students (experiences, outcomes, demographics, development), faculty (preparation, tenure, satisfaction), administrative leaders (career tracks, leadership style), organization (culture, structures, change), governance and finance (state oversight, boards of trustees, faculty governance), policy (national, state, institutional), and teaching (curriculum, pedagogy, technology). (p. 133)

Given that sexual and transgender identities were only included in two articles within the student-centered journal publication, it is clear that we are limiting the scope of quantitative research across social identities. Nowhere in these journals is there quantitative research that examines faculty, administration, organization, finance, policy, or teaching through the lens of sexuality or transgenderism. Furthermore, none of the 373 quantitative studies in the tier-one higher education journals included ability in their analyses.

These findings are astonishing and unacceptable given the importance of quantitative scholarship in advancing institutional, state, and national policies in higher education and student affairs (Stage, 2007). Sexual, transgender, and disability identities permeate all facets of higher education, including all constituents (students, faculty, administration, alumni), policy, and teaching. The five aforementioned tier-one journals in higher education and student affairs are the leading scholarly voices in our fields. Unfortunately, due to the subject and content of quantitative analyses, these journals are in essence erasing the experiences of several large groups of individuals, namely people with disabilities, transgender individuals, and sexual identity minorities. Consequently, institutional advocacy, policy reform, and resource allocation are all hindered by the absence of quantitative studies that closely examine these populations. Intersectionality calls for scholars to understand the relationship between people and their social locations with specific focus on power and privilege (Mahalingam, 2007). As a scholarly community, we have caught ourselves in a catch-22, whereby these underrepresented groups are underresearched, yet survey developers do not include these demographic questions because of a lack of empirical research on these populations.

Findings from this study demonstrate the high prevalence and use of certain higher education and student affairs survey instruments. As indicated in the results, the 19 most widely used survey instruments permeated one-third of all quantitative studies in tier-one journals. This alone justifies the need to closely examine the ways in which these survey instruments collect demographic data.

Among the widely used surveys from education nonprofit organizations, 12 of the 13 were individual-level surveys. This finding demonstrates the centrality of examining students, faculty, staff, and other constituents in higher education and student affairs. Clearly, demographic variables are essential to comprehensively understanding individual-level outcomes and relationships. As demonstrated in the results, certain education nonprofit organizations control a majority of the widely used survey instruments. To advocate for a more intersectional approach to higher education and student affairs research, change must begin with these organizations. In particular, the Cooperative Institutional Research Program, the National Survey of Student Engagement, the National Opinion Research Center, the Wabash National Study of Liberal Arts Education, and the College Student Experiences Questionnaire Assessment Program must reform their survey designs to be more inclusive of social identities. Not only will this change the statistical analyses possible with these data, but it will also demonstrate a strong commitment to intersectionality and giving voice to all higher education constituents.

As discussed by Cole (2009), scholars do not have to create a new set of methods for incorporating intersectionality into current research. Rather, researchers must reconceptualize the meaning and consequences of social categories. This process begins with revising and incorporating a broader understanding of individual experiences as framed through demographic information and social identities.

Furthermore, higher education and student affairs researchers must advocate for a wider and more intersectional approach to research among journals. The tier-one journals in this study published articles that included demographic information to varying degrees. Table 17.3 provided a comparison of demographic variables included in the most widely used higher education and student affairs instruments from education nonprofit organizations with demographic variables included in articles across the tier-one journals from 2010 through 2012. These findings are not surprising, leading to an understanding of the absence of certain demographic questions. A side-by-side comparison leads to the possibility that the more regularly demographic variables are included in survey designs, the more likely these demographics will be included in quantitative analyses. Especially in *Research in Higher Education* and *Higher Education,* which published 55.50% of all quantitative studies in tier-one journals, we must advocate for a stronger presence of complex social identities and demographics across all empirical analyses.

LIMITATIONS

As previously discussed, I only assessed demographic information collection from education nonprofit organizations. Though it is important to examine federal government surveys in regard to demographic collection, the inaccessibility of the instruments coupled with the near-impossible difficulty of advocating for change made it difficult to include these survey instruments in the analyses. Future studies should explore quantitative survey instruments in education from federal government agencies and ways in which policy makers and advocacy organizations can promote change for more inclusive demographic information collection.

Additionally, I was unable to include class/SES in portions of my analyses because of the uncertainty in how survey instruments operationalized the construct. Because I did not have code books or variable operationalizations for each instrument, I was unable to determine the ways in which researchers quantified class/SES. Future studies should examine class/SES as a quantitative construct to determine valid and reliable ways to include this construct through an intersectional lens.

The instruments examined in this study were used in only about one-third of all quantitative articles published from 2010 through 2012. I consciously decided to include only the most widely used survey instruments to demonstrate the high impact that these surveys have on the field of higher education and student affairs. Needless to say, though, it is important to advocate for an intersectional understanding of demographic information collection with all survey instruments, regardless of the frequency of use. When we create a culture of change and a stronger affirmation toward intersectional perspectives in quantitative designs, our scholarly community will be better prepared to advocate for all higher education constituents across and within social identities.

IMPLICATIONS

Intersectionality offers researchers new ways to operationalize complex social identities. Survey methodologists can modify demographic collection and analytic techniques to facilitate more intersectional research. Dubrow (2008) discussed that for quantitative scholars who want to incorporate intersectional theory with existing survey data, interaction terms are an appropriate way to measure relationships among social identities. Similarly, McCall (2005) advocated for a research design with demographic information as independent variables with main effects and interactions. She termed this technique as the categorical approach to intersectionality, "focus[ing] on the complexity of relationships among multiple social groups within and across analytical categories. ... The subject is multigroup and the method is systematically comparative" (p. 1786). Multiple categories analyze intersections of demographics and categories within, simultaneously examining power and privilege in relation to social identities.

One major issue when conducting survey research is determining the number of participants required to obtain a representative and stable approximation of the population and of subpopulations. There are several risks in using too few participants. Covariation among factor items may not be stable when sample size is low. Further, when the ratio of participants to survey items is low and the sample size is small, chance may influence correlations among items to a fairly substantial degree

(DeVellis, 2003). With small samples, a deviant sample has greater influence and presence than with a larger sample due to randomization and representation. Additionally, a small sample size may not adequately detect a significant effect (Kerlinger & Lee, 2000). With an increased sample size, the sampling distribution narrows and the standard error decreases.

If not enough participants are sampled, the entire population for which the instrument is intended may not be represented. To address this concern, both the sample size and participant composition should be a consideration. Nonrepresentative samples can be different from the intended population in two ways: by the level of attribute present in the sample as opposed to the intended population, and with a sample that is qualitatively rather than quantitatively different from the target population. The latter nonrepresentativeness can result when the sample is unlike the population in important ways (i.e., social identities), thus affecting the underlying causal structure relating variables to true scores and ultimately reliability (DeVellis, 2003). Researchers must take extra care in choosing a sample that closely represents the population for which the instrument is being developed (Ajzen & Fishbein, 1980; Nunnally & Bernstein, 1994). Due to the difficulty in recruiting certain subpopulations, survey methodologists may consider oversampling certain constituencies so there is a lesser threat of nonrepresentativeness. Furthermore, oversampling may provide a sufficient participant yield to conduct analyses using the categorical approach to intersectionality.

As evidenced, quantitative intersectional research does not come without difficulties. McCall (2005) discussed that "it is near impossible to publish grandly intersectional studies in top peer-reviewed journals using the categorical approach: the size and complexity of such a project is too great to contain in a single article" (p. 1787). Quantitative intersectional analyses usually require interaction effects through multilevel or hierarchical designs, providing a more complex estimation and interpretation of results. Still, quantitative scholars must not limit themselves in embracing a more intersectional approach to research in both demographic data collection and analyses. By expanding the scope of demographic variables included in higher education and student affairs research, scholars can have data accessible to conduct intersectional research. Without reforming the ways in which survey methodologists include demographic variables, scholars will continue to perpetuate a culture of exclusion in higher education and student affairs research that ignores various communities and social identities.

CONCLUSION

By approaching demographic information collection from an intersectional lens I hope for this chapter to encourage a new wave and generation of quantitative empirical analyses that examine the intersections of identities and experiences in higher education and student affairs. Such an assertion has the potential to transform the scholarly body of higher education. Though this chapter has only fostered a surface-level dialogue of quantitative intersectional research, these findings and discussions can provide a starting point for higher education and student affairs scholars to advocate for systemic change in quantitative designs and survey instrumentation.

REFERENCES

Adams, M., Blumenfeld, W. J., Castaneda, C., Hackman, H., Peters, M., & Zungia X. (Eds.). (2013). *Readings for diversity and social justice* (2nd ed.). New York, NY: Routledge.

Ajzen, I., & Fishbein, M. (1980). *Understanding attitudes and predicting behavior.* Englewood Cliffs, NJ: Prentice Hall.

Astin, A. (1970a). The methodology of research on college impact (I). *Sociology of Education, 43,* 223–254.

Astin, A. (1970b). The methodology of research on college impact (II). *Sociology of Education, 43,* 437–450.

Astin, A. (1991). *Assessment for excellence: The philosophy and practice of assessment and evaluation in higher education.* New York, NY: Macmillan.

Bray, N. J., & Major, C. H. (2011). Status of journals in the field of higher education. *Journal of Higher Education, 82,* 479–503.

Cole, E. R. (2009). Intersectionality and research in psychology. *American Psychologist, 64,* 170–180.

Crenshaw, K. (1989). Demarginalizing the intersection of race and sex: A black feminist critique of antidiscrimination doctrine, feminist theory and antiracist politics. *The University of Chicago Legal Forum, 139,* 139–167.

Davis, K. (2008) Intersectionality as buzzword: A sociology of science perspective on what makes a feminist theory successful. *Feminist Theory, 9,* 67–85.

DeVellis, R. F. (2003). *Scale development: Theory and applications.* Newbury Park, CA: Sage.

Dubrow, J. K. (2008). How can we account for intersectionality in quantitative analysis of survey data? Empirical illustration for Central and Eastern Europe. *ASK, 17,* 85–100.

Kerlinger, F. N., & Lee, H. B. (2000). *Foundations of behavioral research* (4th ed.). Fort Worth, TX: Wadsworth/Thompson Learning.

Mahalingam, R. (2007). Culture, power and psychology of marginality. In A. Fuligni (Ed.), *Contesting stereotypes and creating identities Social categories, social identities, and educational participation* (pp. 42–65). New York, NY: Sage.

McCall, L. (2005). The complexity of intersectionality. *Signs, 30,* 1771–1800.

Nunnally, J. C., & Bernstein, I. H. (1994). *Psychometric theory* (3rd ed.). New York, NY: McGraw-Hill.

Pascarella, E. T. (1985). College environmental influences on learning and cognitive development: A critical review and synthesis. In J. Smart (Ed.), *Higher education: Handbook of theory and research* (Vol. 1, pp. 1–64). New York, NY: Agathon.

Pascarella, E. T., & Terenzini, P. T. (2005). *How college affects students* (Vol. 2). San Francisco, CA: Jossey-Bass.

Renn, K. A. (2010). LGBT and queer research in higher education: The state and status of the field. *Educational Researcher, 39,* 132–141.

Sanlo, R. (2002). Scholarship in student affairs: Thinking outside the triangle, or Tabasco on canta-loupe. *NASPA Journal, 39,* 166–180.

Stage, F. K. (2007). Answering critical questions using quantitative data. *New Directions for Institutional Research, 13,* 5–16.

Tinto, V. (1975). Dropout from higher education: A theoretical synthesis of recent research. *Review of Educational Research, 45,* 89–125.

Tinto, V. (1987). *Leaving college: Rethinking the causes and cures of student attrition.* Chicago, IL: University of Chicago Press.

Tinto, V. (1993). *Leaving college: Rethinking the causes and cures of student attrition* (2nd ed.). Chicago, IL: University of Chicago Press.

Weidman, J. (1989). Undergraduate socialization: A conceptual approach. In J. Smart (Ed.), *Higher education: Handbook of theory and research* (Vol. 5, pp. 289–322). New York, NY: Agathon.

PART THREE

Praxis

CHAPTER FIFTEEN

No Longer Cast Aside

A Critical Approach to Serving Queer and Trans Students of Color in Higher Education

MEG E. EVANS AND JASON K. WALLACE

Even in our best efforts, higher education professionals overlook and neglect the intersectional needs of queer and trans students of Color (QTSOC) on college campuses. Failing to acknowledge and honor all students' identities lies in direct conflict to the goals of professionals who seek to meet the needs of students from admission to graduation. In this chapter, we discuss the experiences of QTSOC on college campuses by providing practical tips to better serve QTSOC underlining the importance of centering this population in philosophy and praxis.

OUR PHILOSOPHY AND POSITIONALITY

Addressing affirming praxis for serving QTSOC necessitates a discussion of our philosophy when approaching this work. We believe "a diverse student body creates positive learning environments, promotes cross-racial interactions, and is positively associated with student learning outcomes" (Karkouti, 2016, p. 59). The existence of QTSOC on college campuses affords all students the opportunity to engage in ways that not only enrich their learning but texturizes their campus experience. We believe that centering QTSOC in praxis provides permission for all students to live their truth and explore their social identities beyond the context of White, hegemonic environments that higher education promotes. If professionals can engage in praxis that holistically meets the needs of a queer-trans-femme woman of Color, then this praxis inherently liberates people of all gender identities, sexual orientations, gender expressions, and varying racial and ethnic identities.

ME's positionality: I identify as a queer, gender non-conforming White person who is deeply engaged with self-reflection and self-work around racial justice. I recognize I am on a journey to continue to unlearn my socialized patterns of White dominance and fragility. I have worked in higher education for over a decade and deeply believe that we have failed when trying to serve our students who hold multiple minoritized identities.

JW's positionality: As a queer, cisgender, Christian Black man with over eight years of experience in higher education, theory and lived experience inform my lens for praxis. Though I hold salient minoritized identities, which drive my passion for this work, my numerous dominant identities call for me to do my own work to unlearn harmful, cisnormative and patriarchal practices, and leverage my privileges for our collective liberation.

OUR THEORETICAL FRAMEWORK

White institutional presence (WIP; Gusa, 2010), queer theory (Turner, 2000), critical race theory (CRT; Bell, 1987), and intersectionality (Crenshaw, 1991) provide the theoretical framework for our praxis. Embedded ideologies of Whiteness negatively impact campus climate, explicitly for students of Color (Gusa, 2010). Gusa (2010) posits detailed attributes of what she coins as White institutional presence to explain how Whiteness dominates college campuses. Queer theory "critically analyzes the meaning of identity, focusing on intersections of identities and resisting oppressive social constructions of sexual orientation and gender" (Abes & Kasch, 2007, p. 620). Queer theory resists inherent ideas of heteronormativity and postulates that society, particularly people who identify in dominant groups, socially construct both gender and sexual orientation. We also engage concepts from queer scholars of Color using notions of quare theory (Johnson, 2001) to further inform our philosophy. CRT notes that race permeates everything (Bell, 1987). "CRT offers conceptual tools for interrogating how race and racism have been institutionalized and are maintained" (Sleeter, 2017, p. 157). Finally, when discussing intersectionality, Crenshaw (1991) posited that because of Black women's minoritized identities in both race and gender, they experience a unique form of oppression and discrimination. WIP, queer theory, CRT, and intersectionality serve as strategic frameworks to illuminate and validate the necessity for our campuses to engage in this work and help to frame how professionals can learn to work within systems of oppression to meet QTSOC needs.

QTSOC EXPERIENCES IN COLLEGE

QTSOC experience many forms of overt and covert discrimination on college campuses (Brockenbrough, 2015). From racial microaggressions to misgendering, QTSOC find themselves in danger of verbal and physical violence based on their race, ethnicity, sexual orientation, gender identity and/or expression (Balsam, Molina, Beadnell, Simoni, & Walters, 2011; di Bartolo, 2015; Nadal et al., 2011; Nicolazzo, 2015; Sue, Capodilupo, & Holder, 2008). This trauma often leads to mental health issues (Kulick, Wernick, Woodford, & Renn, 2017).

QTSOC often experience racism in what some would consider "safe spaces" for queer and trans folks such as gender and sexuality resource centers, women's centers, and student organizations purposed for queer and trans folks (Fox & Ore, 2010). Conversely, QTSOC experience homophobia/biphobia/transphobia in race-alike spaces such as culture houses, multicultural offices, culturally-based student organizations, and multicultural Greek-lettered organizations (Negrete & Purcell, 2011). Due to the challenges faced by QTSOC, it is imperative that professionals put forth intentional efforts to make certain that students within this demographic feel supported on campus. It is systems of oppression embedded within campus structures that make college campuses uncomfortable and potentially dangerous for QTSOC (Gusa, 2010).

7 TIPS FOR A QTSOC-AFFIRMING CAMPUS

In this section, we offer professionals practical tips to serve QTSOC. By making these intentional efforts, QTSOC will not only feel seen on campus but valued. Though we have witnessed these recommendations work on a variety of campuses, we also name that each institution is different, and the following recommendations may not prove effective for all campuses. Context matters, and we fully recognize that the tides of change roll slowly.

1. White, Straight, and/or Cis Folks: Do Self-work

Society socializes us all to think, act, and react in certain ways, and that socialization is often handed down from generation to generation (Harro, 2000). It impacts ways of knowing and often impacts the ways in which people engage with the world. Often, White professionals do not even know the impact, often negative, they have on students of Color (Gusa, 2010). Before professionals can authentically engage in QTSOC liberation, those with dominant racial, sexual, and/or gender identities must do their own self-work of unlearning racist, sexist, misogynistic, homophobic/biphobic/transphobic beliefs (Linder, 2018).

Be mindful of engaging in self-work at the expense of people of Color and/ or queer and trans people. Instead, engage in workshops, trainings, and webinars where facilitators volunteer their time and expertise and are adequately compensated for their labor. Also, use available resources such as documentaries, books, blogs, and podcasts for further education. The information is out there—find it and use it.

2. Engage New Accountability and Assessment Practices

Before professionals can know what issues to address regarding QTSOC inclusion on campus, they must know what the current lived experience is for QTSOC. Pre-assessments like an office, campus, or community climate survey can help and include contextual factors that are environment-specific. Professionals must engage in continual assessments to meet the needs of QTSOC and decolonize structural barriers while accounting for the principles of CRT, queer theory, WIP, and intersectionality.

Once professionals know the needs of QTSOC, they can look for accountability partners to help meet those needs. Professionals should have an open relationship with their accountability partners as there is a need for comfort in honest disclosure and feedback. This relationship should include regular check-ins with short-term and long-term goals for specifically serving QTSOC. For those who supervise, set specific expectations for direct reports, and then serve as one of their accountability partners to further center QTSOC needs and experiences. Scheduling regular time with an accountability partner is critical to better serving QTSOC (Washington, 2011).

3. Explicitly Name QTSOC Labor

A straightforward way to serve QTSOC is by naming their labor. CRT discusses the importance of offering counternarratives in dominant spaces (Bell, 1987). Many students, faculty, and staff offer mental, physical, and emotional labor by going beyond their role to educate the larger campus community about QTSOC (Abustan, 2017; Aguilar & Johnson, 2017). QTSOC experience both racial battle fatigue (Smith, Allen, & Danley, 2007) and queer battle fatigue (Wozolek, Varndell, & Speer, 2015) which uniquely place them at the intersection of two oppressive systems. Though professionals may not ask for this labor, they often use QTSOC to educate White, cisgender, and/or straight people about their lived experience which is both fatiguing and exploitive (Aguilar & Johnson, 2017). To ask QTSOC to create the environment they need to succeed without asking other students to do the same upholds White supremacy. Avoid tokenizing QTSOC, and give rewards when they serve as educators. Additionally, acknowledge when queer and trans professionals of Color are putting forth this labor–especially when it is not in their job description. Recognize when faculty members mentor QTSOC and take their labor into consideration during the tenure and promotion process.

4. Create an Intentional Space Purposed for QTSOC

All students need spaces where they can feel welcomed, accepted in their fullness, and centered in the vision for the space. Creating a space for QTSOC may mean the creation of a student organization, a student lounge, or simply a discussion group. As in most spaces, those dedicated specifically to QTSOC are impacted by varying power dynamics. It is important honor the tenets of CRT and queer theory by naming, addressing, and interrupting toxic masculinity, anti-Blackness, cisnormativity, xenophobia, misogynoir, biphobia, colorism, and other oppressive behaviors that show up. QTSOC spaces are not exempt from White supremacy.

Remember that QTSOC are not a monolith. Like all other students, QTSOC needs vary from student to student; however, unless spaces are created that center QTSOC, those specific needs will likely go unvoiced and unnoticed. It is important to recognize that QTSOC support and affirmation cannot, and often does not, happen in identity-based offices/centers alone. "LGBT campus centers are often critiqued for being White-centric, and multicultural centers are often critiqued for being heteronormative and cisnormative" (Johnson & Javier, 2017, p. 5). If QTSOC are experiencing campuses this way and not finding places where they can engage in their fullness, what can institutions do on both a macro and micro level to more fully embrace QTSOC?

5. Develop Purposeful Collaborations and Partnerships

Professionals seeking to center the experiences of QTSOC must not forget the importance of network building (Kezar & Lester, 2009). Collaborations and partnerships proven effective in serving QTSOC include student affairs practitioners and administrators, faculty from varying academic departments, student organizations, community organizations, and staff from non-profits focused on gender, sexuality, or racial justice. In the early stages of collaboration, it is important to be purposeful when identifying partners (Kezar & Lester, 2009). Not everyone will see the importance of centering their praxis, at least in part, around QTSOC, nevertheless interest convergence may prove effective (Bell, 1995). Who are the other professionals who can place a critical eye to programming, policies, and office norms?" It may be best to initially select collaborative partners that already exhibit an interest in partnering or at least demonstrate an interest in serving minoritized students. Selection of these partners may start with those who have already established a commitment to QTSOC through research, praxis, or engagement.

Once professionals identify initial collaborators, a snowball type strategy might be used—gaining subsequent collaborations through current participants and collaborators (Kezar & Lester, 2009).

6. Make Strategic Professional Hires

Hiring professionals who not only display certain diversity competencies but can speak to specifically serving QTSOC is imperative (Kayes, 2006). For new hires to be open to this learning and collaboration, there is a need for diversifying search committees to include queer and trans professionals of Color and other professionals who recognize the need and desire a diverse campus. Many universities publish guidelines for hiring managers to help reduce bias (Kayes, 2006). These guidelines could serve as a model that centers queer and trans people of Color more specifically to ensure a more just and equitable search process.

When asked to be on committees, it is of crucial importance to use CRT to be reminded that Whiteness is pervasive (Bell, 1987) and name the who and what is missing on those committees. Who is being asked to sit on and chair committees? What practices are in place to help remove bias from the selection process? It is critical to be strategic and advertise in places that serve and center queer and trans people of Color—like *Diverse Issues in Higher Education* and the Consortium of Higher Education LGBT Resource Professional's job boards, Facebook groups, GroupMe's for queer and trans people of Color, Twitter, etc. Hiring managers can work with human resources to craft QTSOC affirming statements for job postings. Finally, professionals must make sure policies and practices that seek to center and affirm QTSOC are also in place to help retain queer and trans professionals of Color.

7. Celebrate, Recognize, and Foster Joy as a Form of Resistance

Celebrating, recognizing, and fostering QTSOC joy is, likely, the most powerful form of resistance that we offer to professionals. The lives of QTSOC are more than just the difficult ways in which QTSOC navigate campuses not created for them. By celebrating a new QTSOC relationship, a birthday, a coming out, a passed exam, or simply their existence, professionals resist the racist and heteronormative idea that only White cisgender straight people deserve happiness. Add a black and brown stripe to the rainbow flag and include gender pronouns on door tags, business cards, and name tags. Highlight queer and trans people of Color trailblazers like Marsha P. Johnson, Gloria Anzaldúa, Bayard Rustin, and countless others. To provide a landscape for discussions about queerness outside White dominant structures, explore the cultural nuances of queer identity such as two-spirit in Indigenous culture or hijras in South Asian culture (Hossain, 2012

Lang, 2016). Queer theory (Turner, 2000) gives the permission to be confident in creating the new normal on our campuses and honor QTSOC.

In addition to the small wins, it is important to celebrate the successful matriculation and graduation of QTSOC. Programs like Lavender Graduation should not only exist but include cultural components that specifically honor QTSOC. Consider what it would mean for Lavender Graduation to include a variety of languages, cultural cuisine, culturally-relevant music, and keynote speakers who identity as queer and trans people of Color. Additionally, it is vital that professionals nominate QTSOC for university-wide awards as those who hold dominant identities rarely acknowledge QTSOC labor (Gusa, 2010). Centering joy and celebration in QTSOC praxis can transform the ways in which QTSOC engage on campus.

CONCLUSION

Queer and trans students of Color are not a problem to be solved (Marine, 2011) and it is imperative that professionals work on engaging and centering QTSOC in praxis. By operating outside of a single axis of social identity (Chan, Erby, & Ford, 2017) and utilizing ideas from WIP, queer theory, CRT, and intersectionality, QTSOC may be seen, understood, and honored on campuses. Intention influences impact, yet action has a larger influence. Professionals have the responsibility to lead by example (di Bartolo, 2015) and not just ask the questions that need asked to support QTSOC, but also act in ways that center this population in both philosophy and praxis.

REFERENCES

Abes, E. S., & Kasch, D. (2007). Using queer theory to explore lesbian college students'multiple dimensions of identity. *Journal of College Student Development, 48*(6), 619–636.

Abustan, P. (2017). Collectively feeling: Honoring the emotional experiences of queer and transgender student of Color activists. In J. M. Johnson & G. Javier (Eds.), *Queer people of Color in higher education* (pp. 31–56). Charlotte, NC: Information Age.

Aguilar, D., & Johnson, J. M. (2017). Queer faculty and staff of Color: Experiences and expectations. In J. M. Johnson & G. Javier (Eds.), *Queer people of Color in higher education* (pp. 57–72). Charlotte, NC: Information Age.

Balsam, K. F., Molina, Y., Beadnell, B., Simoni, J., & Walters, K. (2011). Measuring multiple minority stress: The LGBT people of Color microaggressions scale. *Cultural Diversity and Ethnic Minority Psychology, 17*(2), 163–174.

Bell, D. (1987). *And we will not be saved: The exclusive quest for racial justice.* New York, NY: Basic Books.

Bell, D. (1995). Brown v. Board of Education and the interest convergence dilemma. *Harvard Law Review, 93*, 518–533.

Brockenbrough, E. (2015). Queer of Color agency in educational contexts: Analytic frameworks from a queer of Color critique. *Educational Studies, 51*(1), 28–44.

Chan, C. D., Erby, A. N., & Ford, D. J. (2017). Intersectionality in practice: Moving a social justice paradigm to action in higher education. In J. M. Johnson & G. Javier (Eds.), *Queer people of Color in higher education* (pp. 9–30). Charlotte, NC: Information Age.

Crenshaw, K. (1991). Mapping the margins: Intersectionality, identity politics, and violence against women of Color. *Stanford Law Review, 43*(6), 1241–1299.

di Bartolo, A. N. (2015). Rethinking gender equity in higher education. *Diversity & Democracy, 18*(2). Retrieved from https://www.aacu.org/ diversitydemocracy/2015/spring/dibartolo

Fox, C. O., & Ore, T. E. (2010). (Un)covering normalized gender and race subjectivities in LGBT "safe spaces." *Feminist Studies, 36*(6), 629–649.

Gusa, D. L. (2010). White institutional presence: The impact of whiteness on campus climate. *Harvard Educational Review, 80*(4), 464–489.

Harro, B. (2000). The cycle of socialization. In M. Adams, W. J. Blumenfeld, R. Castañeda, H. W. Hackman, M. L. Peters, & X. Zúñiga (Eds.), *Readings for diversity and social justice: An anthology on racism, antisemitism, sexism, heterosexism, and classism* (3rd ed., pp. 15–21). New York, NY: Routledge.

Hossain, A. (2012). Beyond emasculation: Being Muslim and becoming *Hijra* in South Asia. *Asian Studies Review, 36*(4), 495–513.

Johnson, E. P. (2001) "Quare studies, or (almost) everything I know about queer studies I learned from my grandmother. *Text and Performance Quarterly, 21*(1), 1–25.

Johnson, J. M., & Javier, G. (Eds.). (2017). *Queer people of Color in higher education.* Charlotte, NC Information Age.

Karkouti, I. M. (2016). Black students' educational experiences in predominantly White universities A Review of the related literature. *College Student Journal, 50*(1), 59–70.

Kayes, P. E. (2006). New paradigms for diversifying faculty and staff in higher education: Uncovering cultural biases in the search and hiring process. *Multicultural Education, 14*(2), 65–69.

Kezar, A., & Lester, J. (2009). *Organizing higher education for collaboration: A guide for campus leaders* San Francisco, CA: Jossey-Bass.

Kulick, A., Wernick, L. J., Woodford, M. R., & Renn, K. (2017). Heterosexism, depression, and campus engagement among LGBTQ college students: Intersectional differences and opportunities for healing. *Journal of Homosexuality, 64*(8), 1125–1141.

Lang, S. (2016). Native American men-women, lesbians, two-spirits: Contemporary and historical perspectives. *Journal of Lesbian Studies, 20*(3–4), 299–323.

Linder, C. (2018). *Sexual violence on campus: Power-conscious approaches to awareness, prevention, and response.* United Kingdom: Emerald.

Marine, S. B. (2011). "Our college is changing": Women's college student affairs administrators and transgender students. *Journal of Homosexuality, 58*(9), 1165–1186.

Nadal, K., Wong, Y., Issa, M., Meterko, V., Leon, J., & Wideman, M. (2011). Sexual orientation microaggressions: Processes and coping mechanisms for lesbian, gay, and bisexual individuals *Journal of LGBT Issues in Counseling, 5*(1), 21–46.

Negrete, N. A., & Purcell, C. (2011). Engaging sexual orientation and gender diversity in multicultural student services. In D. L. Stewart (Ed.), *Multicultural student services on campus: Building bridges, re-visioning community* (pp. 81–93). Sterling, VA: Stylus.

Nicolazzo, Z. (2015). *"Just go in looking good": The resilience, resistance, and kinship- building of trans college students* (Doctoral dissertation). Retrieved from http://www.ohiolink.edu/etd/

Sleeter, C. E. (2017). Critical race theory and the Whiteness of teacher education. *Urban Education, 52*(2), 155–169.

Smith, W. A., Allen, W. R., & Danley, L. L. (2007). Assume the position … You fit the description": Psychosocial experiences and racial battle fatigue among African American male college students. *American Behavioral Scientist, 51*(4), 551–578.

Sue, D. W., Capodilupo, C. M., & Holder, A. M. B. (2008). Racial microaggressions in the life experience of Black Americans. *Professional Psychology: Research and Practice, 39*(3), 329–336.

Turner, W. B. (2000). *A genealogy of queer theory.* Philadelphia, PA: Temple University Press.

Washington, J. (2011). Preparing diversity change leaders. In D. L. Stewart (Ed.), *Multicultural student services on campus: Building bridges, re-visioning community* (pp. 81–93). Sterling, VA: Stylus.

Wozolek, B., Varndell, R., & Speer, T. (2015). Are we not fatigued?: Queer battle fatigue at the intersection of heteronormative culture. *International Journal of Curriculum and Social Justice, 1*(1), 1–35.

CHAPTER SIXTEEN

When Sisters Unite

Overcoming Oppression to Persist and Thrive in a PhD Program

PATRICIA P. CARVER, TAMEKKA L. CORNELIUS,
AND KRISTIE S. JOHNSON

The pursuit of a Doctor of Philosophy (PhD) is a daunting task. It is a lonely journey, or so it was explained that way at our doctoral orientation. Your work is yours alone. Your survival, success, or failure is yours to celebrate or to lament. Yet, for Black women, fighting lonely battles in the world of academia is not new. Throughout history, Black women have exhibited resilience in surpassing barriers of discrimination and achieving insurmountable accomplishments.

For instance, educators such as Hallie Quinn Brown, Anna Julia Cooper, and Mary McLeod-Bethune, all of whom challenged the educational system on behalf of Black women. They understood that *intersectionality*, while not formally named, influenced Black women's lives. Kimberlé Crenshaw (1989) introduced the term intersectionality to articulate the marginalization and systematic oppression Black women have faced for centuries due to their intersecting racial, gender, and class identities, among other marginalized identities.

While society would like to think that there are no differences between Black and White women or between Black men and Black women, differences do exist (Rosales & Person, 2003). Rosales and Person (2003) suggest that Black women are grouped with White women in issues of sexism and grouped with Black men with regard to issues of race, thereby deeming Black women as invisible in both situations. Because of this flawed perception, Rosales and Person suggest that Black women in graduate school settings are often overlooked for collaboration efforts in research, teaching assignments, and other opportunities that are afforded to White women and men of Color graduate students.

In concert, Howard-Hamilton (2003) suggests that Black women have been, and continue to be, overlooked in the academy causing them to lack encouragement in pursuing higher levels of education. For instance, Black women are hampered by microaggressions, unjust negative stereotypes, and other racial deprivations that cause them to be considered "peripheral participants" (Howard-Hamilton, 2003 p. 24) by other students, staff, and faculty. Data substantiate Howard-Hamilton's claim, as Black women are not achieving PhDs at the rate proportionate to our representation in the population. According to the 2010 U. S. census, Blacks are the second largest demographic group making up approximately 6.8% of the total population and 13.3% of women (United States Census Bureau, 2017). In contrast, in 2017, Black women made up 3.96% of all PhDs and only 9.6% of women who are PhDs (United States Census Bureau, 2017).

Since society has been slow in developing mechanisms to assist Black women when coping with systemic oppression and marginalization, particularly in educational settings, Black women have often formed their own avenues of support. More specifically, the networks available to Black women PhD students and graduates are limited and Black women in PhD programs have often had to depend upon themselves and each other to thrive and maintain success.

Historically, Black women have looked to their ancestors as examples of formed their personal circle of power, endurance, and influence. This support i the role that *sister circles* have played in Black women's lives throughout history (Neal-Barnett et al., 2011). Neal-Barnett and colleagues (2011) note that sister circles have been in existence for centuries, filling in where mainstream society ha left Black women to fend for themselves. A sister circle is a group of likeminded women who lovingly support one another, while providing a sense of community These circles offer a network and friendships between Black women that lend support, encouragement, and a kindred spirit where there may otherwise be none. For Black women in PhD programs, sister circles provide necessary networks to help Black women progress through the PhD journey by providing support and representation that is offered because of invisibility. The support offered in sister circles is invaluable as they celebrate Black womanhood instead of requiring Black women to attempt to do the impossible and choose between Blackness, woman-hood, or other marginalized identities as disregarding any part of who they are adds to vulnerabilities with regard to racism and sexism (hooks, 2003).

Black women have depended upon sister circles to maneuver them through the rough times and patches in their lives. This coping strategy has been used especially in higher education where many women of Color feel isolated due to their small numbers, particularly at predominantly White institutions (PWIs). Croom Beatty, Acker, and Butler (2017) discussed two such PWIs who established sister circles to help women in responding to racist, sexist attitudes at their respective schools. Forming sister circles have proven to be a major catalyst for success whe embarking on the journey of securing a PhD in an educational system not created with the interest of Black women in mind. For example, women at the University of Iowa formed the "#SisterPhD" sister circle (McCloud, 2017, para. 6) and the "Great Eight" sister circle (Logue, 2016, para. 3) was instituted at Indiana University to support Black women through their PhD programs. Groups such as these support women in the lonely existence of a PhD program and play a vital role in the success of Black women who may not otherwise have a confidant to share their struggles and successes—this is why we created our sister circle. There are many stories of strong, successful Black women who have survived systematic oppressions within higher education settings; however, their stories are often left untold. Our sister circle—that we formed as we pursue PhDs in higher education—has decided to share our story, not only because it is cathartic, but also to help other women who are journeying through their PhD programs as well.

PC'S STORY

The pursuit of a PhD has come later in life for me. This endeavor comes after spending over 16 years teaching at a university. Although the idea of being a PhD was never a significant goal, the opportunity was there, and it was too difficult to ignore. After completing the PhD program, my aspirations will not change, as I will continue on the same trajectory—teaching in the classroom. Although my cohort as a whole has been supportive, forming the special bond with the other Black women in the program was a natural process. By the middle of the first semester, we knew that there was a need for support and we converged together.

The start of our sister circle began informally as we communicated with one another about class assignments, lending minor support, and forming study partners when needed. We knew it was important to encourage each other through words and in action. It did not take us long to bond as a sisterhood as we progressed through the program. We have lived through births, deaths, illnesses, and the occasional "I'm ready to quit the program" dilemma. The one caveat I do know is that without the other Black women in the program, my journey would not have been as seamless or tolerable. The love and support received from these women are immeasurable.

As I am writing, we have made it through three years of this intense journey without the privilege of having one Black woman standing in front of the class. Some might argue that there have been Black men and White women, but it is not the same. I wanted to hear from other sisters who have made the successful academic journey that I am on; however, this did not happen. The oversight is especially disheartening when Black women make up almost 40% of our cohort. Yet, no one seems to have noticed or cared except for my sisters and me. However, it should not have surprised me, as there were other signs that the program did not understand the importance of African American lecturers or the needs of the Black women in the program. For instance, in one class, our professor posted a reading list of at least 50 books for the class to read and none of the authors were Black women. He may have felt he passed the "diversity test" by offering Black men and White women authors; however, he left out a large segment of the student population—us. Our professor may not have been aware of intersectionality or the importance of the framework for Black women in student development. These kinds of incidents are what make my sister circle so important in grounding and supporting one another.

As another example, my sister circle was there to support me when a faculty member proposed that my dissertation topic concerning Black women students was not scholarly enough. He did not see the importance of Black women not having anyone to date romantically on a predominantly White campus. My sisters even laughed and became indignant with me when the same professor recommended I read the writings of a White feminist theorist to ground my studies once he finally came around to agreeing to my topic. My sisters also shared my disbelief and angst when a White male student proposed that I choose which was the more important cause—my gender *or* my race; he suggested that it was too much to ask for equity in both arenas. I still cringe over that encounter as he made it seem like such a simple and seamless decision to make. However, my sister circle got it, and they get me. They share in the indignities that have held Black women back for so long.

What astounds me most is that we could not be more different. We are all of different generations, in different phases in our lives, and have unique life goals. Yet, we have formed this unbreakable sister circle. Maybe it is because those shared intersecting characteristics of race and gender are our strongest bonds. It could be that no one understands the trials and tribulations of being a Black woman better than a Black woman.

My sister circle has been invaluable to me. The sisters have helped me weather through the storms of my PhD program. I knew that there was a special bond because, although we are in different phases of our lives and will go on different paths, it was easy for us to connect as a sisterhood. As we are ending our journey, I know that these women will be in my corner from here to eternity. They know my weaknesses, and instead of trying to gain from them, they have gathered around me to give me their strengths. When I fall short, they fill in the gaps, ensuring that I become stronger.

TC'S STORY

My PhD journey began after an eight year hiatus from the classroom. After receiving my master's degree, I began working as a student affairs professional with the prospectus of obtaining a PhD in the future. That opportunity came in 2015 with the design of a new PhD program at the institution of which I was employed. From the beginning, I was met with opposition to even apply to the program by my White counterparts. Entry into the program required the approval of a supervisor or department head. At the time I was the only Black woman in a department of ten and was supervised by a White man who was currently a student in the PhD program that I was considering. When approached with my desire to apply to the PhD program, I was told that the department did not think that now was the right time and that I should wait another year to become more familiar with my job duties before pursuing this advanced degree.

I experienced a range of emotions. I felt hurt by the rejection, disappointed in the potential delay, and angry at the dismissal of my desire to further my education. I knew I could do this, but I could not help to feel a tinge of inadequacy. As the only Black woman in the department, the department's response to my request left me feeling vulnerable to *imposter syndrome*. Clance and Imes (1978) describe imposter syndrome as the lack of an internal sense of success despite earned scholastic honors and professional recognition and intelligence. I do not attribute these feelings to me being a Black woman, but rather because I was the only Black woman in that particular space and was being told by the majority that I was not ready, that somehow I was lacking.

Determined, I applied for a different position within the university and secured a new role in a new department. My new supervisor, a Black woman with a doctorate, was aware of my goals, met with me to discuss them, and signed off on the PhD application less than one month into my new role. I was accepted into the program and later discovered that the vice president of my new department, a White woman, was shocked to learn that I had been accepted into the program; she too thought that I needed to wait. At this point I felt confused, but I also felt validated. A Black woman saw potential and promise wherein her White counterparts felt trepidation and apprehension. What was it that the Black woman saw in me that the White man and White woman did not? This vast contrast between my interaction with a Black woman versus two White colleagues was my introduction to the importance of a kindred support system.

My sister circle has provided that for me. From the moment we met and looked around the room, we knew that we were it. As the only three Black women in the program, we knew that we would need to provide the backing, encouragement, and emotional assistance to one another that no one else could. We often spoke our own language because our experiences and oppressions are unique to Black women. For example, asking each other, "Does this make sense?" before a presentation, or, "Did he/she say what I think they said?" after a questionable comment from a colleague was normal and understood without question. In addition to our non-verbals, the exchange of a glance during a class discussion on gender bias or after a discouraging comment that only another Black woman could understand often reassured me. There is no competition among us. We share notes, serve as our own proofreaders and editors, share scholastic joys, familial lows, and everything in between. I am eager to make history with my sisters as the first three Black women to graduate from the PhD in higher education program at our institution.

Without my sisters, this journey would have been lonely and wearisome. I receive scholarly feedback and advice for written assignments and affirmation for my thoughts and ideas. Outside of the classroom, I know they are just a text or phone call away when I need to vent about the latest suspicion of gendered racism, a microaggression, or when I want to share with them a victory that occured during the workday. Befriending my circle has been a refreshing necessity and one that I do not take for granted. I am looking forward to our group paving the way for a broader representation of diversity within our field.

KJ'S STORY

After exploring a few doctoral programs, none felt interesting or compelling enough to make the major commitment that is required of a PhD program. It would be nearly a decade after receiving my master's degree in international development and social change that I would begin my doctoral program. However, it was not without some challenges.

While family, many friends, and close colleagues cheered me on, there were several coworkers and acquaintances who inquired if it was really necessary to have *another* advanced degree and others incorrectly assumed that it must be an online degree that I was pursuing as a Black woman. While there is nothing wrong with pursuing an online degree, these statements are microaggressions grounded in racism, classism, and elitism towards me, a self-identified Caribbean-American woman. Interestingly, many of these same individuals started doctoral programs and never finished or simply could not gain acceptance into a doctoral program Yet, they were determined to dissuade me from pursuing my PhD. After meeting the director, I felt encouraged to begin the program.

Once I began the program, I was impressed with the range of diversity which was the vision of the inaugural director. We had several White and six African Americans—three men and three women—with many different experiences. While we all supported one another and got along really well, the bond I shared with the two African American women in my program sustained me. Not only did we support each other academically, but also personally and professionally. My sister circle helped maintain my sanity in very real and profound ways. We have laughed cried with and for each other, whispered prayers of safety and well-being, and held each other's hand in silence when words were insufficient.

These women I call my sisters know my shortcomings, my flaws, my failings, and yet still love me. We have celebrated engagements, birthdays, promotions, publications, awards, and a birth. While it was extremely challenging, I am proud that I was able to stay with my cohort without falling behind on my coursework. This would not be possible without my sister circle. Not only did they allow me to stay at their homes instead of a hotel to save money, but they also selflessly prepared lunches and snacks for me every class weekend to ensure I was eating well. As a result of our deep friendship, our lives are interconnected on many different levels. Not only do we share class notes, we also share cooking recipes, workout routines, books, PhD resources, successes of other Black women in academia, and the best haircare products for natural hair. I cannot articulate the humble gratitude and sincere respect and adoration I feel for these women I call my sisters. My sister circle provided encouragement and support in what could have been a dark and lonely journey. Yet, the desire for Black women to further their education is not strange or unheard of. As a society, it must be remembered that there is not a monolithic narrative that is reflective of all Black women and all of their experiences. In fact, our experiences, as well as our journey to the PhD program, are as diverse as the African Diaspora and reflects our rich and dynamic backgrounds that not only contribute to the classroom but to all of academia and society at large.

CONCLUSION

Our sister circle came both at the right time and in the right space. The fact that the three of us were chosen based on merit to join the first cohort of the doctorate program at our institution was no mistake. In a time and space where we were the only Black women in our cohort and in a program where we were taught for the first two years exclusively by White faculty members at a predominantly White institution, we were our crutch.

We provided the challenge and support we needed to persevere and succeed. We exercised self-care collectively in the form of encouraging messages, opening the doors to our homes to one another on class weekends, critiquing and editing class assignments and papers prior to submiting, and sharing information or advice that may have otherwise been withheld from our White counterparts. We provided reinforcements for one another along the way in the midst of the aforementioned challenges that directly influenced our tolerance to grow professionally and personally and to advance toward our degrees. This resiliency and passion to succeed is what has sustained us throughout the program and we are proud of how much we have accomplished individually and together despite interlocking oppressions working against us.

As we prepare for the end of our PhD journey, we have each made commitments to continue the bond and strength of our circle beyond the classroom. Additionally, we plan to ask the university's administration to provide more support services and resources for Black women pursuing PhDs. For instance, a database of Black women graduates of the program or those at the dissertation stage willing to serve as mentors to new students is a solid example of a resource that could be provided to help other Black women as they begin their journey. While we are capable of navigating the scholastic structure on our own—and often after some trial and error—the university should be supportive in its efforts to make the transition smoother for Black women.

What we have learned from our sister circle is that success has been a two-way, or in this case a three-way, street. It has been a give and take, with each of us having to recognize what we want and what the other needs out of the relationship. Our friendship spans generations, cross state lines, and cross industries; and while we are at different phases of our careers and personal lives, our end goal is the same—to graduate with PhDs. Together, we have created a formula that works for us to march forward towards that goal in the face of adversity and opposition.

Each of us has a story to tell. Stories that include how our identities, as Black women, are tied to the path we have chosen and the struggle to get there due to systemic oppressions. The barriers we have faced as Black women have been covert and overt, yet we have persisted. It is our hope that by sharing our stories, we have provided light into the dark tunnel for another sister who is thinking about or is entrenched in a doctoral program herself; it is our hope that our stories start her sister circle.

REFERENCES

Bandura, A. (1986). *Social foundations of thought and action: A social cognitive theory.* Englewood Cliff, NJ: Prentice Hall.

Bova, B. (2000). Mentoring revisited: The Black woman's experience. *Mentoring & Tutoring: Partnership in Learning, 8*(1), 5–16.

Clance, P. R., & Imes, S. (1978). The imposter phenomenon in high achieving women: Dynamics and therapeutic intervention. *Psychotherapy Theory, Research and Practice, 15*(3), 241–247.

Crenshaw, K. (1989). Demarginalizing the intersection of race and sex: A Black feminist critique of antidiscrimination doctrine, feminist theory and antiracist politics. *University of Chicago Legal Forum, 1989*(8), 139–167.

Croom, N., Beatty, C., Acker, L., & Butler, M. (2017). Exploring undergraduate black womyn's motivations for engaging in "sister circle" organizations. *NASPA Journal About Women in Higher Education, 10*(2), 216–228.

hooks, bell. (2003). *Teaching community: A pedagogy of hope.* New York, NY: Routledge.

Howard-Hamilton, M. F. (2003). Theoretical frameworks for African American women. In M. Howard-Hamilton (Ed.), *Meeting the needs of African American women* (New Directions for Student Services, No. 104, pp. 19–27). San Francisco, CA: Jossey-Bass.

Logue, J. (2016, April 26). The "great" graduating eight. *Inside Higher Ed.* Retrieved from https://www.insidehighered.com/news/2016/04/26/

McCloud, L. (2017, March 30). The importance of a sister circle for Black women pursuing the PhD #SADocsofColor. *Student Affairs Collective.* Retrieved from https://studentaffairscollective.org/sadocsofcolor-sister-circle-black-women-pursuing-phd/

Neal-Barnett, A., Stadulis, R., Murray, M., Payne, M. R., Thomas, A., & Salley, B. B. (2011). Sister circles as a culturally relevant intervention for anxious African American women. *Clinical Psychology, 18*(3), 266–273.

Rosales, A. M., & Person, D. R. (2003). Programming needs and student services for African American women. In M. F. Howard-Hamilton (Ed.), *Meeting the needs of African American women* (New Directions for Student Services, No. 104, pp. 53–65). San Francisco, CA: Jossey-Bass.

United States Census Bureau. (2017, December 14). *Educational attainment in the United States: 2017.* Retrieved from https://www.census.gov/data/tables/2017/demo/education-attainment/cps-detailed-tables.html#

CHAPTER SEVENTEEN

Intersectional Praxis
IN Higher Education
AND Student Affairs
Supervision

SCOTT BURDEN, JIMMY HAMILL, AND CHELSEA GILBERT

Intentional application of intersectional theory and research is of utmost importance in all aspects of work in higher education; however, this framework is rarely applied outside of the realm of student experience, and even more infrequently invoked in the context of supervisory relationships. Supervision has tangible implications for the field of higher education and student affairs; supervisors are rarely given the training and preparation necessary in order to supervise effectively (Calhoun & Nasser, 2013); supervisees are disproportionately disillusioned and dissatisfied with the quality of supervision provided to them (Renn & Hodges, 2007); and, perhaps most importantly, a lack of effective supervision is one of the principal factors for attrition in new student affairs professionals (Barham & Winston, 2006; Creamer & Winston, 2002; Tull, 2006). Despite these clear indicators that supervision is a critical factor when it comes to retention of student affairs professionals, there is a dearth of literature on effective practices in student affairs supervision (Shupp & Arminio, 2012). Of the sources that do exist, few take into account the ways that identity, experience, and systems of power and privilege impact supervisory relationships (Clayborne & Hamrick, 2007).

In this chapter, we respond to this gap in the literature by providing examples of an intersectional, multi-level supervisory framework. Ultimately, we aim to cultivate an awareness of the importance of intersectionality as a critical framework for supervision in the context of student affairs and higher education. In order to do this, we share examples of our implementation of the framework of intersectional feminist supervision at Lehigh University in the context of a resource center for students, faculty, and staff who identify as lesbian, gay, bisexual, transgender, queer, questioning, intersex, asexual, and other genders and sexualities (LGBTQIA+). Specifically, we focus on our efforts to destabilize hierarchical structures in the context of professional staff, graduate student, and undergraduate student supervision. Finally, we provide practical strategies and resources for intersectional praxis in supervision that can be utilized by practitioners in their own spheres of influence.

CONTEXT

We are professional staff members at Lehigh University in the Pride Center for Sexual Orientation and Gender Diversity (the Pride Center). Lehigh University is a medium-sized, R2 research institution located in Bethlehem, Pennsylvania. The student body is comprised of high-achieving students who are predominantly white[1] and from the tri-state area (New York, New Jersey, and Pennsylvania). The Pride Center works to create a campus environment where people of all genders and sexualities can thrive as their full, authentic selves. We focus on providing community-building and support for LGBTQIA+ students, faculty, and staff as well as education for the campus community.

Collectively, we represent three levels of supervision—a director, an associate director, and a graduate assistant. We all identify as white, queer, and cisgender and differ in our gender identities, socioeconomic backgrounds, and spiritual/religious affiliations. Our current undergraduate student staff team of eleven includes six who identify as people of Color, and three who identify as trans and/or nonbinary. As a staff team, we actively recognize and acknowledge difference in our social identities and experiences as well as our corresponding positionalities. The concept of positionality states that an individual's position and sense of who they are in relation to others deeply informs their relationships, communities, and the spaces that they occupy (Avci, 2016). We further explore the ways in which our positionalities and identities inform our relationships and our supervision strategies in this chapter.

THEORETICAL FRAMEWORK

Our guiding theoretical frameworks for our supervisory practice include intersectionality, self-authorship, and feminist praxis in supervision. Intersectionality highlights the complex matrices of identity and power that collide within individuals' lived experiences (Crenshaw, 1991), thus challenging supervisors to more closely attend to their staff members' particular vantage points and embodied realities. Specifically, intersectionality encourages supervisors to reflect on their own positions in relationship to staff members and to make collaborative decisions with this awareness in mind.

Our supervisory practices with our student staff are also informed by self-authorship theory and the learning partnerships model. Self-authorship used in learning, as explained by Baxter Magolda (1999), is an example of constructive-developmental pedagogy. This pedagogical approach to learning is intended to promote conditions where self-discovery and development can be fostered. By way of the learning partnerships model, Baxter Magolda (2004) asserts that learning must be situated within the learners' context and that knowledge accumulation and learning is shared between all. This desire to mutually construct knowledge together as a team intentionally usurps power dynamics and directly relates to our supervisory strategies by way of feminist praxis.

The tenets of feminist praxis in supervision (Porter & Vasquez, 1997), most commonly applied in counseling settings, offer a valuable framework for the higher education supervisory context (Fullerton, 2017). Feminist praxis in supervision envisions supervisor-supervisee relationships as collaborative (Porter, 2009); emphasizes the importance of awareness of and attention to power dynamics (Gentile, Ballou, Roffman, & Ritchie, 2009); attends to social context and systemic oppression (Szymanski, 2003); incorporates intentional reflexivity into daily practice (Porter & Vasquez, 1997); and, leverages the supervisory relationship as an avenue for social change (Gentile et al., 2009). As higher education steadily becomes more diverse, it is increasingly critical that intersectional praxis be a key part of supervisory practice (Clayborne & Hamrick, 2007).

Combining the frameworks of intersectionality, self-authorship, and feminist praxis in supervision, we as a Pride Center staff strive to practice what we are calling *intersectional feminist praxis in supervision*. For us as supervisors, it is an ethical imperative to cultivate a critical consciousness, to understand our supervisees' lived realities, and to create a more equitable environment in which they not only exist but also thrive.

PRAXIS

Just as we ground our supervisory framework in intersectional feminist theory, we strive to actively ensure that our supervisory practices are reflective, critical, and liberatory. Because of this, we see our efforts as perpetual works in progress—never "arriving" at perfection but rather in the constant process of becoming. Below, we illustrate several examples of our supervisory practice through the lens of feminist praxis in supervision, with the caveat that each of these examples are, by necessity, dynamic and ever-shifting based on our continued inner work.

Collaborative Relationships

Our work in the Pride Center is rooted in collaborative relationships amongst both professional and student staff. For us, collaborative relationships are defined by the ideology that everyone is both a learner and a teacher. This stems from our belief that all members of our community are capable of contributing equitably and across lines of difference in order to promote the collaborative relationships that are imperative to our work. There are several ways in which our attempts to build collaborative relationships influence our team. First, we approach decision-making collaboratively as we strive to approach strategic planning, problems, and challenges in a manner that values the synergistic contributions of each individual. Secondly, we center collaborative relationships in both the process and content of our curricular approach to Pride Center programming and student development. All of our programmatic, student staff, and student intern efforts are grounded in goals, objectives, assessment, and intentional reflection, all of which were developed collectively by our director, associate director, and graduate assistant. We also empower all members of our staff team to contribute to our various curricula, and consistently seek feedback from them to ensure that we are developing effective programs and meeting the needs of our various constituents.

The development of collaborative relationships is also evidenced in our work with the structure of our staff professional development model. During the academic year, we meet weekly as a professional staff team. These meetings alternate on a weekly basis; the first week is dedicated to updates and collective problem solving while the other week focuses on professional development. We have incorporated a shared responsibility model for professional development that requires each staff person to alternate taking the lead on professional development for the week. In doing so, we have been able to further commit to the work of collaborative relationships and actively work towards contributing to our culture of teaching and learning regardless of title or level within a hierarchy. Through trust-building and intentional dialogue, our work is increasingly effective by way of our ability to hold one another accountable. Ultimately, we all feel empowered to contribute and make decisions as a team, and as such, our work is elevated in order to better serve all of our constituents.

Awareness of and Attention to Power Dynamics

We also prioritize an awareness of and attention to power dynamics in our supervisory relationships. Because we inhabit an inherently hierarchical system both in the context of our institution as well as within higher education more broadly, is critical that we name and intentionally strive to disrupt those hierarchies whenever possible. For us, this concept of power sharing is a consistent, daily practice that reveals itself in subtle yet impactful ways. For example, in divisional meetings where directors of departments are expected to share updates, our director intentionally shares the space with the rest of our team, ensuring that all voices are elevated and recognized as important carriers of knowledge. In workshops and training sessions, we pay careful attention to whose names are listed first; recognizing that titles play a role in power dynamics, we intentionally list our director last and the person with the least amount of hierarchical power first. Addressing power dynamics also plays out in our advocacy efforts on behalf of our supervisees. We consider it our duty as supervisors to not only actively seek out compensation and recognition for our supervisees, but also to create opportunities for them to serve on committees of influence, speak at high-profile events, and build relationships with key stakeholders. Finally, we strive to disrupt the ways that information is used as currency by modeling transparency to the greatest extent possible.

Transparency recently became especially important as our office transitioned to a new division and reporting structure. In transitions such as these, it has been our experience that information is often passed down in a *funnel*-type model; senior administrators with large amounts of information about the rationale and details of a change pass down pieces to leaders of departments, who then pass down pieces to their supervisees, and so on. In this way, front-line employees, graduate students, and undergraduate students are commonly left without the information they need to properly process and understand the change, or worse, are given no information at all. In order to remain attentive to these dynamics, our director consistently took questions and concerns on behalf of our team to her supervisor and relayed this information promptly through team meetings. She also hosted a town hall event for students where updates were shared along with an open question-and-answer period. These efforts are ongoing and cumulative, and they have resulted in multi-directional trust-building over time. Ultimately, we have learned that awareness of and attention to power dynamics must be a constant process, and that it is not only possible, but critical, that we infuse these practices into our supervisory relationships.

Attending to Social Contexts

We attend to social contexts consistently in our team meetings, where we openly have conversations about broader systems of oppression that relate to campus challenges we are facing. It is our position that higher education reinforces dynamics of inequity and oppression, both at individual institutions as well as in its broader structures. One way we examine our institution's participation in these systems is through a weekly meeting with our student interns (staff members who receive class credit for their work in the Pride Center). In these meetings, we follow a curriculum that begins with theoretical examinations of power and moves throughout the semester toward praxis-based responses to violent power structures; we include the work of scholars and activists such as Angela Davis, Janet Mock, and Kimberlé Crenshaw along with advocacy and activism strategies from organizations such as Southerners On New Ground (SONG). Throughout our conversations, we work in tandem to examine various social contexts, ensuring that each person contributes their own knowledge and experiences along with their corresponding limitations, and ultimately moving to the ways in which these theories implicate our structures and work as a Pride Center. We empower interns to use these strategies within their own semester-long projects, which have ranged from the creation of a peer education group to video projects providing allyship tips.

To further empower our student staff, we provide opportunities for them to facilitate conversations surrounding social justice and identity, which we call *Lunch and Learns*. In these programs, students research a particular question they would like to explore through an hour-long conversation over lunch with other students. Topics in these conversations are meant to move beyond introductory discussion of identity to examine new and underrepresented intersections and experiences. Previous discussions have included allyship with indigenous communities, wage gap inequity for transgender folks, and strategies for activism. Staff members provide introductory resources to help students begin their research, and students then find more sources to create talking points and questions for conversation. We stress to students that their role in the space is not to be an expert, but rather to be a facilitator that opens up possibilities for dialogue. Through these supervisory practices, we are striving for radically transparent spaces that raise our consciousness about our participation in and resistance to structures of oppression within and beyond higher education.

Intentional Reflexivity

To promote reflexivity, a process that is defined by England (1994) as "self critical sympathetic introspection" (p. 244), we engage in a 360 review process each semester in which feedback is shared with each member of our team in a multidirectional manner; this allows us to disrupt power dynamics common in performance review processes where feedback is restricted to a supervisor's evaluation of a supervisee. This process is inclusive of undergraduate, graduate, and professional staff as we seek to promote a culture of feedback that leaves space for reflection and affirmation. The 360 review process also provides our student staff the opportunity to evaluate our professional staff team. This exercise has empowered our students to have open and honest conversations throughout the year knowing that there is a culture of intentional reflexivity in our office. For our professional staff team, we complete online evaluations and provide both qualitative and quantitative feedback. Each of us is expected to evaluate one another and also seek feedback from at least two other peers or colleagues to allow for critical reflection. Once the results of these evaluations are gathered, we engage in an open and honest dialogue amongst all of the professional staff to examine our strengths and growth edges. In a similar process for our student staff, each of our student staff members evaluates three of their peers in addition to our professional staff team using a 360 evaluation process that incorporates the use of competencies in which we ground our work with student staff.

Additionally, in order to incorporate intentional reflexivity throughout the year, each member of our team has weekly or bi-weekly one-on-one meetings with their supervisor. These one-on-one meetings are often utilized to provide updates and share out any needs or concerns. That said, it is also imperative to utilize these spaces to provide the opportunity for reflection. For our team, this can take many forms: conversation about future goals/directions, inquiring about life outside of work, bringing in current events to discuss their professional and personal impact, and navigating tension that exists within our institution.

For example, our associate director and director recently engaged in a conversation around their future goals. This conversation was important as it highlighted the specific need to support one another in the present while simultaneously keeping an eye on future career aspirations. Due in large part to this conversation, action items were created to ensure that both our associate director and director were situating themselves well for a successful career in higher education and were supporting one another throughout that process. This conversation is important as it highlights the specific intention that is necessary for such relationships to succeed. These are just a few of the ways in which intentional reflexivity is utilized within our context of supervisory relationships. By way of incorporating these practices, we have built better relationships as a staff team, we have been able to engage conflict with humility, and we have seen our work be positively influenced.

Pursuit of Social Change

Finally, we pursue social change in our professional development efforts, which most recently have been focused on the pursuit of racial justice, both individually and collectively. This developmental work around racial justice was part of a broader focus for the Pride Center's work during the 2017–2018 academic year. Given the high-profile incidents of white supremacy and anti-Blackness that took place after the 2016 presidential election, we felt that it was critical to intentionally dive deep into racial justice praxis as a team. One of our core commitments as a center states that all oppressions are interlinked and that liberation for LGBTQIA+ communities cannot be achieved unless liberation for all marginalized communities is achieved. Racial justice has been, and continues to be, a core part of our work; however, this intentional focus gave us the opportunity to challenge ourselves and grow in our understanding and practice of racial justice, intentionally leverage Pride Center resources in support of people of Color, and focus our programming purposefully on topics that relate to racial justice. Throughout all of these efforts, we explored racial justice through the lens of the Grassroots Institute for Fundraising Training's (n.d.) 4 I's of Oppression, examining the ways that we both perpetuate and resist white supremacy on *internal, interpersonal, institutional,* and *ideological* levels.

Both our professional staff and student staff meetings incorporate professional development around our center's theme for the year. One of our student staff members is responsible for organizing monthly discussions for the rest of our student staff team that challenges them to think deeply about the year's theme. For example, our conversations around racial justice were inspired by readings, videos, and other multimedia that focused on issues such as toxic masculinity, self-care, hip hop feminism, and Black identity. Carving out time for these student-led discussions each month in student staff meetings has been an important way for us to model how supervision can advance social change in the context of antiracist efforts. In regard to our professional staff, we dedicate two meetings each month to professional development conversations. By rotating responsibility for leading these meetings, we hold all members of our team accountable for their own development as well as the development of our team. Though setting aside time to have these intentional conversations is sometimes challenging, we have found that it is incredibly powerful to have authentic, vulnerable conversations around race, gender, sexuality, and other aspects of identity across supervisory lines. Though this process, we have deepened our commitments to racial justice as well as our relationships with one another.

LESSONS LEARNED

The work of liberation within higher education is ongoing and we learn new lessons each day about how our own supervisory practices either contribute to or impede liberatory efforts. Flexibility and adaptability have been key as we strive to create what SONG calls "alchemy: a magical process by which something of little value is made into something of great value," as opposed to chemistry, "a process that many see as putting together a formula that, if followed correctly, comes out the same every time" (Page, Pharr, Helm-Hernandez, & Breedlove, n.d., p. 1) Rather than provide concrete recommendations to practitioners seeking to implement principles of intersectional feminist praxis in their supervisory contexts, we instead close with final takeaways from our own process. These are not intended to be formulaic, but rather generative, sparking new and innovative ideas to transform our institutions for the better.

Early on in our process, we learned the necessity of owning our own positionality and its corresponding impact in our supervisory relationships. For us, it has been especially critical that supervisors initiate these conversations about race, class, gender, sexuality, and other social identities in ways that disrupt power dynamics and provide space for supervisees to share their own identities and experiences. Additionally, we have increasingly learned that institutional hierarchies require creative strategies that often mean rethinking the way things have always been done. Disrupting and resisting these hierarchies has required innovation and critical perspective-taking that has not always been easy but has been incredibly worthwhile as a result of the trust-building and deepening of relationships that occurred. Finally, we are always learning and re-learning the value of all voices and all experiences in the process of creating and distributing knowledge. By empowering our supervisees—both students and professional staff—as co-creators in our strategic plans, our decisions, our programming, and our curriculum, we are reminded of how much we can learn from one another regardless of our position in the institutional hierarchy. As we go forward in our journeys, we hope to always be reminded that, as Warner (2016) stated, "the spirit of learning [is a] route to liberation" (p. 3) and that transforming our systems always begins with transforming ourselves.

NOTE

1. The authors have intentionally chosen not to capitalize "white" and/or "whiteness" as a means to resist white supremacy.

REFERENCES

Avci, O. (2016). Positionalities, personal epistemologies, and instruction: An analysis. *Journal of Education and Training Studies, 4*(6), 145–154.

Barham, J. D., & Winston, Jr., R. B. (2006). Supervision of new professionals in student affairs: Assessing and addressing needs. *College Student Affairs Journal, 26*(1), 64–89.

Baxter Magolda, M. B. (1999). *Creating contexts for learning and self-authorship: Constructive-developmental pedagogy*. Nashville, TN: Vanderbilt University Press.

Baxter Magolda, M. B. (2004). Self-authorship as the common goal of 21st-century education. In M. B. Baxter Magolda & P. M. King (Eds.), *Learning partnerships: Theory and models of practice to educate for self-authorship* (pp. 1–36). Sterling, VA: Stylus.

Calhoun, D. W., & Nasser, R. M. (2013). Skills and perceptions of entry-level staff supervision. *Georgia Journal of College Student Affairs, 2013*, 20–34.

Clayborne, H. L., & Hamrick, F. (2007). Rearticulating the leadership experiences of African American women in midlevel student affairs administration. *Journal of Student Affairs Research and Practice, 44*(1), 123–146.

Creamer, D. G., & Winston, R. B. (2002). Foundations of the supervised practice experience: Definitions, context, and philosophy. In D. Cooper, S. Saunders, R. B. Winston, J. Hirt, D. Creamer, & S. M. Janosik (Eds.), *Learning through supervised practice in student affairs* (pp. 1–34). New York NY: Brunner-Routledge.

Crenshaw, K. (1991). Mapping the margins: Intersectionality, identity politics, and violence against women of Color. *Stanford Law Review, 43*(6), 1241–1299.

England, K. V. L. (1994). Getting personal: Reflexivity, positionality, and feminist research. *Professional Geographer, 46*(1), 241–256.

Fullerton, C. (2017). *Incorporating feminist praxis into supervising #SApros*. Session presented at the NASPA Annual Conference, San Antonio, TX.

Gentile, L., Ballou, M., Roffman, E., & Ritchie, J. (2009). Supervision for social change: A feminist ecological perspective. *Women & Therapy, 33*(1–2), 140–151.

Grassroots Institute for Fundraising Training. (n.d.). *The four I's of oppression*. Retrieved from http://www.grassrootsfundraising.org/wp-content/uploads/2012/10/THE-FOUR-IS-OF-OPPRESSION-1.pdf

Page, C., Pharr, S., Helm-Hernandez, P., & Breedlove, C. (n.d.). *Alchemy: The elements of creating collective space*. Retrieved from http://southernersonnewground.org/wp-content/uploads/2012/12 SONG-Alchemy-The-Elements-of-Creating-Collective-Space.pdf

Porter, N. (2009). Feminist and multicultural underpinnings to supervision: An overview. *Women & Therapy, 33*(1–2), 1–6.

Porter, N., & Vasquez, M. (1997). Covision: Feminist supervision, process, and collaboration. In Worell & N. G. Johnson (Eds.), *Shaping the future of feminist psychology: Education, research, and practice* (pp. 155–171). Washington, D.C.: American Psychological Association.

Renn, K. A., & Hodges, J. (2007). The first year on the job: Experiences of new professionals in student affairs. *Journal of Student Affairs Research and Practice, 44*(2), 367–391.

Shupp, M. R., & Arminio, J. L. (2012). Synergistic supervision: A confirmed key to retaining entry level student affairs professionals. *Journal of Student Affairs Research and Practice, 49*(2), 157–174.

Szymanski, D. M. (2003). The feminist supervision scale: A rational/theoretical approach. *Psychology of Women Quarterly, 27*(3), 221–232.

Tull, A. (2006). Synergistic supervision, job satisfaction, and intention to turnover of new professionals in student affairs. *Journal of College Student Development, 47*(4), 465–480.

Warner, J. (2016, January 25). Learning is liberation. *Inside Higher Ed*. Retrieved from https://www.insidehighered.com/blogs/just-visiting/learning-liberation

CHAPTER EIGHTEEN

Innovations IN Student Affairs

Applying an Intersectionality Framework to Stakeholder Personas

NATESHA L. SMITH, THOMAS J. HOLVEY,
AND NURAY SEYIDZADE

An often-discussed concern amongst higher education administrators is identifying strategies to create programming as a comprehensive portfolio of services
providing holistic opportunities of personal and academic growth for students
(Harper, 2008). Despite this aspiration, universities and colleges seem unable
to cultivate such programming without a unifying idea or approach to development and service delivery. Already available to higher education professionals are
Council for Advancement of Standards in Higher Education (CAS), professional
guidelines (e.g., NASPA-Student Affairs Administrators in Higher Education),
university-wide initiatives, and division mission statements. However, missing is
a comprehensive articulation of various populations' (i.e., stakeholders–students,
faculty, community partners) needs, objectives, and challenges.

In this chapter, we propose the use of intersectionality-informed constructed stakeholder personas (CSPs) as a unifying strategy in the development
and facilitation of student affairs services on higher education campuses. CSPs
are "data-based archetypes that [identify] the needs of different groups in the
design process" (Ortbal, Frazette, & Mehta, 2016, p. 231). Although a somewhat
new concept in student affairs praxis, CSPs are a well-documented and established tool for marketing in higher education and other industries (e.g., business,
healthcare; Friess, 2012; Hanover Research, 2014). Using intersectionality-
informed CSPs in higher education, beyond marketing, is an innovative solution
to help student affairs professionals strengthen the efficacy of student programs
and services for diverse student populations. Following is an introduction to

CSPs as a framework for application in student affairs practice and exploration of intersectionality in the development of CSPs. When illustrating the application of intersectionality in developing CSPs, we focus student personas for increased understanding. A brief statement of how the process can be applied to the creation of personas for other primary stakeholder groups, faculty, and community partners, is provided in the final sections of the chapter.

UNDERSTANDING PERSONAS

Personas are fictitious user representations created through the analysis of real user data (Thoma & Williams, 2009). Introduced by Alan Cooper (1999), a software designer, personas are a common marketing tool historically used to represent the goals of users (Ortbal et al., 2016). To construct accurate and appropriate personas for an area of interest, professionals must assess data (e.g., institutional, program specific) to discover numerous factors comprising the identities of common users (e.g., demographics, developmental goals). Using this information, several personas can be created to represent the ideal user for a service. Personas include a name, demographics, goals, interests, and often a visual embodiment of the user (Thoma & Williams, 2009). Individuals can reuse personas to have a better understanding of who ideal users are and how marketing and programming can be designed to target particular populations. Although sometimes confused with stereotypes, these representations are no assumptions but rather rooted in extensive existing data. The method of constructing the persona decreases the tendency to use stereotypes to identify the characteristics of common users (Yström, Peterson, von Sydow, & Malmqvist 2010). While the original tool, created by Cooper is still utilized, many scholar have expanded the personas method to include a multitude of factors involved in persona creation, apart from users.

Ortbal et al. (2016) introduced the idea of constructed stakeholder persona (CSPs). Rather than focusing on users (i.e., students), consideration is given to the needs of multiple stakeholders to ensure the program design will be accurate, comprehensive, and profitable (Ortbal et al., 2016). Similarly, higher education administrators creating CSPs should first identify the various stakeholders involved in a program/service. Once these stakeholders are identified, administrators can research the geographic, demographic, and psychographic data for the stakeholders allowing them to create several personas for each stakeholder group (Ortbal et al., 2016). CSPs' greatest value is their ability to be replicated and used across projects with similar stakeholders (i.e., student affairs divisions or departments). Since this method is low cost and requires less time than common program development tools, CSPs are useful for professionals with limited resources (Ortbal et al., 2016).

INTERSECTIONALITY

Kimberlé Crenshaw's (1989) intersectionality framework is often used to better understand an individual's societal experiences due to the integration of the individual's multiple, interlocking social identities. The framework is useful for challenging existing program and service delivery practices, to challenge how various student experiences were excluded from the original development of certain services, and to address the ever-evolving needs of diverse student populations. In particular, the framework allows for an intentional examination of overlapping systems of oppression within the higher education landscape that further marginalize student populations.

With roots in Black feminist thought, this framework has been used to help students understand various identities through restorative justice circles which allow individuals to discuss their perspectives and share conflicting views (Sinclair-Chapman, Eloi, & King, 2014); through transformative education (Tharp, 2017); queer people of Color spaces; lesbian, gay, bisexual, and transgender interpersonal violence services; and, Black men's leadership programs (Linder, 2016). Frequently, the framework is used to focus on providing marginalized groups space to discuss experiences, while encouraging majority group members to reflect on their beliefs and contributions to systems of oppression. Although helpful, these programs seem to focus on marginalized students' experiences with oppression in a greater context rather than addressing how these students may be marginalized by other efforts of campus administrators to address their academic needs and goals. Utilizing an intersectionality framework with CSPs may help combat this issue by bringing together what is known about students' development, complex intersectional experiences, and needs within a postsecondary institutional context.

INTERSECTIONALITY-FRAMED CONSTRUCTED STAKEHOLDER PERSONA

The focus of this section is the creation of CSPs for student populations. In particular, we situate the discussion of CSP construction within the context of theory-to-practice models and describe the usefulness of creating a CSP that reflects the intersection of multiple interlocking identities at the micro-level (i.e., individual student). The desired outcome of the CSP is to reveal social inequalities in service delivery at the social-structural level (i.e., institution) and consider ways in which resources can be better allocated. This section concludes with an outline of how to create a student intersectionality-framed CSP. Following the detailed steps of the outline will be further discussion of how the persona can be used across functional areas in student affairs.

Theory-to-Practice

To gain relevant understanding of college student diversity, practitioners need to challenge their assumptions about the college experience, engage in reflexivity, and apply knowledge from empirical research on college students' needs and development (Reason & Kimball, 2012). Many of the theory-to-practice models developed to guide this work "[are] either too exacting, too fragmentary, or both, to be of much use in addressing the challenges" faced when confronting the complexity of today's college students' experiences (Reading & Kimball, 2012, p. 360).

One of the most comprehensively designed theory-to-practice models is Reason and Kimball's (2012) model that considers *formal theory, institutional context, informal theory, practice,* and *reflection on/in action.* Formal theories importance is reinforced by the Council for the Advancement of Standards (CAS) in Higher Education; by providing unified understanding and centralized language for engaging student affairs departmental or divisional goals. Institutional context considers the perceptions and constructed knowledge of members within the institutional community. In particular, how those elements inform the ways in which developmental goals and students' needs are institutionally supported and achieved. Central to understanding informal theory is recognizing it is a convergence of practitioner positionality, institutional context, and interpretation of formal theory. Practice is the application of informal theory. Reflection includes consideration of one's individual interactions with students and evaluation of the effectiveness of intentionally designed policies, practices, and programs (i.e., assessment).

Although the aforementioned model is more comprehensive than others, knowledge of the college student populations' complexity is not captured in the design of the model. It is not enough to introduce multiple sociocultural formal theories at the onset; there should also be a more nuanced inclusion of students complexity in the theory-to-practice model's consideration of institutional context as well. This is where an intersectionality-framed CSP can be invaluable: serving as a lens through which the complexity of college students can be critically examined.

An intersectionality framework differs from other approaches that consider the complexity of identity as additive. For example, the creation of a Latinx student center that emphasizes ethnic identity development and may or may not consider including workshops or programs discussing socioeconomic differences or gender identity which could lead to Latinx queer students from lower socioeconomic backgrounds feeling excluded. Additionally, additive approaches can lead to competition amongst marginalized populations for institutional resources and prevent groups from working together to overhaul the educational system. Using an intersectionality framed CSP, within an established theory-to-practice model, highlights the interconnectedness between students' social locations and will likely prevent program development benefitting a subset of the college student population.

There are four aspects involved in developing an intersectionality-framed CSP within the institutional context of Reason & Kimball's (2012) theory-to-practice model:

- Shared Planning Processes: Input is needed from across functional areas within the student affairs division. However, basic considerations of team dynamics and size need to be taken into account. One approach could be to identify a core team of six to eight persons, with peripheral members who engage as needed in the development and implementation processes.
- Institutional Considerations: Understanding the institutional type, resource allocation, push/pull factors, etc., can help student affairs divisions to establish centralized learning outcomes to communicate how the division wants to contribute to students' development while at the institution.
- Collected Data: At a minimum, most institutions have internal mechanisms for tracking demographics and retention rates. These data, coupled with patterns of engagement, needs' surveys, academic goal assessments, and knowledge about motivations for attending college will help in building comprehensive personas.
- Values, Beliefs, & Perceptions: Analysis of espoused versus enacted values at the macro (i.e., institutional, divisional) and micro levels (e.g., administrators) will be invaluable to the process. (pp. 367–368)

t is important to recognize persona development is an intentional, time-intensive process. However, there have been several studies documenting the usefulness of the approach (e.g., Adlin & Pruitt, 2010; Madsen et al., 2014). Additionally, the information included from the four aforementioned components will fluctuate depending on the goals of the student affairs division and the target group for which the personas will be created.

Stages of Persona Development

The pre-development stage of creating a student persona, requires identified members of the team to meet to identify the problem(s), discuss what data is available to help understand and solve the problem(s), and determine if creating constructed personas will be helpful to solving the problem(s). After this initial discussion, the team enters stage one by identifying assumptions being made (about the problem and those involved) and developing a strategy to collect missing data. At this stage, it is important to know what is happening and why those things might be happening; so both quantitative and qualitative methodologies should be used (e.g., cluster analysis, focus groups, interviews, multilevel modeling). The collected data will help administrators better understand students' needs and differences. In the second stage—which occurs once data have been collected and compiled—the team should decide how many personas to create, which attributes and qualities to include in the persona, and determine how to validate the personas. At this stage using an intersectional framework requires intentional consideration of marginalized/oppressed attributes and qualities to stave off continued systemic exclusion. The last two stages involve developing a strategy for disseminating the personas across the functional areas and determining how best to use the personas in developing new initiatives, designing collaborative opportunities, and evaluating existing services. Some questions to consider at each stage of the persona development process are listed in Table 18.1.

Table 18.1. Questions to Consider.

Stages of Persona Development	Potential Questions to Consider
Pre-Development: Identify Problem & Available Resources	– What are the goals of the organization? Whose values are communicated through these goals? What problems currently exist in relation to these goals? – Which students are most at-risk of being affected by these problems? – What are ways in which the organization has tried to address these problems? What resources were used? What resources are still available?
Stage 1: Determine Assumptions & Data Collection Strategy	– How are different functional areas thinking about students? What are they thinking? How are thoughts being communicated? – How is student information currently involved in the program design and development processes? Whose being privileged in these processes? – Which student qualities, attributes, behaviors, and goals does the organization need to know more about to solve the problems?
Stage 2: Persona Creation and Validation	– How much data should be included in the personas? Which aspects are most useful when considering existing functional areas/services? – How many personas are needed to portray the complexity of the target population's needs and experiences? – How will the personas be cross-checked and validated? What biases about the target population have been revealed?

Stages of Persona Development	Potential Questions to Consider
Stage 3: Disseminating the Personas	– How does each functional area/service contribute to addressing the specific needs and experiences communicated in the personas? – What are the opportunities for collaboration/partnership across functional areas?
Stage 4: Using Personas to Develop, Design, & Evaluate	– Which existing services are redundant, outdated, or marginalizing? – How might existing services be re-imagined using the personas?

Once the stages have been completed, the process of creating additional target personas is made easier within a particular user group. For example, the first round of this process may result in the creation of seven to eight personas as a base reflection of student diversity. With an intersectionality framework, these created personas would represent multiple marginalized identities (e.g., a Multi-racial, first-generation transgender student) to be considered across student service delivery and design. The idea is to move away from the single frameworks targeting only small factions of student populations on campus: the intent is not to eliminate community spaces for marginalized populations. Instead, the ideas of this chapter are about increasing inclusive practices for improved efficiency of service delivery/design.

Although this process requires considerable time and effort for data collection, analysis, and documentation, CSPs are a powerful communication tool administrators can use to generate and engage diversity, as opposed to statistical summaries that lack nuance and complexity. Because the personas do not represent any one student and contains key differentiating characteristics from an amalgamation of students within specific learner populations, administrators can better focus on important characteristics instead of superfluous details.

Benefits/Drawbacks

Utilizing CSPs to develop programs and services has the potential to increase campus engagement, while improving the experience of marginalized students. Additionally, CSPs can be used to ensure programs align with the institutional mission and broker partnerships with academic affairs' units. The creation of CSPs also functions as a replicable format and a structured approach for student affairs professionals to use regardless of institutional type (Ortbal et al., 2016). While institutional context will influence students' experiences differently, CSPs are more concerned with reaching the target group they were created to serve, which is the primary purpose of student affairs functional areas.

CSPs are a guide used to understand students' potential needs and motiva-tions. They "are never expected to be a single, fully correct representation of all members of [a] group" (Ortbal et al., 2016, p. 231). Because groups' needs evolve routine examinations of programs/services are needed to modify the CSP. Using CSPs could also marginalize certain subgroups of a program's target group if all important variables, when constructing the persona, are not considered. For exam-ple, a program targeting first-generation students omitting students' familial status may marginalize students with familial responsibilities. These students will have different needs, motivations, and responsibilities beyond academics, influencing their experience with the program compared to first-generation students without similar responsibilities.

Because personas blend together characteristics of many users, it can be chal lenging to identify which and how many individuals each persona represent (Chapman & Milham, 2006). There is also a propensity for designers to want to base their understanding of users on stereotypes and not the actual users (Turne & Turner, 2011). This can be mitigated by considering institutional context at the onset, ensuring data drives the development of the persona, and validating the per sona. The latter can prove difficult, as personas emerge from the data collected and decisions made by the design team (Chapman & Milham, 2006). At each stag of the persona development process, the team makes conscious decisions about which aspects of the users to include in the personas based on which aspects con sidered important in addressing the problem. Although validity can be established with expert review (Yström, et al., 2010), assessments regarding the effectivenes of newly designed or reimagined services for the intended user are additional mea sures for implementation.

CONCLUDING THOUGHTS

By using an intersectionality framework to develop the constructed personas, we ar showing how cultural traits and data points can be used to improve service design delivery for campus populations excluded in the original design of student affair divisions. With the evolving diversity of student populations and increasing eco nomic uncertainties on college campuses, student affairs divisions have to learn to be more intentional and cost-effective with service delivery and support. We sug gest the creation of intersectionality-informed constructed stakeholder personas a a unifying approach to meet the needs of the diverse, complex student population.

Future research about the usefulness of CSPs in the design of student affair initiatives and student support services is warranted. Additionally, the concept c intersectionality-framed CSPs should be expanded to consider other university stakeholders, such as faculty and community partners. In particular, the four-stage process outlined for developing constructed stakeholder personas can be engaged to consider concerns or problems regarding the lack of collaboration between academic affairs and student affairs. By creating and understanding the purpose of CSPs, from a psychosocial perspective, student affairs professionals can better equip themselves with a unifying strategy in the development and implementation of programs for students with varying intersecting identities: programs and services based on real, current information rather than assumptions and preconceived opinions.

REFERENCES

Adlin, T., & Pruitt, J. (2010). *The essential personal lifecycle: Your guide to building and using personas.* Burlington, MA: Morgan Kaufmann.

Cooper, A. (1999). *The inmates are running the asylum.* Indianapolis, IN: Sams.

Crenshaw, K. (1989). Demarginalizing the intersection of race and sex: A Black feminist critique of antidiscrimination doctrine, feminist theory, and antiracist politics. *University of Chicago Legal Forum, 1989*(8), 139–167.

Friess, E. (2012). Personas and decision making in the design process: An ethnographic case study. *Proceedings of the SIGCHI Conference on Human Factors in Computing Systems,* 1209–1218.

Hanover Research. (March, 2014). *Trends in higher education, marketing, recruitment, and technology.* Washington, DC: Author.

Harper, S. (2008). *Creating inclusive campus environments: For cross-cultural learning and student engagement.* Washington, DC: NASPA.

Linder, C. (2016). An intersectional approach to supporting students. In M. Cuyjet, C. Linder, M. F. Howard-Hamilton, & D. L. Cooper (Eds.) *Multiculturalism on campus: Theory, models, and practices for understanding diversity and creating inclusion* (2nd ed., pp. 66–80). Sterling, VA: Stylus.

Madsen, A., Mckagan, S., Sayre, E., Martinuk, M., Bell, A., Park, C., & Sayre, E. (2014). Personas as a powerful methodology to design targeted professional development resources methodology: Creation of personas. In J. Polman, E. Kyza, D. O'Neill, I. Tabak, W. Penuel, A. Jurow, … L. D'Amico (Eds.), *Proceedings of the International Conference of the Learning Sciences: International Society of the Learning Sciences* (pp. 1082–1087). Denver, CO: International Society of the Learning Sciences.

Ortbal, K., Frazette, N., & Mehta, K. (2016). Constructed stakeholder personas: An educational tool for social entrepreneurs. *Procedia Engineering, 159,* 230–248.

Reason, R. D., & Kimball, E. W. (2012). A new theory-to-practice model for student affairs: Integrating scholarship, context, and reflection. *Journal of Student Affairs Research and Practice, 49*(4), 359–376.

Sinclair-Chapman, V., Eloi, S., & King, S. (2014). The women of Color circle: Creating, claiming, and transforming space for women of Color on a college campus. In D. Mitchell, Jr., C. Y. Simmons, & L. A. Greyerbiehl (Eds.), *Intersectionality and higher education: Theory, Research, and Praxis* (1st ed., pp. 219–228). New York, NY: Peter Lang.

Tharp, D. D. (2017). Exploring first-year college students' cultural competence. *Journal of Transformative Education, 15*(3), 241–263.

Thoma, V., & Williams, B. (2009). Developing and validating personas in e-commerce: A heuristic approach. *Proceedings of the 12th IFIP TC 13 International Conference on Human-Computer Interaction: Part II* (pp. 524–527). Berlin, Germany: Springer.

Yström, A., Peterson, L., Von Sydow, B., & Malmqvist, J. (2010). Using personas to guide education needs analysis and program design. *Proceedings of 6th International CDIO Conference*. Montreal Canada: École Polytechnique.

CHAPTER NINETEEN

Intersectionality AS Praxis FOR Equity IN STEM

A WiSE Women of Color Program

DAWN R. JOHNSON, MICHELLE M. BLUM,
KATHARINE E. LEWIS, AND SHARON W. ALESTALO

The participation of women and underrepresented racial and ethnic groups in science, technology, engineering, and mathematics (STEM) fields remains a persistent social justice issue for educators and policymakers. Black, Latina, and Indigenous women earned 12.6% of bachelor's degrees in STEM in 2014 and accounted for just 7% of faculty at all ranks in STEM departments in the United States (The National Science Foundation [NSF], 2017). As women of Color at all levels of the academy navigate STEM departments, labs, classrooms, and other social and academic spaces, research documents consistent patterns of exclusion from White peers and faculty. Women of Color faced racialized and gendered stereotypes; coped with discouragement and lack of support from faculty; experienced both hypervisibility and invisibility; and felt a diminished sense of belonging and need to constantly prove themselves among faculty and peers (Foor, Walden, & Trytten, 2007; A. Johnson, 2007; D. Johnson, 2012; Ko, Kachchaf, Hodari, & Ong, 2014; Malone & Barabino, 2009). Women of Color experience belonging to and persistence in STEM when they have strong identities as scientists/engineers, are involved in STEM-related professional clubs, feel confident in their academics, participate in research programs, and interact with faculty and peers outside of class (Carlone & Johnson, 2007; D. Johnson, 2012; Espinosa, 2011; Rodriguez, Cunningham, & Jordan, 2017).

Over the past 30 years, colleges and universities have developed women in science and engineering (WiSE) programs to recruit and retain women in STEM fields (Fox, Sonnert, & Nikiforova, 2011). These programs offer activities such a peer mentoring, tutoring, study spaces, career workshops, faculty mentoring, clus tered housing in residential halls, and social activities (D. Johnson, 2011; Fox et al. 2011). There is evidence, however, that WiSE programs struggle with garnerin the participation of women of Color (D. Johnson, 2011) and there is little in th published research on how WiSE programs address the needs of women of Colo who experience STEM learning environments at the intersections of race an gender. This chapter describes the work of WiSE Women of Color in STEM, a intersectional mentoring and community building program for women of Colo in STEM majors at Syracuse University, a private research university located i central upstate New York.

WOMEN OF COLOR IN STEM AND INTERSECTIONALITY

Malcom and her colleagues (1976) first articulated the intersectional experience of women of Color in STEM as the *double bind* of gendered racism. *Intersection ality*, coined by critical legal scholar Kimberlé Crenshaw (1989), is a framewor useful in recognizing and centering the systemic disadvantage experienced b women of Color, by analyzing how race, gender, socioeconomic class, sexua orientation, disability status, and other social identity group markers interloc as socially constructed systems and structures of power and inequity (Dill & Zambrana, 2009). Intersectionality examines the complexity of inequity withi institutional systems and structures (e.g., education, government, media) an specific social, educational, historical, and geographic contexts, by analyzing th junctures of multiple social groups (e.g., queer women of Color; poor disable women) rather than focusing on a singular group analysis (e.g., women onl Crenshaw, 1991; Dill & Zambrana, 2009). Finally, by centering the experience of women of Color, intersectional analyses can result in the transformation c systems of inequity through education, policy, and advocacy (Crenshaw, 199 Dill & Zambrana, 2009).

Recent scholarship on women of Color in STEM has utilized intersectior ality as a guiding and analytical framework (e.g., see Espinosa, 2011; Ko et a 2014; Rincón & Lane, 2017; Ro & Loya, 2015; Rodriguez et al., 2017). Th framing has contributed greatly to STEM education research by disaggregatin the experiences of women of Color from White women and men of Color an drawing attention to the interlocking nature of racism and sexism in STEM environments (D. Johnson, 2012). Lastly, intersectional frameworks have bee used in discussions on policy and practice transformations that would suppo greater equity in STEM fields for women of Color (e.g., Armstrong & Jovanovi 2017; A. Johnson, 2006).

EVOLUTION OF WISE WOMEN OF COLOR IN STEM
AT SYRACUSE UNIVERSITY

WiSE Women of Color in STEM (WWoC STEM) is a program that is part of the campus-wide WiSE program at Syracuse University (SU WiSE). In 1999, faculty founded SU WiSE with three key goals: (1) increase retention and representation of women in STEM, (2) sponsor a lecture series to highlight women scholars, and (3) create advising and mentoring programs. SU WiSE provides support to women faculty and students from the schools and colleges of Engineering and Computer Science, Arts & Sciences, Information Studies, and Education. Activities offered through SU WiSE include mentoring and networking programs for faculty and post-doctoral scholars, undergraduate research awards, an aspiring professionals program for graduate students, and an annual lecture featuring a female STEM scholar. Faculty leaders oversee and implement the varying initiatives and receive a small stipend for research or professional development activities.

Intersectionality as Praxis

In the fall of 2014, a Black woman majoring in chemistry initiated WiSE Women of Color in STEM (WWoC STEM) to build community with other women of Color in science to combat the isolation she experienced in the predominantly White and male learning environments of her major. To illustrate this structural isolation, in 2016, there were 166 full time undergraduate students enrolled in the physical sciences (of which chemistry is a part) at Syracuse (Integrated Postsecondary Educational Data Systems [IPEDS], 2016a). Among these students, seven were Black/African American women. This is reflective of national patterns of degree attainment of Black/African American women in the physical sciences, who represented 3% of bachelor degrees awarded in these fields in 2014 (NSF, 2017). WWoC STEM engages undergraduate, graduate, and post-doctoral women from underrepresented racial and ethnic groups in STEM (defined by the NSF [2017] to include Black/African American, Latina/Hispanic, Native American, Alaskan Native, and Pacific Islander). However, women of Color from other racial and ethnic groups, including international students, have found community in WWoC STEM. With an approximate annual enrollment of 180 undergraduate women from underrepresented racial groups in STEM (among 2,100 full time undergraduates in STEM [IPEDS, 2016a]), 163 women have participated in WWoC STEM programs and events in the last four years.

The small number of women of Color on faculty in STEM at SU necessitated a collaborative approach across race and ethnicity, academic discipline, and academic position, to work with women of Color students in developing the program. The WWoC STEM advisory group began as a collaboration among Black women faculty in physics and higher education, and a White woman faculty member in mechanical engineering. Since then, the leadership team has grown to include Latina (in biology), White (in biology) and Asian (in mathematics) women faculty, and three graduate women of Color who serve as mentors. Two White women provide part-time administrative support for both SU WiSE and WWoC in STEM, and undergraduate women of Color with work-study funding assist with planning events, connecting with students, facilitating programs, maintaining the program's web site, and providing additional staff support. The leadership team meets at the beginning of every semester to plan the calendar of events

Grounded in themes drawn from research, WWoC STEM endeavors to empower women of Color through building community, fostering sense of belonging, and promoting academic, professional, and interpersonal excellence. Meetings and activities are planned for 3–4 times per semester, and senior undergraduate students and graduate student mentors frequently facilitate programs and lead discussions. Events have included panels on undergraduate research experience and the graduate school application process, a screening and panel discussion of the film "Hidden Figures," and virtual panels featuring women of Color professionals in STEM fields. Student-led discussions have focused on topics such as experiences with bias, strategies for support and success, the imposter syndrome, self-care, and building relationships with faculty.

At the conclusion of program gatherings and events, students completed an evaluation form to assess the impact of the activities on program outcomes. Using a response scale where 1 equals strongly disagree and 5 equals strongly agree, participants responded to a variety of items as indicated in Table 19.1. WWoC STEM appears to foster important outcomes, particularly with respect to an increased sense of belonging in STEM; feeling supported in the STEM journey; connecting with other women of Color; and, strengthened commitment to the institution and continuing in STEM. Areas for improvement include strengthening students interest in graduate school and increasing connections with faculty on campus.

Open-ended comments underscore the impact of WWoC STEM. One student noted:

> I love how this program brings us all together to get a chance to build a community of support. It's hard to find women of Color in STEM, so to have a space where all of them can be in the same space at the same time is great!

Another student expressed a similar sentiment stating, "I wanted to connect with other women of Color who know the struggle. I wanted to have people who understand what it is like being a STEM major on this campus." With respect to learning from WWoC STEM events, one student wrote that she learned "[h]ow to email professors, how to interact with them, and how to go about getting research opportunities [and] letters of recommendations," while another indicated learning "[w]hat imposter syndrome is and that I wasn't alone in what I was feeling. I'm glad [WiSE] put on the event and gave me insight on this phenomenon [and] advice to handle it." Finally, a quote from one of our founding students sums up the importance of WWoC STEM:

> As an undergraduate, having a space where I was empowered and mentored by WOC in STEM allowed me to overcome imposter syndrome, find professional opportunities and succeed as a bioengineer. Now I am able to do the same for my mentees.

Table 19.1. WiSE Women of Color in STEM Program Outcomes: 2014–2018.

	Mean
Increase sense of belonging	
I am more comfortable being in a STEM major	4.34
I am more confident that I belong in STEM	4.41
This event increased my sense of belonging	4.47
Build community of women of Color in STEM	
I feel supported in my journey to become a scientist/engineer	4.70
I feel I have more peers who I can go to for information	4.20
I feel connected with faculty, graduate mentors, or other resource people that help me in the future	4.24
I have strengthened existing relationships with people I have met through WiSE	4.20
There was sufficient opportunity to connect with other women in STEM	4.72
Increase career planning knowledge and skills	
My interest in pursuing research opportunities is stronger	4.30
My interest in pursuing post graduate education is stronger	4.01
My interest in pursuing a STEM career is stronger	4.38
Increase professional and academic knowledge and skills (not subject specific) that support persistence	
My intent to continue in STEM is stronger	4.43
My intent to graduate from SU is stronger	4.48

Source: Authors.

CHALLENGES AND FUTURE DIRECTIONS

Many of the challenges faced by WWoC STEM relate to institutional structures and systems that do not easily accommodate the intersectional, multi-disciplinary, and collaborative nature of the program. The most persistent challenge is the lack of women of Color faculty at SU. Recent faculty data indicated that among all faculty across all disciplines, 71% of tenure and tenure-track faculty are White, and only 4% are women of Color from underrepresented racial/ethnic groups (IPEDS,

2016b). WWoC STEM keenly feels this faculty shortage, with few women of Color in STEM available to serve the program in leadership and mentoring capacities. While students of Color in STEM benefit from having mentors with whom they can relate to connect with (Griffin, Pérez, Holmes, & Mayo, 2010) women of Color in STEM often find that White male faculty are unwilling or unable to mentor them (A. Johnson, 2007), and thus are denied the advantages of mentoring relationships when few faculty of Color are available. While we aim to build a pipeline to develop women of Color faculty, this is a long-term effort requiring commitment from multiple parts of the university. In the meantime WWoC STEM works to build a network of faculty allies among White people and men of Color invested in the success of women of Color.

Consistent institutional funding is another challenge faced by WWoC STEM. SU WiSE began with money from the NSF and struggled to secure consistent institutional financial support once the funds were expended, which is often the case for mentoring programs serving underrepresented groups (Haring, 1997 2009). Neither SU WiSE nor WWoC STEM fit easily into silo-like institutional budget models and organizational structures because the programs serve individuals at all points in the STEM pipeline (faculty, undergraduates, graduate students post-doctoral scholars) and across several university schools, colleges, and institutes. As a result, core program faculty have had to advocate for the continuation of funding on an annual basis, and in some years, WWoC STEM programming has been delayed until funds were allocated to SU WiSE. Consistent and timely funding allows WWoC STEM to recruit student participants early in the academic year and secure their involvement, as they manage academic demands, family and personal responsibilities, and other leadership roles on campus.

Reaching the students that WWoC STEM aims to serve is another challenge While WWoC STEM has attracted many students to its programming over the past four years, there are also women of Color who do not participate in the program. Outreach happens by word of mouth, recruitment of students during new student welcome week, and posting event flyers around campus. Assistance with outreach is needed from the registrar to provide lists of potential students, and from faculty to refer students and promote the program in their classes. Additionally, efforts are needed to find out why some women opt not to participate in the program, which may be due to lack of awareness of the group, lack interest in the programming, or support from other campus programs for students of Color in STEM. Students may also be reluctant to get involved in a group for women of Color, as it may accentuate their minoritized status (Seymour & Hewitt, 1997) This emphasizes the need for university resources to cover issues of importance for women of Color in overall STEM programming activities.

Students, staff, and faculty have identified several areas for future programming for WWoC STEM. The program recently received a grant from the university to develop a "resiliency network" of students, and faculty and staff allies to learn about the impact of racial and gender bias in the learning environment, develop strategies for resilience, and to interrupt and address bias when it occurs. SU WiSE piloted a summer research program, prioritizing women of Color, to provide opportunities for students to experience full-time research and build strong connections with faculty mentors on campus. This inaugural effort was a collaboration with the Louis Stokes Alliance for Minority Participation (LSAMP) program on campus. There are plans to expand the research program into the academic year, prioritizing women of Color with work-study funding so they can have a paid research experience that will build their resumes, enhance lab skills, and strengthen interests in graduate school.

Other areas of future programming include connecting with women alumni in STEM during a biannual reunion weekend held for alumni of Color, and working collaboratively with the multicultural affairs office, other campus-based programs for underrepresented students in STEM, and student chapters of the National Society of Black Engineers and the Society of Hispanic Professional Engineers. Students also want to deepen their awareness of various resources on campus and have greater faculty involvement. As discussed earlier, such efforts require dedicated and permanent institutional financial and human resources.

CONCLUSION

In the 2018 spring semester at Syracuse University, video footage from a national engineering fraternity group was made public in which several male students unleashed a barrage of slurs targeted at students of Color, women, disabled students, queer students, and Jewish students. These events serve as a reminder of the intersectional nature of oppression, the need for programs such as WiSE Women of Color in STEM, and the importance of institutional attention to climate issues in STEM. While we have systematically and positively impacted the success of women of Color students on the campus, there is more work to be done. The commitment to equity in STEM requires an intersectional approach, and WiSE Women of Color in STEM at Syracuse University continues in this work.

REFERENCES

Armstrong, M. A., & Jovanovic, J. (2017). The intersectional matrix: Rethinking institutional change for URM women in STEM. *Journal of Diversity in Higher Education, 10*(3), 216–231.

Carlone, H. B., & Johnson, A. (2007). Understanding the science experiences of successful women of Color: Science identity as an analytic lens. *Journal of Research in Science Teaching, 44*(8), 1187–1218.

Crenshaw, K. (1989). Demarginalizing the intersection of race and sex: A black feminist critique of antidiscrimination doctrine, feminist theory and antiracist politics. *University of Chicago Legal Forum, 1989*(8), 139–167.

Crenshaw, K. (1991). Mapping the margins: Intersectionality, identity politics, and violence against women of Color. *Stanford Law Review, 43*(6), 1241–1299.

Dill, B. T., & Zambrana, R. E. (2009). Critical thinking about inequality: An emerging lens. In B. T. Dill & R. E. Zambrana (Eds.), *Emerging intersections: Race, class, and gender in theory, policy, and practice* (pp. 1–21). New Brunswick, NJ: Rutgers University Press.

Espinosa, L. L. (2011). Pipelines and pathways: Women of Color in undergraduate STEM majors and the college experiences that contribute to persistence. *Harvard Educational Review, 81*(2) 209–241.

Foor, C. E., Walden, S. E., & Trytten, D. A. (2007). "I wish that I belonged more in this whole engineering group": Achieving individual diversity. *Journal of Engineering Education, 96*(2), 103–115.

Fox, M. F., Sonnert, G., & Nikiforova, I. (2011). Programs for undergraduate women in science and engineering: Issues, problems, and solutions. *Gender & Society, 25*(5), 589–615.

Griffin, K. A., Pérez, D., Holmes, A. P., & Mayo, C. E. (2010). Investing in the future: The importance of faculty mentoring in the development of students of Color in STEM. In S. R. Harper & C. B. Newman (Eds.), *Students of Color in STEM* (New Directions for Institutional Research No. 148, pp. 95–103). San Francisco, CA: Jossey-Bass.

Haring, M. J. (1997). Networking mentoring as a preferred model for guiding programs for underrepresented students. In H. T. Frierson (Ed.), *Diversity in higher education* (pp. 63–76). Greenwich, CT: JAI Press.

Haring, M. J. (2009). The case for a conceptual base for minority mentoring program. *Peabody Journal of Education, 74*(2), 5–14.

Integrated Postsecondary Education Data System. (2016a). *Syracuse University, institutional profile, fall enrollment 2016.* Retrieved from https://nces.ed.gov/ipeds/datacenter/Facsimile.aspx?unitid= acb4b1afacae

Integrated Postsecondary Education Data System. (2016b). *Syracuse University, institutional profile, Human resources 2016–17.* Retrieved from https://nces.ed.gov/ipeds/datacenter/Facsimil. aspx?unitid=acb4b1afacae

Johnson, A. C. (2006). Policy implications for supporting women of Color in the sciences. *Journal Women, Politics, & Policy, 27*(3–4), 135–150.

Johnson, A. C. (2007). Unintended consequences: How science professors discourage women of Color. *Science Education, 91*(5), 805–821.

Johnson, D. R. (2011). Examining sense of belonging and campus racial diversity experiences among women of Color in STEM living-learning programs. *Journal of Women and Minorities in Science and Engineering, 17*(3), 209–223.

Johnson, D. R. (2012). Campus racial climate perceptions and overall sense of belonging among racially diverse women in STEM majors. *Journal of College Student Development, 53*(2), 336–346.

Ko, L. T., Kachchaf, R. R., Hodari, A. K., & Ong, M. (2014). Agency of women of Color in physics and astronomy: Strategies for persistence and success. *Journal of Women and Minorities in Science and Engineering, 20*(2), 171–195.

Malcom, S. M., Hall, P. Q., & Brown, J. W. (1976). *The double bind: The price of being a minority woman in science.* Washington, D.C.: American Association for the Advancement of Science.

Malone, K. R., & Barabino, G. (2009). Narrations of race in STEM research settings: Identity formation and its discontents. *Science Education, 93*(3), 485–510.

National Science Foundation, National Center for Science and Engineering Statistics. (2017). *Women, minorities, and persons with disabilities in science and engineering: 2017* (Special Report NSF 17–310). Arlington, VA: Author. Retrieved from www.nsf.gov/statistics/wmpd/

Rincón, B. E., & Lane, T. B. (2017). Latin@s in science, technology, engineering, and mathematics (STEM) at the intersections. *Equity & Excellence in Education, 50*(2), 182–195.

Rodriguez, S., Cunningham, K., & Jordan, A. (2017). STEM identity development for Latinas: The role of self- and outside recognition. *Journal of Hispanic Higher Education.* Advance online publication. doi.org/10.1177/1538192717739958

Ro, H. K., & Loya, K. I. (2015). The effect of gender and race intersectionality on student learning outcomes in engineering. *The Review of Higher Education, 38*(3), 359–396.

Seymour, E., & Hewitt, N. M. (1997). *Talking about leaving: Why undergraduates leave the sciences.* Boulder, CO: Westview Press.

Editor Biographies

EDITOR

Donald "DJ" Mitchell, Jr., PhD served as editor for the second edition of *Intersectionality & Higher Education: Theory, Research, & Praxis*. Mitchell is full professor of education and chair of the M.Ed. in Higher Education Leadership and Social Justice program in the Annsley Frazier Thornton School of Education at Bellarmine University in Louisville, Kentucky. His scholarship theoretically and empirically explores race, gender, underrepresented identity intersections and intersectionality in higher education settings. Mitchell has produced over 50 scholarly publications, including serving as lead editor for *Student Involvement and Academic Outcomes: Implications for Diverse College Student Populations* (with Krista Soria, Elizabeth A. Daniele, and John Gipson) and as lead editor for the first edition of *Intersectionality & Higher Education: Theory, Research, &Praxis* (with Charlana Y. Simmons and Lindsay A. Greyerbiehl), both published by Peter Lang in 2015 and 2014, respectively.

Mitchell is recipient of the Ethnographic and Qualitative Research Conference's 2016 McGraw Hill Distinguished Scholar Award; the American College Personnel Association's 2015 Emerging Scholar Award; Grand Valley State University's 2015 Distinguished Early-career Scholar Award; the Multicultural/Multiethnic Education Special Interest Group of the American Educational Research Association's 2014 Dr Carlos J. Vallejo Memorial Award for Emerging Scholarship; the American College Personnel Association's Standing Committee for Men and Masculinities 2014 Outstanding

Research Award (with Dr Darris R. Means); and, the Michigan College Personnel Association's 2013 John Zaugra Outstanding Research/Publication Award. He was also awarded the Center for the Study of the College Fraternity's 2012 Richard McKaig Outstanding Doctoral Research Award for his dissertation, "Are They Truly Divine?: A Grounded Theory of the Influence of Black Greek-Lettered Organizations on the Persistence of African Americans at Predominantly White Institutions."

Mitchell earned a bachelor of science in chemistry from Shaw University, the first historically Black institution in the South; a master of science in educational leadership from Minnesota State University, Mankato; and a PhD in educational policy and administration with a concentration in higher education from the University of Minnesota—Twin Cities.

ASSOCIATE EDITORS

Jakia Marie served as associate editor for the second edition of *Intersectionality & Higher Education: Theory, Research, & Praxis*. Marie is currently a PhD candidate in Pan-African studies at the University of Louisville in Kentucky. A native of Muskegon, Michigan, Marie is a first-generation college student who earned a BA in liberal studies and MEd in higher education with a concentration in college student affairs leadership, both from Grand Valley State University (GVSU) in Allendale, Michigan.

Marie received the 2016 GVSU Graduate Dean's Citation for Outstanding Graduate Publication for her thesis titled, "Racial Identity Development of African American Students in Relation to Black Studies Courses" that was published in *Africology: The Journal of Pan-African Studies*. Marie's research focuses on identity, immigration, global Blackness, and culture.

Tiffany L. Steele served as associate editor for the second edition of *Intersectionality & Higher Education: Theory, Research, & Praxis*. She earned her BA in psychology from the University of Michigan in 2014 and her MEd in higher education with an emphasis in college student affairs leadership from Grand Valley State University (GVSU) in 2016. She is currently a PhD student in the Higher Education and Student Affairs program at The Ohio State University. She also serves as a graduate administrative associate for the Office of Diversity and Inclusion.

Steele received the 2015–2016 GVSU College of Education Dean Award for Outstanding Thesis, the 2016 GVSU Graduate Dean's Citation for Outstanding Thesis, and the 2016 GVSU Graduate Dean's Citation for Academic Excellence. She was also recognized as an emerging leader by "Who Who in Black Columbus." Steele's research interest focuses on the retention of minoritized staff members and students at predominantly White institutions with an emphasis on the lived experiences of Black women.

Author Biographies

Sharon W. Alestalo is program director for Syracuse University's Women in Science & Engineering (SU WiSE). Her professional career has primarily focused on efforts to address diversity and inclusion. Her career trajectory includes 10 years as a rehabilitation counselor for people with disabilities, 15 years as an executive director of a youth organization focusing on gender equity, and 10 years at SU WiSE supporting the success and persistence of women (first-year to faculty) in science, technology, engineering and mathematics disciplines. Alestalo is experienced in the design and evaluation of unique, evidence-based programs that address participant strengths and challenges.

Allison Daniel Anders, PhD is assistant professor in Educational Foundations and Inquiry at the University of South Carolina. Her areas of interest include contexts of education, the everyday experiences of targeted youth and the systemic inequities they navigate, and qualitative research methodologies. Her research includes work with incarcerated youth, children with refugee status, and lesbian, gay, bisexual, transgender, and queer youth.

Michelle M. Blum, PhD is assistant teaching professor of Mechanical Engineering at Syracuse University. She earned dual bachelor's degrees in physics and mechanical engineering from the State University at Albany and Rensselaer Polytechnic Institute. She then earned her MS and PhD from the University of Notre Dame. Blum's research in engineering education focuses on studying the impact of hands-on activities, professional skills development and inclusion and outreach activities. She received the 2016 Syracuse Universit Meredith Professorship Program Teaching Recognition Award, 2017 Syra cuse University College of Engineering & Computer Science Dean's Awar for Excellence in Engineering Education, and 2017 Technology Alliance c Central New York College Educator of the Year.

Scott Burden serves as associate director of the Pride Center for Sexual Orienta tion and Gender Diversity at Lehigh University in Bethlehem, Pennsylvania Scott was born and raised in the great state of Michigan, where he began hi journey into the work of inclusion and equity. Scott did his graduate work a Grand Valley State University studying in their master's program for colleg student affairs leadership where he deepened his passion for social justice. I his role at Lehigh, Scott works towards campus reform and educating stu dents, staff, and faculty about intersectional social justice.

Patricia P. Carver is a PhD candidate in the Leadership in Higher Education pro gram at Bellarmine University located in Louisville, Kentucky. She receive her bachelor's degree in accounting from the University of Louisville an her MBA from Bellarmine University where she is currently an instructor i the Rubel School of Business. Her present research interests include Blac women and how their intersecting roles impact them in business and edu cational settings. Her past research includes student perceptions of entrepre neurship, profitability, and business size, as well as the effects of study abroa on undergraduate college students.

Kelly E. Cichy, PhD is associate professor of Human Development and Fami Studies at Kent State University. Her research examines the links betwee social relationships and health. Specifically, her research agenda focuses o understanding: (a) stress processes within families and the health implic tions of daily stressful experiences (e.g., conflict, social support demands); an (b) racial disparities in health and well-being. In addition to her main lin of inquiry, her research examines best practices in mentoring and program ming to promote undergraduate research, particularly for underserved stude populations.

Jasmine D. Collins, PhD received her PhD in educational organization and lead ership with a concentration in higher education from the University of Illino at Urbana-Champaign and remains there as assistant professor of Agricultur Leadership Education. Collins uses critical theories to understand person sociopolitical, and campus racial climate factors that influence college studen experiences, broadly—and leadership development, more specifically. Sh hopes that her work on this interface between social identity and structures oppression will guide efforts to ensure equitable access to effective leadership opportunities for marginalized students.

Tamekka L. Cornelius is a PhD student in the Leadership in Higher Education program at Bellarmine University located in Louisville, Kentucky. She serves as inclusion manager for Norton Healthcare. Prior to this role, Tamekka worked in student affairs and services for over 10 years at various institutions, including Miami University, the University of Cincinnati, the University of Kentucky, and Bellarmine University, where she served as the inaugural director of the Office of Identity and Inclusion. Tamekka received her bachelor's degree in justice administration and a master's in college student personnel, both from the University of Louisville.

James M. DeVita, PhD is an associate professor of Higher Education at the University of North Carolina Wilmington. James also serves as the associate director of Applied Learning Initiatives at UNCW, and is co-editor of the *Journal of Effective Teaching in Higher Education.* He has presented at numerous international conferences, and published over 20 peer reviewed publications to date. James currently teaches graduate-level courses that focus on student learning and development, social justice topics in education, and research methods. His research examines the experiences of targeted populations in higher education and scholarship on teaching and learning.

Antonio Duran is a doctoral candidate at The Ohio State University in the Higher Education and Student Affairs program. Antonio's research interests include examining the lives of queer students of Color from asset-based perspectives, as well as understanding the experiences of educators who engage in critical pedagogy. As a queer Latino man, Antonio draws upon his personal narratives as a driving force to add to scholarship on collegians with multiple marginalized identities. He hopes that his research and community engagement will contribute to the creation of equitable and just communities on college campuses.

Chinasa Elue, PhD is assistant professor of Educational Leadership and Higher Education at Kennesaw State University. Her research agenda focuses on issues of educational access and equity for underserved student populations across the P-20 continuum. Specifically, her research agenda focuses on (a) the college choice decisions of marginalized student populations and the different factors that impact their college choices; (b) issues of educational access for immigrant student populations; and (c) how law and policy, research, and practice connect to explore issues that impact the educational opportunities for marginalized populations.

Meg E. Evans is a PhD student in the College Student Affairs Administration at the University of Georgia (UGA). Prior to her time at UGA, Meg worked at Carnegie Mellon University, Guilford College, and Warren Wilson College. Meg also currently holds an executive board position for the Consortium of Higher Education LGBT Resource Professionals. Meg has a bachelor's in outdoor leadership from Warren Wilson College in North Carolina and a master's in community leadership from Duquesne University in Pennsylvania.

Jason C. Garvey, PhD is assistant professor of Higher Education and Student Affairs in the Department of Leadership and Developmental Sciences at the University of Vermont. His research examines student affairs and college classroom contexts with focus on assessing and quantifying student experiences across social identities, with particular attention to queer and trans collegians. Prior to his faculty appointment, Garvey worked in student services across a variety of functional areas, including academic advising, lesbian, gay, bisexual, transgender, and queer student involvement and advocacy, undergraduate research, and student affairs assessment.

Chelsea Gilbert is a scholar-practitioner with a passion for empowerment and curriculum development at the intersections of multiple identities. Originally from Georgia, Chelsea did her graduate work at Merrimack College in North Andover, MA, where she focused her scholarship and practice on transgender campus inclusion. In her current work at Lehigh University's Pride Center for Sexual Orientation & Gender Diversity, she builds coalitions across campus to improve policies and practices, as well as empowers students, staff, and faculty to create a more inclusive institutional community. She also facilitates workshops across the country for educators, administrators, and students.

Rose Ann E. Gutierrez is a doctoral student in the Graduate School of Education and Information Studies in the Social Sciences and Comparative Education Division at the University of California, Los Angeles. She is a research associate for the Institute for Immigration, Globalization, and Education and Center for the Transformation of Schools. Her research interests are racism, immigration, and social stratification in education. She received her bachelor degree from the University of Richmond in sociology with double minors in women, gender, and sexuality studies and studio art and master's degree at Seattle University in student development administration.

Jimmy Hamill is pursuing his PhD in English literature at Lehigh University in Bethlehem, PA. His research uses intersectional methods to examine the relationship between queer and religious communities, and he is deeply invested in social justice pedagogy within the classroom. Jimmy previously received his MA at Lehigh, where he focused his scholarship in queer fiction and theory. In his current role as the graduate assistant in Lehigh University's Pride Center for Sexual Orientation & Gender Diversity (Pride Center), Jimmy provides educational and theoretical resources that inform the conversations and workshops put on by the Pride Center.

Thomas J. Holvey is a graduate student in State University of New York (SUNY)-Binghamton's student affairs administration program. He has worked as a peer tutor and as a research assistant in a clinical psychology laboratory focusing on mood disorders, where he worked with undergraduate students with varying levels of depression. He is currently a member of SUNY-Binghamton's student conduct board.

Shadab Fatima Hussain is a doctoral candidate pursuing a degree in developmental and psychological sciences at the Stanford Graduate School of Education. She has extensive experience working in student affairs positions and supporting student communities through leadership positions on committees which advocate for student issues. Her main research interests surround the positive social/emotional and academic development of undergraduate students, with a particular focus on those students who have a bicultural heritage.

Susan V. Iverson, EdD is professor of Higher Education Leadership at Manhattanville College. Iverson's research interests focus on: equity and diversity, status of women in higher education, feminist pedagogy, and the role of policy (e.g., sexual violence) in shaping problem representation. She has two co-edited volumes: *Feminist Community Engagement: Achieving Praxis* (Palgrave, 2014) and *Reconstructing Policy Analysis in Higher Education: Feminist Poststructural Perspectives* (Routledge, 2010). Prior to becoming faculty, Iverson worked in student affairs administration for more than ten years. Iverson earned her doctorate in higher educational leadership, with a concentration in women's studies, from the University of Maine.

Romeo Jackson is a Black, queer, non-binary femme, feminist dedicated to intersectional justice and cross movement building. Currently, they study Anti-Blackness and settler colonialism within a higher education context with an emphasis on the experiences of queer and trans students of Color. Named one of the National Black Justice Coalition's 2015 "100 Black Lesbian, Gay, Bisexual, Transgender, Queer, Gender Non-confirming and/or Same-gender Loving Leaders to Watch," Romeo is committed to uplifting and empowering queer and trans people of Color through a Black queer feminist lens.

Dawn R. Johnson, PhD is associate professor and chair of the Higher Education department at Syracuse University. She is a co-principal investigator for the

Upstate New York Louis Stokes Alliance for Minority Participation program and a faculty co-director for Women in Science & Engineering (WiSE) Women of Color in Science, Technology Engineering, and Mathematics (STEM). He research focuses on under-represented students of Color in STEM, including the experiences of women of Color, and teaches on student development in college. Johnson earned her PhD in counseling and personnel services from the University of Maryland, MEd in counseling and psychological services from Springfield College, and AB in anthropology from Bowdoin College.

Kristie S. Johnson is a PhD student in the Leadership in Higher Education program at Bellarmine University in Louisville, Kentucky. She received her master's degree in international development and social change from Clark University, her bachelor's degree in Asian studies from Florida State University, and her associate's degree in foreign languages from Edison Community College. She is the director of grants at Marian University where she identifies funding to support underrepresented students. As a Fulbright Scholar, her research focused on the Uyghurs, an ethnic minority group. Her current research includes concepts of global citizenship and leadership traits of foreign-born university presidents.

Ashley P. Jones is a doctoral candidate in the Program in Higher Education Leadership at University of Texas at Austin. She earned a BS in business administration from Georgetown College and MEd in college student personnel from the University of Louisville. Ashley's background is in student affairs with most recent roles in residence life. Her dissertation research focuses on the intersections of spirituality and sexual orientation for lesbian, gay, bisexual and queer/questioning undergraduate students. Ultimately Ashley hopes that her work as a scholar-practitioner contributes to informing identity development models and educational practices that promote inclusive campus environments for all students.

Susan R. Jones, PhD is professor in the Higher Education and Student Affairs program in the Educational Studies Department at The Ohio State University. Her research interests include psychosocial perspectives on identity, intersectionality and multiple social identities, service-learning, and qualitative research methodologies. She has published over 25 journal articles, 2 book chapters, and 5 books, including as co-author of *Identity Development of College Students* (Jossey-Bass, 2013) and *Negotiating the Complexities of Qualitative Research: Fundamental Elements and Issues* (Routledge, 2006, 2nd edition published in 2014). Jones is one of the co-editors of the 5th and 6th edition of *Student Services: A Handbook for the Profession* (Jossey-Bass, 2011, 2017).

Katharine (Kate) E. Lewis, PhD is professor of Biology at Syracuse University (SU), faculty co-director of SU's Women in Science & Engineering Program and director of SU's Neuroscience Integrated Learning Major. She obtained a BA (with honors) in natural sciences from the University of Cambridge, followed by a MA in women's studies from the University of Westminster and a PhD in genetics and developmental biology from University College London. She was also a Kennedy Scholar at Harvard University for a year where she studied mainly women's studies and the intersections of gender and race and a postdoctoral fellow at the University of Oregon.

Emily P. McClaine is a success coach in the Office for Inclusive Excellence at Slippery Rock University. Her scholarly interests include access and opportunity in education and strategies to support historically underrepresented college students. She holds a Master of Education in higher education administration and student personnel with certificates in college teaching and career and academic advising from Kent State University, as well as a Bachelor of Arts in English from Duquesne University. In her practice with students, she focuses on fostering intrinsic motivation, inviting self-exploration, and empowering perseverance and resilience as they strive toward their personal and professional goals.

Ryan A. Miller, PhD is assistant professor of Educational Leadership (Higher Education) at the University of North Carolina at Charlotte. His research agenda focuses on student development and the conditions for creating inclusive campus cultures in higher education. Ryan's study on the intersectional identities of lesbian, gay, bisexual, transgender, and queer students with disabilities received the 2016 Melvene D. Hardee Dissertation of the Year award from NASPA | Student Affairs Professionals in Higher Education. Prior to becoming a faculty member, Ryan worked professionally in higher education (student affairs and diversity and inclusion) for eight years. He holds graduate degrees in education from The University of Texas at Austin and Harvard University.

Samuel D. Museus, PhD is professor of Educational Studies at University of California, San Diego. He is also founding director of the National Institute for Transformation and Equity at Indiana University. Museus has produced over 250 publications and conference presentations focused on diversity and equity, campus environments, and college student outcomes. He has produced 10 books, including *Creating Campus Cultures: Fostering Success among Racially Diverse Student Populations*, *Asian American Students in Higher Education*, and *Racism and Racial Equity in Higher Education*. Museus has previously received

several national awards in recognition of the impact of his scholarship, includ
ing the Association for the Study of Higher Education Early Career Award in
2011, and the NASPA George D. Kuh Outstanding Contribution to Researcl
and Literature Award in 2014.

Z Nicolazzo, PhD is assistant professor of Trans* Studies in Education in th
Center for the Study of Higher Education at the University of Arizon;
Nicolazzo's research focuses on discourses of gender in higher education, wit?
a particular emphasis on affirmative and resilience-based research alongsid
trans* students. Nicolazzo's first book, *Trans* in College: Transgender Student
Strategies for Navigating Campus Life and the Institutional Politics of Inclusior*
details an 18-month critical collaborative ethnography with trans* collegians

Christa J. Porter, PhD is assistant professor of Higher Education Administratio
at Kent State University. Her primary line of inquiry examines the devel
opment and trajectory of Black women in higher education. Specificall
she explores identity development and socialization processes of Black col
lege women and faculty. Additional lines of inquiry include college studer
development theory and critical qualitative methodology. Her service to th
academy is guided by co-constructive and transformative frameworks and he
praxis is grounded in Black feminist thought, intersectionality, and critic;
theories.

Leah J. Reinert, PhD started Everyone Needs an Editor: Academic Editing an
Consulting in 2017. They have experience in higher education and studer
affairs graduate programs as an instructor and researcher and in higher educ;
tion policy as a research and program assistant with the Midwestern High
Education Compact. Leah's research explores the use of strategic silence in tr
career negotiation and management of women faculty. Their other researc
interests include equity, inclusion, and LGBTQA issues in higher educatic
and intercultural and inclusive teaching and learning. Leah earned their Ph?
in higher education from the University of Minnesota in 2016.

Natasha A. Saelua is a doctoral candidate at Indiana University's Wright School e
Education, completing her degree in higher education. Her research interes
are culturally relevant education and service-learning and culturally enga;
ing campus environments. Saelua earned a BA in history and MA in Asi;
American studies at University of California, Los Angeles. A proud "milita:
brat," she is a first-generation Pacific Islander and traces her roots to Tutui?
American Samoa.

Gabriel R. Serna, PhD is assistant professor of Higher, Adult, and Lifelong Ed
cation at Michigan State University. His research interests include high

education economics and finance, college-going and choice, undocumented students, student price responsiveness, college and university fiscal administration, and enrollment management. His interest in intersectionality stems from both personal experiences and scholarly examination of the relationships between social constructions of identity and economic theory and methodology. He holds a PhD in education policy from Indiana University Bloomington, an MPP in public finance from the Martin School of Public Policy & Administration at the University of Kentucky, and a BBA in economics from New Mexico State University.

Nuray Seyidzade is a graduate student in the student affairs master's program at State University of New York-Binghamton. As an undergraduate student of human development, she focused on matters of social justice and the intersections of various social identities. She plans to continue working with students of diverse backgrounds in her future career as a student affairs professional.

Natesha L. Smith, PhD is assistant professor of Student Affairs Administration at the State University of New York—Binghamton. Having worked in Middle Eastern, East Asian, Caribbean, and North American higher education settings, Smith's research interests are a reflection of her cultural immersion experiences and work as a student affairs administrator/faculty member. Her research explores organizational culture, internationalization, and identity intersections.

D-L Stewart, PhD is professor in the School of Education and co-coordinator of Student Affairs in Higher Education and affiliated faculty in the Center for Women's Studies and Gender Research at Colorado State University. He focuses most intently on the history and philosophy of higher education, as well as institutional systems and structures that affect the postsecondary experiences, growth and development, as well as success of minoritized students. D-L examines these topics through intersectional, critical, and poststructural frameworks that incorporate ableism, religious hegemony, and classism alongside racism, patriarchy, as well as anti-queer/trans antagonism.

Daniel Tillapaugh, PhD is assistant professor and chair of the Department of Counselor Education in the Graduate School of Education at California Lutheran University. He graduated with a PhD in leadership studies at the University of San Diego and an MEd in counseling and personnel services from the University of Maryland. Tillapaugh's research interests are related broadly to intersectionality within higher education, particularly intersections of sexuality and gender on student development.

Jason K. Wallace is a doctoral student in the College Student Affairs Administra tion PhD program at the University of Georgia (UGA). Prior to pursuing hi studies full-time, Jason worked as assistant director of Multicultural Service and Programs at UGA. He has also worked at the University of North Texa at Dallas, Texas Christian University, and Tarrant County College. Jaso holds a Bachelor of Science in advertising and public relations, and a Mas ter of Education with an emphasis in educational administration, both from Texas Christian University.

Charmaine L. Wijeyesinghe, EdD is an author and consultant with over 35 year of experience working with colleges, universities, and organizations on issue of social identity and inequality, organizational change, and intersectional ity. She held positions in student affairs administration at the University c Massachusetts Amherst and Mount Holyoke College, and served as nationa trainer for program staff and boards of the National Conference for Commu nity and Justice. Her publications include two editions of *New Perspectives o Racial Identity Development* (NYU Press), the New Directions for Studer Services volume *Enacting Intersectionality in Student Affairs* (Jossey-Bass), an book chapters and articles on intersectionality, Multiracial identity, and soci justice practice.

Cobretti D. Williams is a doctoral candidate and research assistant at Loyo University Chicago. Currently, he is the editorial assistant for the *Journ of Student Affairs Research and Practice* and the editor-in-chief for the *Jour nal on Critical Scholarship in Higher Education and Student Affairs*. Throug his research, Cobretti employs critical queer and feminist epistemologies t understand the experiences of women of Color in higher education.

Printed in Australia
AUHW021242270921
352714AU00068B/699

9 781433 1653